Rugby's Class War

Bans, boot money and parliamentary battles

David Hinchliffe M.P.

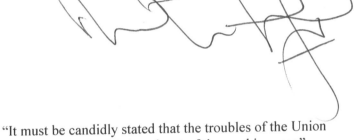

"It must be candidly stated that the troubles of the Union
commenced with the advent of the working man"

Arthur Budd, President of the Rugby Football Union 1888-89

LONDON LEAGUE PUBLICATIONS LIMITED

Rugby's Class War
Bans, boot money and parliamentary battles

A CIP catalogue record for this book is available from the British Library.

First published in Great Britain in October 2000 by:
London League Publications Ltd, P.O. Box 10441, London E14 0SB

ISBN: 1-903659-00-0

Cover design by: Stephen McCarthy Graphic Design
                          46, Clarence Road, London N15 5BB

Printed and bound by: Redwood Books, Trowbridge, Wiltshire.

Cover photos: Wigan versus Bath: Mike Haddon
                          Bath versus Wigan: Gerald Webster / *Rugby Leaguer*

The source of much of the information in the chronology was *Rugby's Great Split* by Tony Collins and the *Rugby League Fact Book* by Robert Gate, Guinness Publishing Ltd, 1991.

The quote on the title page is from page 11, *Garry Schofield's Rugby League Masterpieces*, by Garry Schofield with Neil Hanson, London, 1995

This book is dedicated to all the ordinary, decent people who have developed, defended and sustained the sport of Rugby League Football throughout its existence and to all who will also do so in the future.

The George Hotel, Huddersfield, where the 1895 meeting of the clubs that formed the Northern Union was held (Photo: Peter Lush)

Foreword

I had a wonderful career in Rugby Union. From playing for the junior team in our village, Resolven, five miles from Neath, I joined Swansea and then played for Neath. I won 13 Welsh caps in the front row, and was in the 1987 World Cup team, when we finished third. That was a tremendous squad, with Jonathan Davies and many other excellent players. Seven of them eventually "went north" to play Rugby League. I enjoyed playing Union in a working class environment in South Wales. A big influence on me was Mel James, who was from the same village and also went north to play for St Helens. He was a local hero and would tell us about his League experiences when he came home.

So in September 1987, at the age of 23, why did I switch to Rugby League and sign for St Helens? People told me that when you finished in Rugby Union, in those 'amateur' days, you had nothing to show for your career, except maybe financial hardship, arthritis or a serious injury. They said, if you have the chance, go north and secure your future. "Caps don't pay the mortgage" I was told.

I had been approached by Rugby League clubs from the time I played for the Welsh Youth team, when I was 17. Warrington, Widnes and Halifax all spoke to me at different times. They were keen to sign younger players - it was cheaper for them!

I had watched Rugby League on television - the BBC2 Floodlit Trophy and the Challenge Cup Final. To me it was the ultimate challenge as a rugby player - so different, so hard. The only thing to match it was being selected for the British Lions - the one Union honour I had missed out on. But I felt it was the right time to "go north" - even though it meant leaving home. The north of England seemed a long way away.

I was also offered £25,000 a year to play Union in France at that time. However, I took a similar deal from St Helens, but with a four year contract. I wanted to be paid for what I was good at and I fancied playing League. There was far more chance to handle the ball and make tries in League than in Union.

I had a wonderful time at St Helens, outstanding really. We played in two Challenge Cup Finals, won the John Player Trophy and were in the Premiership at Old Trafford. What was most rewarding was winning the respect of my fellow professionals and the supporters. The money was a factor in my original decision to go north, but gaining respect as a player was the real reward.

I was over 19 stone when I played League and played a physical game. There were bullies in some teams and often I would sort them out - sometimes "getting my retaliation in first".

When my contract finished at St Helens I needed a break from the game. League is played at a higher speed than Union, there are more collisions and it is more damaging. My knees were injured and my body needed to recover. When I first went home I couldn't run two laps round the field.

But after a year off, I was fit again and wanted to play. I had offers from League, even one to go back to St Helens, but I thought - why not go back to Union? Other people were being allowed to return to senior Rugby Union after playing League in some countries, or being allowed to play for local sides in others. In South Africa, France and New Zealand, people were flouting the rules. It was double standards.

To help me, I got a solicitor, Tim Jones, who was brilliant. We worked out a plan of attack to get me reinstated. But we hit brick walls. We would ask the WRU for a meeting, and they would refer the matter to the International Rugby Board, who only met once a year.

So we considered bringing a case of "restraint of trade" against the WRU. We could have gone to court and asked friends I had played with: have you ever been paid for playing Rugby Union? It was common knowledge that players were paid in Wales at that time. But to do this would have cost me many friends, so I was not keen.

Some journalists helped my campaign, particularly Gareth Roberts from the *Western Mail*. Some people were critical of me for having earned money, and then wanting to return to Rugby Union, but I had honestly earned my money - it was others who had been "illegal".

I approached my local M.P., Peter Hain, for help. He was superb and could put pressure on in the right places. He took me to see Iain Sproat M.P., the Sports Minister and he said that Rugby Union was wrong and should change their rules.

We decided to use the media and make a fuss. Peter Hain M.P. and David Hinchliffe M.P. were very good, raising the issue in Westminster and getting the Inland Revenue interested in the payments being made in Union.

The Union authorities then agreed that former League players could be reinstated after a three year break. In fact, I had started playing Union in France in 1993. I was recruited to Grenoble by Jacques Fouroux, but that stopped when a Welsh journalist who was on holiday went to a match, saw me playing and recognised me. It was on the 6.00p.m. television news and the WRU contacted the French Rugby Federation and I had to stop playing. When I was allowed to play again, I went back to Grenoble. I was playing and coaching in Canada at the time, Grenoble tracked me down and I played a couple of seasons in France. After Union went open in 1995, I played for Swansea and Bridgend and got back into the Welsh squad, although I didn't win any more caps. I did some coaching at Neath last year, but now I have a young family and run a big sports pub in Neath which together take all my time. Maybe in the future I will get involved in coaching again.

I will always remember the words "Stuart Evans is banned" when I was playing in France. I'm glad that now players can play Union or League whenever they want and players of both codes will not face the battles I did to play the game of their choice. This book tells the important story of some of those battles.

Stuart Evans
September 2000

Stuart Evans played Rugby Union for Neath, Swansea, Bridgend and Grenoble, and won 13 caps for Wales. In Rugby League, he played 80 games for St Helens from 1987 to 1991, scoring seven tries and appeared in the 1989 Challenge Cup Final.

Introduction

The saying that sport and politics should not mix has become one of the most well worn clichés of the modern world - and you can be sure the people who have proclaimed it loudest and most often have been those with most to hide. Sadly, but inevitably, sport can never exist in a vacuum. We may all like to imagine those days of innocence, remembering that sport was created as a leisure activity to provide healthy enjoyment and entertainment, but there can be no doubts now that people's behaviour and attitudes in their sports mirror the society in which they exist.

When David Hinchliffe and his fellow Members of Parliament formed the All Party Parliamentary Rugby League Group they did, indeed, create - if you'll pardon the pun - a political football. But there was not a trace of them trying to use sport as a political tool. Quite the opposite, they found themselves in the unique sporting situation of trying to right an unforgivable wrong, of trying to give a voice in the nation's corridors of power to a certain, and very clearly defined, group of disenfranchised citizens of the United Kingdom.

Of course, if this involved any one of a thousand social or community issues, it would be considered as the normal right and proper duty of Members of Parliament to be addressing them. Legal requirements and moral codes have come to ensure that law abiding citizens should not be disadvantaged or discriminated against because of their colour, creed, race, religion or political beliefs. So, to find that M.P.s were having to defend the human rights of individuals just because they had chosen to play a particular sport, seems to be incredible - a story so ridiculous it could not be true.

Sadly, this story was all too true. In the pages that follow, David Hinchliffe gives an insight to the political battles that were still having to be fought on behalf of Rugby League as recently as the final decade of the 20th century. Battles that no other sport has ever had the misfortune to find itself having to endure directly because of the actions and prejudices of those involved in another sport.

Imagine the public reaction if, for example, individuals were forbidden from playing tennis because they had also played badminton, from cricket because they had played hockey or from football because they had played basketball, purely because the domineering sport in question was so anxious to stop people having the opportunity to sample the delights of another. The outcry from influential media and public figures would have been so vociferous and immediate, that any attempts to bully and intimidate - especially children in schools for heaven's sake - would rapidly have been exposed and forced to stop.

But not so in the world of rugby. Why did it take almost 100 years for Rugby League to be allowed to break down the barriers put up against it by Rugby Union?

The answer, of course, as David Hinchliffe immediately recognises, lies in the murky waters of the British class system. Because no other sport has been so clearly, and uniquely, identified with one specific class as Rugby League has with the so-called working class. The game was unequivocally born because of the needs of working men who were employed in the industrial towns of the north of England in the latter years of the 19th century. And throughout its history it has maintained a blue-collar identity, a symbol of pride for those close-knit communities that support it so passionately.

But, instead of being recognised for the courageous and honest motives those brave men of 1895 brought to the game of rugby, their actions were perceived as a rebellious act of treachery never to be forgiven by the Rugby Union establishment. And, because that establishment were part of the ruling class, it was always their version of history that came to be written.

For people like David Hinchliffe and myself, who grew up in communities where Rugby League was such an integral and respected part of our lives, it was hard - later in life and a few miles further away from home - to believe why so much hostility existed towards our game. Whilst we could understand why Welshmen would be upset with Rugby League from a sporting viewpoint because so many talented players had left Wales to go and play the "northern game", we could never appreciate the bitterness against us in human terms from people who were quick to claim working class roots and socialist beliefs. We could never understand why their bitterness was not targeted against their own Rugby Union game which constantly turned its back on their own people - virtually forcing players to accept the opportunities offered by Rugby League - just so that it could continue to doff its cap to the ex-public schoolboys at Twickenham.

Especially in the first half of the twentieth century, during the depression years, it was money from northern Rugby League clubs that put food on the tables for plenty of working class families in Wales. The wealthy Rugby Unions, apparently, would rather have let its less privileged players and their families starve than be seen to be sacrificing their so-called "amateur principles."

In 1995, when Rugby Union finally decided to admit that the principles Rugby League believed in fully 100 years before were all right after all, no apology was forthcoming on behalf of all those individuals who had suffered at the hypocritical hands of Rugby Union throughout the 20th century.

Now, as professional Rugby Union falls over itself to recruit coaching and playing expertise from Rugby League, giving the impression that rugby's class war is finally over, it is important that the road to here - as described by David Hinchliffe - is set down in print, so that future generations can have no doubts about the truth.

So much of this story I know only too well from personal involvement. As a grammar school boy in a rock solid Rugby League town in the north of England, I was denied the opportunity to play the game that was such a big part of our heritage and, instead, forced to play Rugby Union. In the year 2000, this is still the case in so many schools - so much for that bit of rugby's class war being over. Can you imagine schoolboys in South Wales being told they cannot play Rugby Union, but must instead only play League?

As a youngster I read in a newspaper comments from the president of the South African Rugby Union in which he described anyone involved in Rugby League as being "a reptile" - and wondered if that meant people like me, or my elderly aunt who made the tea and sandwiches at my local club?

While at college in Oxford, in the absence of any Rugby League in those days, I played a few games of Union - until I let it be known I had played League (obviously only at the lowest level of amateur football) - and was curtly asked not to turn up anymore. I was involved with the fledgling Oxford Rugby League team when Bob Mahuta was banned by the local Rugby Union, prompting one of the earliest media storms to blow up. This was rugby's class war in action.

I spent time with the French international League star Jean-Marc Bourret the very weekend he was agonising over whether to take the fortune offered to him to switch to (amateur) Rugby Union back in 1980.

In the May 1984 edition of *Open Rugby* we first published Trevor Delaney's plans for a "Freedom in Rugby" campaign. Later, in March 1985, I was one of the people who attended the inaugural meeting of the campaign, symbolically held at the George Hotel in Huddersfield. I took with me that day a friend from France, Robert Fassolette. As the year 2000 approached, Robert was still campaigning to see if the "Treize Actif" movement he formed would be able to achieve any positive results in trying to gain recompense for the destruction and outlawing of the Rugby League game by the Vichy government during the war - a sporting atrocity brought about directly by Rugby Unionists seeking to destroy Rugby League. You see, rugby's one-sided war has not been restricted to battlefields in the United Kingdom.

Now, in the year 2000, we can enjoy widespread Rugby League for students and in the armed forces - areas of society that were, for so long, regarded as out of bounds to the game. Those are areas which have directly benefited from the sacrifices made by the people who fought, and won, rugby's class war. Sadly, it appears that the inability of Rugby League's own leaders to agree among themselves since the barriers finally came down may mean that the game that had right on its side is likely to fail to take advantage of its new found freedom, and instead it is Rugby Union which could enjoy all the future benefits.

Being so specifically identified as a working class game - something that was a great strength for Rugby League throughout most of its first century - may now, tragically, prove to be its downfall. I dearly hope not, but a changing society has brought a different urban landscape to many of the communities on which Rugby League's foundations were built. The game can and does continue to play a very valuable role for young people in areas of social depravation, but so many foundations are being chipped away - the global picture is the one that counts in sport now, as small town loyalties and traditions mean little anymore.

But rugby's class war had to be fought - on behalf of every schoolboy, student and would-be amateur Rugby League player. I only hope those who now have been given freedom in rugby can still pick up the ball and run with it.

Harry Edgar
Harry Edgar was the founder and publisher of the former *Open Rugby* magazine. He is a widely respected Rugby League journalist and author who has written extensively on the game.

Preface: The emperor's new clothes

"If all the Rugby Union clubs face problems in the immediate future, what about the game of Rugby League? Played as a major sport in only a handful of countries, it now faces a real crisis." It was the BBC's Rugby Union correspondent, Ian Robertson, reporting on *Radio Five Live* that the International Rugby Football Union Board, meeting in Paris in late August 1995, had taken the historic decision to allow professionalism in the Union game. His comments epitomised everything Rugby League had had to put up with for the previous 99 years and 364 days. After almost a century to the day from the 1895 breakaway by the Northern Union clubs, which led to League's decision to go down the professional road, Rugby Union's decision to do exactly the same was presented by the BBC as a defeat for Rugby League.

Robertson - like so many in the establishment media in my opinion - was too deeply rooted in Union's antipathy for League to offer a remotely objective view of the background to that day's decision. The reality was probably far too painful for him because Union had been living a lie for years. Its central principle of "amateurism" - which had caused the original split in 1895 - had been conclusively proved to be the sporting equivalent of the "Emperor's New Clothes".

While some commentators expressed surprise at the Paris decision, the International Rugby Board could have done little else. A whole series of different elements had come together recently to bring matters to a head. The growing commercialisation of Union, with sponsorship and television deals, had brought unprecedented finance into the game. Those players not already in receipt of financial benefits as a direct result of their activities on the field began to demand their share of the new goodies. However, the continued exclusion from Rugby Union of players associated with Rugby League had been the subject of intense political debate and serious threats of legal action, with Union "shamateurism" increasingly exposed for the hypocrisy it was.

But, as Union took this inevitable step, Rugby League was indeed facing a real crisis, but for very different reasons than those suggested by Robertson. The advent of the Murdoch-backed Super League, with suggested club mergers and a move to summer rugby, had plunged the followers of the code into an unprecedented internal battle for its very soul.

This book is a personal reflection on some of the remarkable events that saw the two rugby tribes conclude their bitter one-hundred-year war only to descend into acrimonious conflict within their own separate ranks over fundamental questions concerning the future of each game. It describes the banning of myself and others of my generation from Rugby Union for what was until fairly recently the cardinal sin of playing Rugby League as an amateur, and the impact such bans have had on the wider development of the 13-a-side game.

It examines the growing challenges to the attitudes which underpinned the proscription of League players by the Rugby Union authorities and analyses in detail the parliamentary campaign which contributed to the eventual achievement of free movement between the codes in recent years.

While the book broadly pursues an evolutionary course in offering my own account of some quite profound changes, I make no apology for occasionally reverting to earlier events of note in an effort to put some of the developments I describe in their proper perspective. I also make no apology for dwelling on certain issues which I believe to have had particular significance. The lengthy description of the parliamentary battle to overturn the ban on playing Rugby League in the armed forces is needed to demonstrate the lengths to which some found it necessary to go to prevent men in the forces enjoying the 13-a-side game. The tremendous growth of Rugby League in the forces vindicates the work that was done to secure the right to play it.

Similarly, the detailed discussion of the efforts made to establish the Inland Revenue's position on alleged earnings by "amateur" Rugby Union players is included because of its significance to the eventual formal professionalisation of their game.

Throughout the book I make no secret of my deep affinity with Rugby League and readily concede that the evaluation of developments in Union since the changes of 1995 frequently rely on the thoughts and comments of others a good deal closer to that code than I have ever been. While the conclusions I reach about the future direction of both codes of Rugby are written from an unashamedly League perspective, I hope they will stand the test of more objective analysis.

If there was any one underlying motive for writing this book, in the light of the comments by Ian Robertson and others like him, it was simply to put the record straight. Perhaps some, for the first time, will hear the other side of this important story.

David Hinchliffe M.P.
October 2000

Rugby League's working class roots: The plaque by The Railway Hotel
in Featherstone (Photo: Peter Lush)

About the author

David Hinchliffe has been the Labour M.P. for Wakefield, where he was born and raised, since 1987. He was a Shadow Health Minister during the last Parliament and has been Chairman of the Commons Health Select Committee since 1997. This is his first book although he has had articles, mainly on health and social policy, published in a number of periodicals and newspapers including *The Guardian* and *The Independent.*

Away from politics he has had a lifelong interest in sport, and particularly Rugby League, following the fortunes of Wakefield Trinity R.L.F.C. since he was a child. Before entering Parliament he played hooker for a number of amateur Rugby League clubs and also, despite that code's ban on Rugby League players at that time, some "illicit" Rugby Union.

Among his other interests are tracing the history of the Hinchliffe family and travelling the inland waterways of Yorkshire on his narrowboat. He lives in Wakefield with his wife Julia, teenage children, Robert and Rebecca and dog Seth.

Acknowledgements

This book has been very much a team effort and it is frankly impossible to thank all those who have assisted and encouraged me during its writing. But I would like to place on record my particular gratitude to John Blanchard who, along with my late father, took me to my first Rugby League match well over forty years ago; to the late Richard Clarkson for his early advice and enthusiasm for the idea of such a book; to Maurice Oldroyd and the British Amateur Rugby League Association for sharing their knowledge of the subject matter and allowing me access to press files and correspondence; to colleagues past and present at the Rugby Football League, especially archivist Tony Collins, for advice and support; to the numerous Rugby League and Rugby Union writers and correspondents whose thoughts I have quoted and in particular Neil Hanson, Dave Woods, the staff of *Rugby League World* (formerly *Open Rugby*), *League Express* and the *Rugby Leaguer*, and to the House of Commons library for access to research material and press data.

I want to especially thank Tony Pocock for his lengthy, good humoured and patient assistance in putting the book into a reasonably coherent form and Ros Sanderson, Sarah Johnson and Julia Hinchliffe for typing the text and improving the English.

I am most grateful as well to Stuart Evans for his foreword and to Harry Edgar for writing the introduction. A particular debt of gratitude is owed to Peter Lush, Dave Farrar and Michael O'Hare for their hard work in editing the final version, to Huw Richards for his advice on Rugby Union and Rugby League, to Glyn Robbins for commenting on an early draft, to the photographers for their assistance in providing the photos, to the publishers London League Publications Ltd and the book's printers, Redwood Books.

Last, but by no means least, I want to thank Julia, Robert and Rebecca for their patience and support when my limited time at home has so often been spent researching and writing this book.

David Hinchliffe M.P.
October 2000.

Guide to initials

Rugby League:
ARL   Australian Rugby League
ARLFC Amateur Rugby League Football Club.
BARLA British Amateur Rugby League Association - the ruling body of
          amateur Rugby League.
NFP   Northern Ford Premiership
RFL   Rugby Football League - the ruling body of professional rugby league.
RLC   Rugby League Conference
RLFC   Rugby League Football Club.
SLE   Super League Europe

Rugby Union:
IRB   International Rugby Football Union Board - Rugby Union's international governing
            body.
RFU   Rugby Football Union - English Rugby Union's governing body.
WRU   Welsh Rugby Union - Welsh Rugby Union's governing body.
SRU   Scottish Rugby Union - Scottish Rugby Union's governing body.
RUFC   Rugby Union Football Club
EPRUC English Professional Rugby Union Clubs Ltd
EFDR   English First Division Rugby

Rule changes

From 1895 to 1908, Rugby League was moving away from its Union roots and made important changes to the rules. that clearly differentiated it from Union. Scrummaging was reduced and kicking had a lesser role with handling in the ascendancy, to make a more attractive game to watch and help draw better crowds.

Points scoring and line outs: In 1897 all goals were worth two points. The line-out was abolished.

Thirteen players: The reduction from fifteen to thirteen players a side was introduced in 1906.

Play the ball and ball-back: The "play the ball" was introduced in 1906. It was different from today's game with the ball always heeled back to a colleague, because the tackled player could be surrounded by other players. The "ball-back" rule prevented kicking directly into touch from open play. If the ball did not bounce play was bought back to where it was kicked. This reduced the number of scrums and amount of touch kicking. These were major changes from Rugby Union.

Loose-heads: In 1907, one of the more defining rulings occurred with the defining of the scrummaging rules and the defending side being allowed the "loose-head" in all cases, before this apparently some sides packed all their players in the front row.

Tries are the aim not goals: In 1908 a fundamental change from the old rules of 1897 saw the object of the game being changed. In the old rule Law 1 (unchanged from Union) the emphasis had been on goal scoring. The rule was changed to "The object of the game shall be to cross an opponent's goal-line to score tries and kick the ball over the cross bar and over the posts".

(With thanks to on an article in *Code 13* Number 9 by Trevor Delaney and *Rugby League - An Illustrated History* by Robert Gate)

Contents

1: They play for exercise not exhibition

It is some testimony to the British class system that it was 1995 before the sport of Rugby Union began to dismantle the regulations on "amateurism" which had caused the great split with what became the separate sport of Rugby League 100 years earlier. It is indeed quite remarkable that despite the huge social changes of the 20th century and the consequent movement away from the division between "gentlemen and players" in a whole range of sporting activities, Rugby Union's rigid class barriers remained in place almost to the millennium.

There are some who will maintain that a century of Union-League conflict was nothing to do with social class. History, however, will prove they were wrong. Even the *Encyclopaedia Britannica* suggests: "Class solidarity and exclusiveness led to the invention of the amateur rule, originally formulated in the 1870s to prevent the participation of all those who worked with their hands."[1] Tony Collins's recent book *Rugby's Great Split* also strongly demonstrates the role that class divisions played in the formation of the Northern Union in 1895, which became the Rugby Football League in 1922.

The problem was that what had been the sporting preserve of public schools had in late Victorian times spread to the masses. And in the industrial north of England, in particular, the working man perfected the art of rugby football in a way that attracted huge crowds. In asserting that "they play for exercise not exhibition",[2] the Huddersfield headmaster, the Reverend Frank Marshall, might have been speaking of the England Rugby Union team of the early 1990s. But he was pinpointing one of the earliest divisions in attitude towards rugby football because League valued exhibition alongside exercise from the outset.

It was Marshall, brought up in the Midlands, who spearheaded the investigation and punishment of northern players and teams who breached the proscription on professionalism laid down by the Rugby Football Union in 1886. That proscription, which also forbade the broken-time payments increasingly being made in the north to compensate players who were prevented by their playing commitments from working on Saturdays, combined with the desire for competition amongst the northern clubs, led to the great split. Prior to 1886, as Tony Collins has outlined, Rugby Union had no rules on amateurism or professionalism. He explains that they accepted that "gentlemen" could claim their expenses, as amateur cricketers did. But he says that their attitude to working class players was shown by Harry Garnett, a leading figure in Yorkshire rugby at that time, who "suggested that if working men couldn't afford to play, they shouldn't play at all".[3] The Northern Union, which became the Rugby Football League in 1922, would never be forgiven by the Rugby Union establishment for what happened in 1895. The new code in the north had not only unceremoniously buried the amateur principle, its establishment was also deemed to have prevented the continued success of the England Rugby Union side. Geoffrey Moorhouse summed it up in *A People's Game*, his official history of Rugby League: "Having been outright or joint champions five times between the 1882-83 season and that of 1891-92, England were not to get so much as a sniff of the title for another eighteen years, which was largely attributed to an absence of its best players, who were otherwise engaged in the north," he wrote. "The bitterness that this engendered, added to the affront of having been snubbed by the very people one normally patronised, explains a great deal of the hostility that was to flow from the parent game to its offspring in subsequent decades."[4]

I had slipped into the middle of this affair half a century later by an accident of birth. I came into the world at a hospital just a few streets away from Wakefield Trinity RLFC's famous Belle Vue ground. The grounds and gardens of the now closed Manygates Hospital - where my son and daughter were also born - are so close that they were illuminated when Trinity's floodlights were turned on.

While I have no memory of ever being without Wakefield Trinity and Rugby League, my actual introduction to Belle Vue probably took place when I was about eight years old. One Saturday afternoon, along with my parents, I was visiting some family friends, John and Mary Blanchard, who lived at Portobello, less than half a mile from the Trinity ground. John had suggested to my father that we went to watch the Trinity match that day and I took my first short walk to the ground that was soon to become a sort of second home for me.

I was pushed to the front of the terracing on the Wakefield side of the old west stand and peered up at the giants in red and blue. It was a very different game in those days and the tank-like players that performed under the unlimited tackle rule would have no place in the modern game.

This was my first experience of being part of a big crowd and sharing with them a common and strictly partisan passion for the success of our team. Coming from a teetotal family of non-smokers it was also my first experience of beery breath and tobacco. There were other smells that were to become associated with my Saturday afternoons. There was the smoke from the engine sheds and the nearby power station, but more than anything there was the smell of wintergreen. It was to be some years before I knew the source of that aroma but as a small boy the smell of it had quite magical associations with the explosive action and excitement that was to become such a crucially important part of my life.

I began to live for Saturday afternoons, not knowing at the time that I was witnessing, at first-hand, what was perhaps the greatest era in the history of Wakefield Trinity. I could not have known that the side that was developing in front of my eyes would go down in the annals of the game as one of the finest, perhaps even the best, in the world.

The atmosphere of Rugby League matches in those times was captured in the film *This Sporting Life*. I recently showed the video of it to my children, partly to show them the Trinity ground of those days. I was in the crowd when the matches were filmed at Belle Vue. The famous British actress, Glenda Jackson, made her first appearance on screen in the film, playing a barmaid. In 1992, she was elected as a Labour M.P.. I said hello to her when I bumped into her in the Commons. "We made our screen debuts in the same film," I said, "but your career took off and mine didn't." She looked puzzled, but laughed when I explained I had been in the crowd watching the great Trinity players.

As I grew older and my dad had to work on Saturdays I was allowed to go to Belle Vue without my parents. I remember the match-day routine as if it happened only yesterday, even though it is now nearly 40 years ago. By 1.15 on a Saturday afternoon Wakefield's Kirkgate Bridge was filled with a steadily flowing stream of folk bedecked in red and blue. We passed various pubs that were full of drinkers who would eventually make their way up Doncaster Road, stopping at the gents at the corner of

Sugar Lane. We would buy a programme from the seller by the cemetery and then it was on to the schoolboys' entrance by St Catherine's Church. The money taken at those turnstiles went to Wakefield Schools Rugby League in those days and they were usually operated by teachers whom we knew.

You could cheerfully say "Hello, sir" on Saturday afternoons but this arrangement caused no end of problems in the days before floodlights when cup replays were held on Wednesday afternoons in term time. On those occasions dozens of us would hop off school and scale the gate at the back of the old west stand. I never recall getting into trouble at school over this because there was a kind of silent acknowledgement among many of the teachers that quite frankly we had got our priorities absolutely right.

The actor, playwright and Rugby League enthusiast Colin Welland once wrote about having taught at a Rugby League pitch with a school built round it[5] and this was my school to a tee. Virtually all the male teachers, from the headmaster down, at Lawefield Lane County Primary School in Wakefield were League fanatics. There was even one woman teacher who coached Rugby League, something very rare in the 1950s. They might not have got me through my 11-plus, the exam that decided at the age of 11 whether you went on to a grammar or secondary modern school, but I came away from there with something of much greater importance - a sporting passion that steered me through adolescence and kept me (by and large) clear of trouble with the law and into adulthood.

It was at that school that I was taught the basics - the 3Rs and RL. Frankly, I excelled at none of them but mastered the RL basics sufficiently well to justify a place on the left wing of the school team. I went through an entire season of school fixtures without actually receiving a pass - a far cry from today when even the youngest players can spin the ball along the line. In those days if the ball got as far as the centres it was a remarkable achievement. But I remember some great matches and a feeling of immense pride in wearing the school colours of black and white. Possessing the school jersey gave the chosen few a feeling of great distinction. When you took it home for washing it was not hidden in your satchel but hung on your back, tied around your neck along with your boots, for all to see.

After I had failed my 11-plus I lost a number of good mates to Rugby Union at the Queen Elizabeth and Thornes House grammar schools. In those days usually only Union was played at grammar schools and the game of Rugby League was deprived of some pretty talented prospects as a consequence. As I reached adolescence, I was formally certified as non-academic and moved to a secondary modern school. But in one of my earliest encounters with the British class system in sport I found that one side effect of academic failure was that my new school played Rugby League.

I spent some three years at the Cathedral Church of England Secondary Modern School playing in the school team once again, but for some reason I found myself at the age of 14 leaving a year early and beginning a two-year GCE O-level course at Wakefield Technical and Art College. It was not long before I was in like-minded company with the formation of a college under-17s Rugby League side. I was at least a year younger than most of the other players and, after being in the second row of the Cathedral School team, I found myself converted to hooker, more because of insufficient size for other scrum positions than any merits as a number 9.

Although we had one or two players of ability the rest were of a similar standard to me and it would be an understatement to say we did not make much of a mark. Our opponents included Wakefield Trinity and Featherstone Rovers Juniors and a Castleford under-17 team that included a youngster tipped for future prominence who went by the name of Roger Millward. If we kept our opponents down to 50 points we were having a good week. It was more often over 70. At just 15 years old in the under-17s side, I was learning Rugby League the hard way.

For a period I was the club secretary, my first ever experience of the game's administration. I had to go to Monday night meetings in a smoky back room of the Albion public house on Stanley Road. Here we dealt with disciplinary matters, refereeing appointments and fixture arrangements.

I was to meet for the first time some of the stalwarts of the game in my home town, such as Harry Consterdine and George Gledhill and others who gave a lifetime of service to running the sport in various capacities. It was the boundless enthusiasm of such people that kept the amateur game's flame flickering through some pretty desperate years before the British Amateur Rugby League Association was eventually formed in 1973. Despite the efforts of such as Harry and George, the amateur game was frankly a shambles in terms of its organisation. The public impression of strong Rugby League roots beneath the professional clubs in areas such as Wakefield was a long way from the true picture. It was woefully weak and very often, in my personal experience anyway, unable to offer even the most basic facilities of a changing-room and a bath.

The late 1960s in Wakefield saw the formation of a number of pub sides, which initially played Sunday afternoon friendlies. With the eventual move of professional matches from Saturday to Sunday, in Wakefield and elsewhere, the Sunday leagues were formed and had to start their matches at 11a.m. Why those Sunday leagues suddenly developed at that time is something of a mystery. As the 1970s neared, the sport as a whole was in every other way in serious decline. The attendances of professional clubs were on the slide and in many areas amateur Rugby League was virtually non-existent. Wakefield was always described as a hotbed of Rugby League but at that time it was the home of only two amateur clubs.

The lack of playing opportunities for those who had enjoyed Rugby League at school meant that the majority gave up the game for good when they left and in some instances exceptional talent was lost for ever. The better players graduated to the junior and intermediate sides of Trinity and other professional clubs while some went on to play Rugby Union for the first time in their lives. The Colts sides at the Sandal and Wakefield Rugby Union Clubs offered regular playing opportunities at well-organised clubs with good facilities. What was on offer on the field may have been profoundly inferior to League, even in the days of League's unlimited tackles, but at least there was a changing room, a bath and some beer and grub after the match.

Trinity's achievements

However, I suppose Trinity's achievements in the late 1960s were a continual reminder that there was really only one "proper" form of rugby. The acquisition from Featherstone Rovers of that marvellous footballer Don Fox, joining his brother Neil at Belle Vue, contributed significantly to two successive championship final victories in 1967 and 1968 as well as the infamous 1968 Wembley appearance. That final is remembered as the "watersplash" final. The Wembley pitch was flooded and had it not been the Challenge Cup final the game would never have been played. It is, of course,

4

one of the most infamous finals in history. Don Fox won the Lance Todd Trophy for the man-of-the-match, but missed a conversion in front of the posts in the last seconds that would have won the game for Trinity. However, I believe Wakefield were robbed by a penalty try being given to Leeds for obstruction earlier in the game.

Trinity's successes boosted the local fortunes of Rugby League no end and led to a number of people, including myself, starting to play the game again.

I reckon I must have been around 19 or 20 when I had my first ever game of Rugby Union. I had attended training sessions in the past at both the Sandal and Wakefield clubs but had never until then turned out for one of their teams. Frankly, some of the personnel at both clubs at that time did not particularly attract me. While their social backgrounds may have been a bit humble by Twickenham's standards, the educational path to both clubs at that time seemed largely that of solidly grammar or private schools. Until recently, the first thing that greeted you at Sandal was an advertisement for private education. But this secondary-modern school lad, increasingly active in the Labour Party, was really only there because they offered regular football and decent facilities for the players.

The extent of that alien territory was soon to become much clearer. Emerging Sunday Rugby League in Wakefield did not go unnoticed at Sandal and, following an early season League sevens tournament, several "twin-trackers" (i.e. people playing both league and union) received letters from the club making it clear they were no longer welcome. While I do not recall getting one of these letters personally it was made very clear to me exactly where I stood because like a number of others I was also playing League on a Sunday morning.

One of the Sandal club officials concerned with the exclusion of League players then was Jack Adams. Many years later, I presented his son Gareth with a memento from Wakefield Council for his selection for an England Rugby Union youth side. I pondered the irony as well some time later when Adams junior moved from Sandal Rugby Union Club to Bath to further his amateur career at a club eventually to be at the forefront of professional Union.

The purge of applying Union's rules on amateurism against League players hit the local press when one Sandal player, John Jackson, who played Sunday Rugby League with the local Black Horse pub team, chose to go public on the nonsense of it all. But local Union officials pointed to the Union rule that explicitly at that time forbade anyone who had played Rugby League over the age of 18 from playing Rugby Union. It did not matter that you had not received a penny for playing League, you were still out for good.

"Rugby lepers"

In some respects the creation of a group of "rugby lepers" assisted the development of local Rugby League, by ensuring that many of us played only one code whether we liked it or not. I always preferred playing Rugby League, but resented the complete lack of basic facilities at many clubs. My team at that time, Flanshaw, for example, had changing rooms but no washing or bathing facilities. We frequently caused great amusement by turning out for a second game - of soccer - on Sunday afternoon, filthy before the match began.

It was this fact more than any other that saw me back playing illicit Rugby Union some time later. With other outcasts from the Union scene in Wakefield, I joined Hemsworth RUFC, a club some seven miles from my home town. Despite seeking anonymity, some of us were recognised by several of their players at our first training session at Hemsworth High School. We had played League against each other on Sunday mornings, because Hemsworth RUFC provided a remarkably large proportion of the players who made up the Hemsworth Miners Welfare Rugby League team.

The great thing about the Hemsworth club was that nobody really bothered about the nonsensical rules regarding Rugby League. Although the club had its origins as Hemsworth Grammar School's Old Boys (Hilmians) and contained graduates, teachers and other professional men, it had a much greater social class mix than either of the two Wakefield Union clubs appeared to have at that time. As a consequence it had a tolerance of players whose background was Rugby League and no one seemed to mind our Sunday morning activities. An added factor was the way the club was run largely by the players. There was no separate brigade of ageing officialdom - Will Carling's "old farts" - concerned with applying anachronistic rules and regulations.

Hemsworth played a mix of other clubs in various part of Yorkshire, from those based in mining villages such as Dinnington, to the second and third teams of more fashionable Union outfits such as Ilkley, Otley, Morley and Headingley. These bigger clubs more accurately represented the real world of Union at the time and articulated the hatred of Rugby League far more clearly in my opinion than petty officialdom at Sandal RUFC. I can recall us being sneered at in more than one clubhouse for wanting to watch the closing stages of a Saturday *Grandstand* Rugby League match on the bar-room television set.

In some respects such treatment ensured that I and my fellow travellers went in harder on the next occasion we played these clubs. It was so obvious that the same class distinction that underpinned attitudes towards Rugby League led as well to a distinct feeling that clubs such as Hemsworth were very much second-class citizens, a kind of Union lower order.

While many of my colleagues could laugh all this off, perhaps my politics led me to take it more seriously. I detested everything the blazer brigade stood for but now, on mature reflection, I am glad I met them. When during later years the sporting world was at a loss to comprehend Twickenham's last ditch defence of a long lost "amateurism" principle, I had no problem understanding why some were denying a reality that was staring them right in the face. I had met them, talked to them, and gained an insight into their very different world.

Nowhere was that world brought home to me more clearly than when I played for Hemsworth away to Otley seconds at the end of one particular season. We were soundly beaten by a much bigger team and I tore some muscles in my side, playing much of the game on the wing.

Recovering in the clubhouse after the match, I noticed a large oil painting over the bar depicting action in a match many years earlier. The club steward serving behind the bar proudly told me that it showed the Roses match in 1893. "Can you see the players whose faces have been painted out? They're the ones who went Northern Union," he said. A fine historic picture of sporting achievement had apparently been tampered with to blot out of existence those members of a cup-winning side who had gone on to play the forerunner of Rugby League. For taking that step they were removed from recollection, as if they had never existed. They had committed the unforgivable.

The story about that picture had a profound and lasting effect on me. I wondered for a long time why those players had chosen to go to the Northern Union. No doubt it was because of the same economic necessity that had resulted in the advent of broken-time payments. Working-class players simply could not afford to miss a Saturday shift to play a game of rugby. These men had probably been painted out of history for feeding their kids. Years later, I found out that the painting out of the players was an oft-repeated and widely accepted myth. As Tony Collins has explained, only two players would have been left in the painting if such alterations had occurred, because the rest played Northern Union, as did the Otley club themselves from 1900 to 1906 before reforming as a Rugby Union club in 1907.[6]

Until then I had never really given much thought as to why there were two codes of rugby. It had seemed essentially a class thing and no more. Secondary-modern children played League; grammar and private schools played Union. It clearly *was* a class issue. That painting may have been nearly 80 years old at the time, but the class attitudes that removed those men from history remained entrenched in Rugby Union rules even in the 1970s. And in some respects, over the period of the 20th century, attitudes had hardened. What had begun as a specific objection to broken-time payments was by then institutionalised in Union rules as a much wider objection to participation of any kind, even as an amateur, in the totally independent sport of Rugby League.

I came home from that match feeling angry at what I had seen and been told. But I also felt angry at myself for having taken part for so long in a sport that quite obviously engendered such attitudes.

I had some good mates at the Hemsworth club but, after Otley, I don't recall ever playing another game of Rugby Union. I joined Walnut Warriors Rugby League Club during that summer, playing on the field next to Sandal Rugby Union club. The Warriors were one of the original Sunday League outfits in Wakefield and they were at the time a well-organised, progressive club. I played with the Walnut until 1979, when I was 29 and by then increasingly active in local politics. The appointment of the older of the Fox brothers - Peter - as coach played a part in my decision to pack it in. He joined 'Nut after being sacked by Wakefield Trinity and immediately instituted training sessions that were much more serious than anything I had previously experienced.

As a consequence of Fox's presence, the club attracted a host of new players and I was moved from hooker to prop, a position for which I was never really big enough. Playing away to Rossington, near Doncaster, on a freezing winter morning, I got a badly gashed left eye and concussion, in a match that was a punch-up from start to finish. I was off the field for treatment for a time, but was sent back on, despite concussion, because we were down to 11 men with no substitutes available. I am convinced to this day that I got hypothermia in the second half of the match. After I had had the eye stitched at Pinderfields hospital in Wakefield, they kept me in for two days' observation. I never played competitive rugby again.

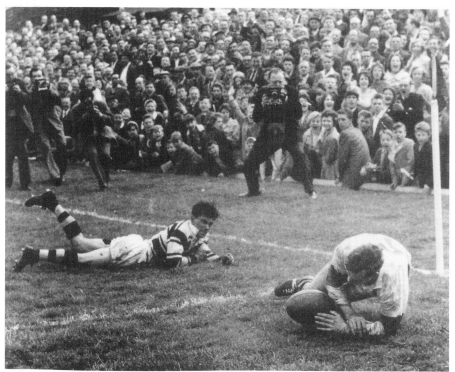

John Etty scoring for Wakefield Trinity against Hull in the 1960 Championship semi-final.
David Hinchliffe is in the front row, to the right of the group of photographers.
(Photo: Courtesy David Hinchliffe M.P.)

1961-1962 Wakefield Trinity team: Record victory: 73-5 against Bradford Northern.
Challenge cup winners - 12-6 against Huddersfield, Rugby League Championship runners-up,
Yorkshire League and County League Champions.
Back row: W.J. Armour (physiotherapist), D.W. Armitage, E.W. Sugden, R. Rylance, J. Ridge,
J. Atkinson, L. Pounder, S. Milner (committee), E. Thomas (secretary).
Centre: J. Booth (baggage), C. Greenwood, J.Prinsloo, M. Kosanovic, G.V. Round, D.
Williamson, A. Firth, D. Metcalfe, J. Wilkinson, B. Briggs, K. Traill.
Front row: F. Smith, A. Skene, K. Rollin, N. Fox, S.H. Hadfield (chairman), D. Turner (captain),
Ald. F. West (president), K. Holliday, G. Oakes, H. Poynton, K. Hirst

2: An Early Call to Arms

The renewed interest in amateur Rugby League in my home area in the late 1960s was reflected elsewhere in West Yorkshire, and the 1970s saw it acknowledged as the "boom sport" of the decade by the Sports Council chairman, Dickie Jeeps. But its expansion on home territory, and particularly further afield, was constantly checked by the Rugby Union ban on even amateurs playing both games.

My treatment and that of my contemporaries at the hands of Sandal RUFC was repeated on many occasions at different clubs and became a particular thorn in the side of those trying to establish Rugby League in other than its traditional areas. When successive governments began increasingly to trumpet the concept of "sport for all" it was understandable that some of those observing the treatment of League players felt it necessary to make political representations over what seemed a marked discrimination against amateurs playing one particular sport.

The opening shot of one very key player in the campaign against Union's attitudes consisted of a lengthy letter sent on 18 October 1972 to the then Conservative Minister for Sport, Eldon Griffiths M.P. Written in his then capacity as press officer of the Huddersfield RL Referees Society, Maurice Oldroyd's representations pinpointed the "blatant discrimination" against amateur Rugby League players contained in the Rugby Union regulations on amateurism: "No person who is or has been associated with a non-amateur rugby club or organisation or an amateur club having any connection with a non-amateur organisation shall participate in the playing, refereeing, controlling, coaching, training, organising or administering of the game."[7]

His letter accepted that the Rugby Union "quite rightly and zealously guards its amateur status against the threat of the 30 non-amateur Rugby League clubs"[8] but pointed out the involvement of professional cricketers in Union and the willingness of the four home countries to play against a French national side containing known ex-professionals. While Oldroyd's acceptance of Union's right to defend itself against a perceived threat from professional Rugby League might now be questioned in the light of known widespread abuses of amateurism in Union itself, it is clear that his wider agenda then included the formal establishment of a separate identity for amateur Rugby League. The establishment of the British Amateur Rugby League Association - with Oldroyd as its national administrator - in 1973 was not only a long overdue attempt to organise the non-professional teams properly but also seen as a means of paving the way for an improved relationship with Union. In the terms used in the Union rule-book BARLA was an amateur rugby organisation administering amateur rugby teams.

While BARLA's early years saw considerable success in increasing the numbers playing the game, Union's rules remained unchanged. They were the subject of a formal meeting in 1975 between BARLA and the Labour Sports Minister, Denis Howell M.P., arranged by Michael Maguire M.P., then Labour M.P. for Ashton-in-Makerfield. During the following year several northern MPs who were backing BARLA's case tried unsuccessfully to meet the Rugby Football Union (RFU) face to face. As a subsequent press report made clear, interesting organisational difficulties prevented their dialogue. "The difficulty," explained the RFU's then secretary, Air Commodore Weighell, CBE, DFC, "is that our Committees all come together on Fridays, and Fridays are no good for MPs."[9]

The continued application of the Union rule quoted above by Oldroyd caused particular difficulties for the rapidly expanding number of colleges and universities taking up League with enthusiasm during the later 1970s. Numerous stories emerged of ban threats by university Rugby Union authorities intimidating League-playing students. A 38-year-old Maori, Bob Mahuta, is recorded as the first martyr to the cause. He had played Union in New Zealand all his life but was banned for good by the RFU for having played one game as a post-graduate student for Oxford University's fledgling amateur Rugby League team.

The growing battleground of university and college rugby was in many respects a consequence of wider developments in secondary education which were breaking down the divisions which I had experienced at school. Colin Welland - an 11-plus success and grammar school educated - noted this point in a *Guardian* article in 1979 which accused Twickenham of operating "Klan techniques" for eighty years. "At eleven, we were already learning to correlate Rugby Union with our social superiority. League, along with soccer, was the council school game, the dinner-time pursuit of men in overalls grunting and cursing on the works waste ground." But comprehensive education, he suggested, was ending all this with both League and Union often available to all. "No longer are the rules by which he kicks a football a refection of a child's social or professional aspirations."[10]

Writing in his annual report for 1979, BARLA's Chairman Tom Keaveney noted: "Regrettably, after seven years of honourable and gentle requests to change the situation, the Rugby Union continues unashamedly to victimise and intimidate any of its members who try to play our amateur sport." [11]

By then there were suggestions that the Sports Council's grants to Rugby Union might be withheld if it failed to alter its rules concerning amateur Rugby League. Its Yorkshire and Humberside Region Vice-Chairman, Bernard Atha, a Leeds Labour Councillor, undertook to look at whether the Sports Council was entitled to make grants to a sport which discriminated against another.

Union's difficulties

Union's own difficulties over its definition of amateurism had led to allegations that the former Wales full-back, J. P. R. Williams, had "professionalised" himself by writing a book; and its continued links with South Africa's apartheid regime had also raised eyebrows with the invitation to that country's Barbarians to tour Britain in 1979.

These developments no doubt contributed to concern and frustration over BARLA's patient diplomatic tactics and by 1980, while talks with the RFU were continuing "on an amicable basis and in a good atmosphere",[12] according to Oldroyd, others were being less polite. Ray French, the former Union and League international forward, argued that "sweet reasonableness" was no good, commenting: "The Union just chews up the words and spits them out."[13] Doug Laughton, the former Great Britain League skipper, was even more direct, saying: "It's time BARLA stopped pussyfooting".[14]

But if BARLA sought an alternative to direct dialogue with the RFU their options were constrained by Union dominance of the sporting and political establishment. The chairman of the Sports Council, Dickie Jeeps, was a former President of the RFU while Hector Munro M.P., the Sports Minister, had held a similar position in Scottish Rugby Union. And despite their involvement in polite dialogue on the issue, the RFU position appeared unaffected by BARLA's clearly independent organisation of amateur Rugby League. Another key figure in the affair - Alex Ramsey, the RFU President - made this clear at the 1980 annual dinner of Roundhay RUFC. Speaking of the amicable negotiations with BARLA, he added: "But we must always recognise that the Rugby Union will never agree to play with or against players who are classified in our interpretation of the word as 'professionals'."[15]

Exactly what their interpretation of "professionalism" was seemed by then to have become increasingly unclear. Some people were asking, for example, how Harlequins had funded the appearance of the All Black forward, Andy Haden, in the 1980 John Player competition and questioning the basis of his contract with the Italian club Gaffe Rima. Apparently he had "rugby player" as his profession in his passport. The French arrangements also caused particular interest when, in December of that year, their international Rugby League centre, Jean-Marc Bourret, was signed by Perpignan Rugby Union club for a reported fee of more than £20,000. The Rugby League magazine *Open Rugby* contrasted Bard's paying off a substantial debt to his former League club within days of joining Union, with amateur League players representing Liverpool University in the John Player Sevens competition requesting that their faces should not to be shown on television because of the fear of a Union ban.[16]

At almost the same time as Bourret was moving between the French codes, the RFU were making noises about relaxing somewhat their attitude towards former amateur League players wanting to play Union. A proposal aired at the RFU's AGM in 1981, for ratification by Union's International Rugby Football Board (IRB), proposed adjustments to the regulations on amateurism which, they argued, lifted all barriers to the movement of amateur players between codes. The acceptance of amateur League players into Union was dependent upon them having "ceased to be involved" in League. Despite protracted negotiations BARLA were no further forward in advancing the interests of those players who in many instances chose to play Union on Saturdays and League on Sundays. Union sources subsequently termed their new position as offering a "controlled gangway" compared to the BARLA aim of a free gangway.[17]

Elements within the Sports Council continued to be unhappy with the Union position. Its Yorkshire and Humberside regional council sent a telegram to the RFU on the day of their 1981 AGM stating that they viewed "with utter dismay" the proposal before the RFU's AGM to include a restrictive clause which would prevent the free movement of players between amateur codes of rugby.[18] In ignoring the regional council's concerns, the RFU was probably unaware that at the same council meeting it was agreed to urge Sports Council sanctions against the RFU and its clubs if the restrictive clause remained.

In March 1983 Union's IRB meeting amended the 1981 position to allow full-time students to play either code of rugby provided it was part of the named sporting activity within their college or university. The "concession" arose following a number of complaints made to the RFU by student bodies and a threat by the British Polytechnic Sports Association to cut off support for Rugby Union after alleged Union interference in the polytechnics' Rugby League competition.

It was business as usual that year at Milton Keynes, where a works' Rugby League team, Wheeler Transport XIII, an applicant for membership of the Southern Amateur Rugby League, which at that time operated in London and the south, folded following Union insistence that players could not belong to both a Union and League club.[19] Such rigid adherence to the amateurism rules, destroying attempts to develop League in non-traditional areas, stood alongside continued evidence during 1983 of a growing disregard of the amateurism rules within Union itself. The autobiography of Peter Wheeler, the England Union skipper, talked openly about boot money;[20] and even the BBC's Union broadcaster, Ian Robertson, was associated with a book alleging that the South Africans had poured something like £40,000 into a tour fund set up for the Rugby Union British Lions in 1980.[21]

The Observer's Rugby Union correspondent, Clem Thomas, wrote that he "could not recall a more unhappy and embattled year" for British Rugby Union. In summarising the events of 1983 he referred to the ongoing controversy over allegations that top Union internationals had been paid for wearing sports gear: "The evidence provided by the involvement of the Inland Revenue, and by the confession of Adidas that most of our leading players had been seduced by commercial interest and had transgressed the amateur laws, was irrefutable." He recalled that after unadvisedly suing the Daily Telegraph, J.P.R. Williams had admitted under oath that he had received beer money from Adidas, and had added: "we all know that he was only one of more than a hundred players involved".[22]

While Williams's situation put the Welsh Rugby Union in some difficulty, they were clearly on more comfortable ground towards the end of the year reminding their clubs in a circular that the amateurism regulations meant "that no amateur Rugby League player may be accepted into membership of a club whilst he is still involved in Rugby League football."[23] A Western Mail article, reporting this development in December 1983, noted that during June 1983, two months after the formation of the Welsh Amateur Rugby League, their paper had been told by the WRU: "that there was no WRU regulation preventing anyone playing both codes at an amateur level."[24] The Wales Amateur Rugby League secretary, Jeff Woods, was reported to be seeking legal advice on the situation and approaching the Sports Council for Wales to establish whether the Union position was contrary to the criteria under which they had received £100,000 in grants.

His concern was that four of the six clubs making up the WARL were university or college sides with some members also playing Union. BARLA saw the letter as contrary to the position of the IRB and a "positive act to stop the growth of amateur Rugby League in Wales, and particularly in the academic centres of the country."[25]

Writing about the WRU action in the Rugby Leaguer, Ray French argued that the statement was particularly designed to frighten students away from League at a time when it was having great success in higher education. He suggested that the WRU knew that their edict had no validity and proposed urgent legal action in the circumstances. "I have good counsel that no Union club, receiving Sports Council grants, can deny even a professional [my emphasis] from joining or taking part. By the very granting of sports aid all the facilities must be open to the public whether they be professional soccer, boxing, cricket (all of which can join a Rugby Union club) or Rugby League."[26]

French's belief that the Rugby Union was on questionable ground in denying even Rugby League professionals access to publicly funded facilities was strongly held and underpinned his growing impatience with the softly, softly approach in the relations between amateur Rugby League and Rugby Union. But the formal dialogue with Union for their permission to play League continued.

In March 1984, replying to a letter from BARLA's Tom Keaveney, the WRU secretary, Ray Williams, advised: "If a university student decides to play for an amateur Rugby League club in his own time and away from the educational system, he can on his return to his university play Rugby Union for his university in the educational system. Conversely, a university student who plays Rugby Union football in his own time and away from his university can play Rugby League in his university without breaking any regulations as far as Rugby Union is concerned."[27]

Attempts to organise Rugby League in the civil service during 1984 resulted in the usual difficulties with Union rules. A letter from the Civil Service Sports Council advised the secretary of the RFU that: "there would appear to be a desire by many Union players also to play Rugby League, within CSSC competitions. Are there any objections to them doing so?"[28] Air Commodore Weighell advised in a letter to the Civil Service Sports Council, dated 11 April 1984: "The simple rule of thumb is that you can't play both games at the same time so you cannot belong to two clubs, one playing Rugby Union football and one playing Rugby League football."

BARLA were frustrated as well by more covert attempts by teachers with a Union background to discourage schoolchildren from playing Rugby League. In May 1984 they were advised by the Sports Council to raise their concerns with Her Majesty's Inspectorate at the Department of Education and Science. Their subsequent representations detailed information concerning such allegations picked up by their National Coaching Scheme, headed at the time by Phil Larder. BARLA conceded the fact that "such attitudes are difficult to prove in substance as often parents are reluctant to pursue the matter for fear of consequences for their children," and drew attention as well to concerns over evidence of university and college students being intimidated by their tutors for wanting to try their hand at Rugby League football.[29]

The continued obstruction of attempts to develop League in schools, colleges, universities and among professional groups of workers led one Rugby League enthusiast to propose in May 1984 that a lobby should be established to take on the Welsh and English Rugby Unions over their attitudes to both amateur and professional Rugby League. In an *Open Rugby* magazine article picking up Ray French's earlier call for a legal challenge, the Keighley-based writer, Trevor Delaney, argued: "The time for discussions is over; it matters not one dot what this and that RU rule might say about the subject. They have been drafted all along to protect the position of the hypocritical body called the RU. The issue now is how we finance Counsel to make the RU come to heel in a Court of Law, if need be to the European Court of Human Rights."[30]

Delaney drew attention to the irony of an organisation called Freedom in Sport being formed with the support of one hundred Conservative MPs to back a proposed Rugby Union tour of apartheid South Africa, referring to the IRB's "apartheid" policies towards Rugby League. Delaney's call to arms, with the proposal for a Freedom in Rugby campaign, embraced a challenge on the professional front as well and was to prove an important milestone in the long road to free movement.

Flanshaw RLFC (1969-1970).
A 20-year old David Hinchliffe is pictured on the bottom row, second from the left. Harry Babbage (back row, second left) won Great Britain amateur honours, Alan Jude (with the ball) played for Yorkshire under-19s, Bob Harrison (bottom row, third from left) played as a professional with Doncaster RLFC. (Photo courtesy David Hinchliffe M.P.)

Walnut Warriors RLFC (1974-1975).
David Hinchliffe is one from the left on the front row. Shortly after this photo was taken, the team was coached by Peter Fox.
(Photo : Courtesy David Hinchliffe M.P.)

3: The Wagon & Horses Four

The King's Arms, Bridlington benefits each year from the influx of summer visitors to the pleasant east coast resort. But the summer of 1984 saw concern in that establishment over difficulties being faced in the setting-up of a Bridlington-based Rugby League team. Having learned of this development, Bridlington RUFC had written to all their playing members warning them of their exclusion from that club if they played for the new League team.

Over in West Yorkshire, four members of the Fairburn-based Wagon & Horses Rugby League team, near Castleford, made the fundamental mistake of being in the team photograph published in a local paper. Officials of Pontefract RUFC discovered they were also playing members of the Rugby League club and gave them each a one match ban.[31]

Alongside other sanctions at the time this penalty seems somewhat lenient but reflects perhaps the more liberal approach to enforcing the Union regulations in areas where League was well established. As I found out at Hemsworth RUFC, the smaller Union clubs frequently turned a blind eye to League 'miscreants' and by the mid-1980s were often themselves increasingly irritated by Twickenham's attitude. At some northern clubs, former Rugby League professionals were quietly playing Union, often using false names, but with their background known and accepted by their team mates.

The case of the Wagon & Horses Four and the King's Arms were precisely the kind of examples of petty interference in sporting rights that Trevor Delaney envisaged a proposed commission could examine in preparing a legal challenge to Union discrimination. In a statement published in the September 1984 edition of *Open Rugby* magazine, he suggested that such a body should involve various parties concerned with Rugby League, including BARLA, to take evidence from those affected, prior to recourse to the courts. He also proposed that pressing the Sports Minister and Public Accounts Committee to freeze Sports Council grants to Rugby Union should be key aims of the Freedom in Rugby Campaign.[32] Support would be sought from political parties and MPs.

BARLA welcomed the support of Delaney's campaign but following discussion of his proposals at its executive committee, wrote to him on 20 November, stating they felt "at this moment in time, with our current negotiations with the RFU, it would be counter-productive to consider challenging the issue in the courts".[33] Significantly, on the very same day, BARLA also wrote to Twickenham requesting a "resumption" of talks with the RFU.[34] They wrote as well to the IRB pressing for a review of the 1981 amendment of the amateurism regulations. In particular they requested the removal of the requirement for a player to have "ceased to be involved in" any other type of rugby before being allowed Union membership.

Bearing in mind the Union's concerns about RFL clubs poaching playing personnel, it is interesting to note that of the 27 players selected for Great Britain's Under-21 RFL side to play France that month, 24 were former BARLA Youth players, who had grown up in Rugby League and developed through that sport rather than in Union.[35]

While BARLA was resisting Freedom in Rugby's overtures to go to law, the leading proponent of such a challenge, Ray French, by now the BBC's Rugby League commentator, found personal cause to study the legalities of the Union position in late

1984. Having, in his teaching capacity, served 23 years on the Lancashire RU Schools' Committee he found himself banned from that committee for no apparent reason. Press reports suggested that the decision to introduce League alongside Union at his school in St Helens was behind his removal[36] and shortly before Christmas it was confirmed that Union regulation 3.9 relating to professionalism had been invoked.[37]

French noted in his *Rugby Leaguer* column that before the England Union trip to apartheid South Africa the RFU had issued a statement which read that they would "play against anyone of whatever colour, race or creed". Not so, he suggested, if you were "British, white and a believer in the integrity of both codes".[38] In consulting his trade union concerning the legal position, French was conscious not only of the continuing slur on Rugby League but also of the possible ramifications for his own teaching career. The RFU ruling was a restriction on his professional ability to take part in full extra-curricular activities.[39]

Early in the New Year, after French had refused to leave a Lancashire RU Schools Committee meeting, a Union retreat was reported with the RFU recommending to their IRB that schoolteachers should be allowed to participate in full at all levels of the Union game in schools. Writing in his local newspaper column, the former England Union captain, Bill Beaumont, commended the RFU on "a good and brave decision."[40]

This was not the first time Ray French had fallen foul of Union's rules for former Rugby League players. In his book *My Kinds of Rugby*, he outlines how he was invited to coach St Helens RUFC, but could not be seen openly in this role at matches. Despite arriving deliberately late for matches, and saying he was there just to watch players he had coached at school, his cover was eventually blown and he resigned, much to the regret of the young players he had been developing for the club.[41]

Former Great Britain international Cec Thompson had a similar experience. After retiring from Rugby League he went to Leeds University as a mature student and became a teacher. He became involved in coaching Union at school and went on an RFU coaching course. He was asked if he had played Rugby League and although he said he was an economist with an interest in rugby, was the only one on the course not to be given a certificate. Thompson was one of the first black players in England and the first to play for Great Britain. On occasions in society he experienced prejudice, but says that on this occasion he was "cold shouldered because I had played the 'wrong' sort of rugby".[42]

Pressure from the likes of Beaumont may have contributed indirectly to a renewed willingness by the RFU to a resumption of dialogue with BARLA. A letter from Air Commodore Weighell of the RFU on 18 February 1985 suggested that a meeting of the two organisations be held later in the year at the East India & Sports Club in St. James's Square, London. It had taken him since November 1984 to respond to BARLA's proposals and the meeting eventually took place on 25 April.

During the intervening period it was business as usual. Cheltenham RUFC refused to allow their council owned pitch to be used for a Rugby League international between the British and French universities because of a clause in the lease which prevented the playing of Rugby League on it.[43] "Fears of reprisals from Rugby Union authorities" were said to be holding back some students from declaring themselves available for that year's Oxford versus Cambridge Varsity Rugby League match and civil servants in the south-west received an official warning via the Civil Service noticeboard of the possible serious consequences of playing Rugby League.[44]

The very obvious progress being made at the time in the establishment of amateur Rugby League in the south, and further north in the Midlands, was evidenced by growing reports of action taken by Union clubs against players involved in League. John Hughes, a promising young prop, was dropped from the Cheltenham and District Combination Under-21s Union side specifically because he had played League. One of the selectors concerned said: "He didn't comply with the rule. You can't play for two codes at once; you must make decisions about one code or the other". When Hughes was asked whether, if such intimidation was removed, there would be increased interest in playing League, he said: "There would be an absolute landslide towards the game".[45]

Representatives of the Redditch Halcyon amateur RL club in Worcestershire detailed in a letter to BARLA, on 14 March 1985, a series of attempts made to threaten and intimidate League players. It alleged that an official of Redditch RUFC had warned a player that his Rugby Union intermediate coaching certificate could be withdrawn if he continued playing Rugby League. Yardley RUFC in Birmingham had posted a press report of the scorers in a Redditch Halcyon RL match on the club noticeboard and verbally warned the players concerned that they could lose their status with the Union club if they continued playing Rugby League. The players were forced into using false names. At Brocksworth RUFC, in Gloucester, a player was asked to think about the possible consequences for the Union club in terms of exclusion from cup competitions if he continued playing League and at the nearby Longleven RUFC a player was warned of a likely ban by the RFU if he continued with similar conduct.[46]

The newly formed Worcester ARLFC were told that their players would not be allowed to share the local Rugby Union club bar and training facilities,[47] while over in Wales access to the Cardiff Athletic Club was even more proscriptive. The *Daily Express* reported that, in applying to join the football section, prospective members were required to declare specifically that they had not "at any time been engaged in the playing, administration, promotion or fostering of Rugby League, or any other professional rugby football".[48]

Such attitudes, according to *The Guardian*'s Paul Fitzpatrick, were the "cheap, shabby reason why Rugby Union has been able to flourish as a national sport while League has largely been confined within its northern boundaries". He quoted BARLA's belief that they represented the last "sporting anachronism of the age".[49]

There were however continued differences over the most effective means of addressing the anachronism. Ray French feared that BARLA were 'stalling' and *Open Rugby*'s Harry Edgar questioned not only BARLA's approach but also that of the Sports Council. He contrasted the treatment of Rugby League players by Union clubs with the reported payment of £250 a week "expenses" to the "amateur" Australian Rugby Union tourists.[50]

BARLA were at the time continuing to press for the amendment of the Union rule paragraph 3.8, requiring their players to have "ceased to be involved" in Rugby League, with letters being sent by Maurice Oldroyd to both the RFU at Twickenham and the IRB on 12 March 1985. The IRB's reply to BARLA on 1 April indicated that the Board had decided that "some review of the regulations was appropriate in the light of developments that appear to be taking place in amateurism in general." They proposed that "principles should be established which are relevant to the playing and administering of rugby football in modern times." The letter, from the Board's secretary, John G. M. Hart, concluded: "I hope you can be patient a little longer."[51]

However, the patience of Rugby League followers was further tested by the revelation at its March meeting in Paris, that the IRB had, for reasons not unconnected with promoting Union in the USA, agreed to allow professional gridiron footballers to play the Union game. It was both "ludicrous and tragic" according to Oldroyd: "Rugby Union players can play every other professional-based sport but Rugby League."[52]

Freedom in Rugby

The men who assembled at the George Hotel, Huddersfield, on Saturday, 30 March 1985 were probably very different in social background from those who had gathered in the same establishment for the breakaway decision of 1895. But, 90 years on, the agenda had a very similar theme - opposition to the Union establishment - with the inaugural meeting of the Freedom in Rugby Campaign.

While the meeting in 1895 brought to Huddersfield club representatives whose concerns were parochial and pragmatic, Trevor Delaney's initiative drew together a number of individuals whose vision for Rugby League was frustrated continually by Union discrimination. With Delaney acting as secretary/treasurer, other officers elected that day included as chairman, Martyn Sadler, a Sheffield university lecturer who subsequently played a key role in founding the *League Express* newspaper. His press officer was Dr Peter Harrison, a York GP, and committee members included Lionel Hurst, a Cheltenham-based solicitor, and two doctors of philosophy, Mark Newbrook and Brian Burkitt.

Collectively they set out to articulate the fact that Rugby League had tolerated Union's rulings for far too long. Their aim was: "To ensure all rugby players and officials the freedom to play, and otherwise be involved in either code of rugby at any time and in any country of their own choosing."[53]

The programme the campaign agreed that day recognised the need to counteract the widespread belief that League was solely a professional sport. They proposed publicising "the nature of both codes", drawing attention to the myth that Union was totally amateur. As well as lobbying politicians and the Sports Council on grants to Union they resolved "to support legal action which is necessary to bring about the aim of the campaign if all other measures fail."

Not long after the campaign's inaugural meeting, Lionel Hurst advised BARLA of a discussion he had had with a Manchester-based QC who had proposed obtaining statements from players who had experienced discrimination, prior to initial representations to the Sports Council.[54] Maurice Oldroyd, who was due to meet the RFU at the East India Club on 25 April, replied two days earlier that BARLA "would like, at this stage, to pursue an avenue of amicable but constructive negotiations". He concluded: "We must complete the round of discussions that we are commencing, and only then will it be possible to decide which course of action to pursue to bring about the result we all so earnestly desire."[55]

An internal Sports Council briefing paper, produced the following month noted that RFU representatives at the recent meeting with BARLA had agreed to put their concerns regarding the eight offending words of paragraph 3.8 to the appropriate sub-committee of the Union. If the revision was accepted by the RFU it would be necessary for 75 per cent of the International Board to agree to the change at their meeting in March 1986. The paper noted that £170,000 in grants was being paid to the RFU and its affiliated clubs in 1983-84. "The legitimacy of these grants are [*sic*] being widely questioned in the press, by politicians and by members of the public," it added.[56]

Continued pressure on the Government over the matter resulted in representations being made to Twickenham by the new Sports Minister, Neil McFarlane M.P., on 15 May. In his reply of 19 June, Albert Agar, the RFU President, argued that BARLA remained very close to the professional game and that "this association with the professional game cannot be reconciled with IRB regulations".[57] Such concerns about this "close" relationship indicated how little the RFU knew about the respective roles of BARLA and the RFL. The distinct lack of such a relationship had been a source of immense frustration to those concerned with the development of Rugby League over many years.

Agar concluded his response to the Minister by assuring him that both "amateur" bodies were "working towards the harmony which hopefully will silence the criticism which is directed at us by those who are ignorant of the true facts and are intent on making mischief."

Accusations of ignorance and deliberate mischief-making became increasingly used as a defence by Union. Brigadier Dennis Shuttleworth, who succeeded Agar as RFU President in 1985, suggested that the Union had not been given sufficient credit for making very significant concessions towards amateur Rugby League. "It is amazing how many people do not realise that the Rugby Union now has no objections to any amateurs of any age playing both games as long as they don't do it simultaneously," he told the *Yorkshire Post*.[58]

The assertion that critics of Union's rules were unaware of the actual position was somewhat wide of the mark as far as the Sports Council were concerned. They were only too aware of the practical implications of Union's rules, despite the supposed concessionary changes. In a briefing note sent from the Sports Council's Yorkshire and Humberside Regional Office on 23 July 1985, prior to a national meeting with the RFU, particular attention was drawn to "the discriminatory nature of the additional law and interpretation of the International Law by the RFU concerning students in higher education". The memorandum, sent from Robin Barron in Yorkshire to Joe Patton at the Sports Council head office, alleged: "This law obviously operates to the benefit of a very, very small minority of gifted academic students. It is extremely discriminatory against those who continue their education within the further education sector and, perhaps, not even in full-time education".[59]

Barron's understandable concern related to the consequences of the IRB's 1983 rule changes, which, in his view, had resulted in students who attended local colleges in their home areas having less freedom to cross codes than those who moved away from home to go to university.

At the start of the 1985-86 season Union came close to League's approach to competition with the introduction of league tables, after years of warning of the inherent dangers of their being part of the slide towards professionalism. A full national league competition and commercial sponsorship followed in 1987-88. While the ethos underpinning Union competitions appeared to be changing, attitudes towards the development of League in non-traditional areas remained unchanged. In August BARLA found it necessary to raise with the chairman of the Sports Council, John Smith, difficulties which had occurred at the Tyneside summer festival Rugby League competition. According to Maurice Oldroyd, "Players who took part were actually scared their names be disclosed for fear of discrimination by their Rugby Union club on their return."[60]

Later that month, Allan Scott, a Northumberland-based schoolteacher, wrote on behalf of Scotswood ARLFC to the Sports Council setting out the difficulties facing those trying to establish League in the north-east. He described their experience of being turned off pitches used by Union teams until Newcastle City Council intervened; and detailed threats to League players concerning the loss of Union club membership. "One player in an academic establishment is very worried about his progress in his academic work because of a warning previously received about playing Rugby League. The establishment in question runs a Rugby Union team and the academic staff run the rugby side." Scott further alleged that he and his club had been subject to spying missions on behalf of Union. "I have received requests of information about amateur Rugby League by supposed interested newcomers. These people have only come along to look at who was playing, make note and return, as I have found out, to their own Rugby Union clubs," he wrote.[61]

"A great delight. First class people."

Representations of this kind to the Sports Council were accompanied by increasing pressure for action from the Freedom in Rugby Campaign and sympathetic correspondents in the national press. In a strongly worded attack on the RFU, the *Mail on Sunday*'s Patrick Collins accused Air Commodore Weighell of playing the role of King Canute. Weighell's defence was that "Rugby League is, in essence, professional ... Not that I've got anything against Rugby League men. I've played with a lot of very good League people in the services. A great delight. First-class people." But, he added: "Our rules stand and we shall not be changing. As for withdrawing the Sports Council grant, I really can't believe it. And now I think I must terminate this discussion." Collins concluded of Twickenham: "... their ranks are closed, their eyes are shut ... and their ears are stuffed with dusty rule books."[62]

Moves to block assistance to Union from the Sports Council were accompanied by growing demands on local authorities to consider whether their support for local Union clubs, using ratepayers' money, was appropriate in view of their discriminatory rules. As a member of the Wakefield Metropolitan District Council, I was criticised by local Union followers for asking whether continued public support for Union could be justified and nine miles up the road in Leeds the city council incurred even more Union wrath by appointing a rugby development officer whose brief solely concerned League.

The row over their decision was deemed to be a positive and deliberate snub to Union because funding had been made available through the Sports Council to ensure that both games were addressed. The matter was raised at the September meeting of the Yorkshire RFU committee but the issue was to go considerably further. By 1 November, Air Commodore Weighell was on the telephone to BARLA. First of all he indicated that the RFU were writing to follow up the April meeting between the two bodies - "news is not good" - then indicated that the RFU were "hot under the collar" over the Leeds appointment which they alleged was "discriminatory"! The RFU had protested strongly to the Sports Council and also complained to the Minister for Sport.

So stirred up was the *Yorkshire Evening Post*'s Union correspondent, Tony Simpson, that he found it necessary to challenge what he saw as common perceptions of Union folk. Critics of Union, he suggested, loved to portray it as a game for "irresponsible, often drunk, always snobby 'hooray Henrys' who all have blue blood, blue suits and blue voting papers". While it was convenient that the Secretary of the RFU happened to be an Air Commodore and there were people "who have the standard issue international match uniform of brogues, twills and sheepskins", the critical rhetoric of Union's opponents was "'as absurd as it is ill-informed".[63]

By bonfire night, Air Commander Weighell's earlier hints to BARLA had been confirmed in a letter which indicated the RFU's inability to meet their request for the deletion of "... and who has ceased to be so involved" from regulation 3.8. These were the words which prevented players playing both Rugby League and Union, for example playing one code on Saturday and the other on Sunday, as I did in my younger days.

Their objection to what they viewed as proposals for a free gangway related to concerns over order in the movement of players, control for disciplinary purposes and the avoidance of the over-playing of young players. Weighell's letter to BARLA emphasised that: "The maintenance and nurturing of club loyalty and standards is a matter of considerable importance to us and in our view would be undermined by a 'free gangway'." He concluded that "the cry of 'discrimination' which is often raised is now unreasonable, emotional, inaccurate and old-fashioned." The RFU intended to do all in its power to keep Rugby Union football "truly amateur".[64]

BARLA's immediate response was a letter to the Sports Council chairman, John Smith, pointing out that they had been "very patient and more than reasonable" in negotiating to bring about an amicable solution. They pressed the Sports Council to reconsider its position in view of the Union intransigence.[65]

The particular frustration of those in development areas was impressed upon the Sports Council by Bristol ARLFC's Dave Smith shortly after the latest Union snub. Having appealed to them over the usual difficulties his club was experiencing within the local Union side, the Aretians, Smith drew attention to the Sports Council grant-aid being available only where the sport was open to all regardless of creed, race or religion. Writing to their Director-General, John Wheatley, he wondered "whether the officers of the Sports Council are culpable in that they dispense money to the RFU which appears to be in contravention of a Royal Charter." Writing with an obviously detailed knowledge of other sports he concluded, "I wonder how well badminton would develop if the Squash Rackets Association told its players they couldn't play squash, unless they promised never to play badminton again."[66]

Maurice Oldroyd picked up this last point in a strongly worded public statement at the end of November in which he indicated that the crux of future discussions with BARLA would be whether the two codes were separate sports. Asserting the separate existence of League, he speculated on what would happen if other organisations followed Union's example. He argued that: "Players would be banned from playing more than one bat-and- ball game... what about soccer and Gaelic football? Australian Rules is played with an oval ball but does the Rugby Union ban their players?"[67]

After the publication of Weighell's response to BARLA as an open letter in *Rugby World and Post*, a Union journal, Freedom in Rugby's Peter Harrison wrote a detailed response alleging that at the age of 18, or, in the case of full time students, the early 20s, "the RFU forces players to choose which game they cannot play".[68] At the same time his colleague Trevor Delaney was in touch with the *Tribunal Arbitral du Sport* in Lausanne in an attempt to establish whether their independent arbitration might be a possibility. The fact that cases coming to the *Tribunal* for decision were brought before it by special agreement between the disputing parties posed fairly obvious problems.

On 27 November 1985, the Welsh Union player, Steve Ford, received a life ban from Union after it emerged that he had played three trial matches as an amateur receiving only expenses with Leeds RLFC in the previous month. His brother, Phil Ford, had previously switched to League and had a successful career, ironically finishing his rugby days in Union after that sport went professional in 1995.

In the same week, the Welsh Union skipper, Terry Holmes, accepted a £100,000 three-year contract with Bradford Northern. The *Mail on Sunday*'s Patrick Collins wrote that, in Union terms, he had concluded "a Faustian bargain with the forces of darkness" and was now banished for good from his former code. In another stinging attack on Union's curious moral ground, he highlighted the way gifted players were attracted to Union clubs on the promise of jobs or houses, star players were receiving illicit fees from sports equipment manufacturers and "many of their brightest and best are being rewarded in readies for after-dinner speaking engagements or schoolboy coaching courses".[69] Jonathan Davies recalls in his autobiography being paid £400 for an after-dinner speech in 1988 "which I did not mention to anyone except the Inland Revenue".[70] The Union authorities did nothing about such activities but turned the likes of Ford and Holmes into persona-non-grata, Collins argued: "A game which willingly, eagerly leaps into bed with Southern Africa will not trust itself to hold the hand of Northern England."[71]

Even the *Sunday Telegraph* found it necessary to make editorial comment concerning Union's treatment of League players. "At best, Twickenham's reasons for perpetuating this injustice are specious: at worst, the ruling is an infringement of individual liberty, and the suspicion must remain that Twickenham's intransigence is based more on ingrained prejudice and snobbery than on the evidence to hand."[72]

In the first of a series of Parliamentary initiatives concerning the RFU's attitudes, the Wigan M.P., Roger Stott, tabled an early-day motion on 11 December 1985, condemning Twickenham's refusal of BARLA's request for a free gangway. Supported by 25 Northern Labour MPs, including Lewis Carter-Jones, a former Welsh Rugby Union referee, representing Eccles, Stott's motion described the RFU attitude as "nothing short of apartheid" and called upon the Minister of Sport to "instruct the Sports Council not to pay more taxpayers' money to the RFU until this unacceptable discrimination ends".[73]

The original purpose of such parliamentary motions was to point to the level of support among MPs for a debate on the subject matter on "an early day" and the support for Stott's call was indicative of concern over the treatment of amateur Rugby League. He subsequently established through a parliamentary question on 16 December 1985, that the RFU and Rugby Football Schools Union had received Sports Council grant-aid for the game in England alone totalling £161,079 between 1980-81 and 1984-85 and capital grants totalling £321,727 for 1983-84 and 1984-85.[74]

While the parliamentary "apartheid" claims were strenuously denied by RFU representatives, the willingness of Sports Council officials to meet the Freedom in Rugby campaign shortly before Christmas 1985, showed that they were now taking the matter very seriously. Press reports indicated that this was the first occasion the Council had officially met members of a pressure group.[75]

The Council was officially represented by Air Vice-Marshal Larry Lamb, formerly of the RFU, John Wheatley, the director-general, and Joe Patton, the officer directly responsible for both codes. Martyn Sadler, Freedom in Rugby's chairman, was positive about the outcome of the meeting: "The points we put to them were that the Rugby Union rules are a restriction on personal liberty, restrict the development of amateur Rugby League and fly in the face of the Sports Council's policy of not granting aid to any body which operates restrictive practices," he said.[76] He understood that the officials would put their case to the full Sports Council in the New Year.

The *Yorkshire Post* reported that if the Sports Council failed to act against the RFU "there are people waiting in the wings to issue writs against both of them".[77] Whether this was completely true is uncertain but the Freedom in Rugby campaign was certainly giving the public the impression of having sought legal advice and believing they had a good case. With the active involvement of solicitor Lionel Hurst they obviously would have had access to well-informed opinion.

In a strongly worded article shortly after the campaign's meeting with the Sports Council, Ray French vented his frustration over the apparent weakness of BARLA's tactics. "BARLA should be ashamed of itself," he said. "You don't knock fortifications down with snowballs - they melt away. And that is all we have been doing for the past ten years."[78] French referred to the various recent national press articles supporting the cause of amateur Rugby League and made particular reference to the interest of the former England Rugby Union player, Derek Wyatt, a leading figure in the campaigns against tours to South Africa (and elected as a Labour M.P. in 1997), who had made clear his belief that Rugby Union should be subject to legal action over its discriminatory practices.

French was probably unaware that BARLA had received advice on the RFU's legal position. Charity law in relation to status within taxation arrangements was considered alongside the restraint of trade issue which was to be touched on again during the next decade. While obviously amateurs had no "trade" as such that could be "restrained" there was some suggestion that any associated consequences of a Union ban might form the basis for a court action.

Both BARLA and Freedom in Rugby were on much firmer ground in believing that the Sports Council had within its power a simpler and cheaper solution, as Sadler had implied after the meeting with their representatives. In early January 1986 the campaign's Peter Harrison followed up their contact with a letter to the Council stating that their representatives had been "alarmed to hear that, although the Sports Council has repeatedly had the problem brought to its attention over the last ten years, discussion in full council has not taken place."

Bearing in mind that the Union-League dispute had already been widely publicised for many years and also been, as Harrison indicated, the subject of numerous representations involving their Regional Councils and even MPs and ministers, it was astonishing that the full council had not considered it. Less charitable sources might have suggested that such consideration had been deliberately avoided through top level Union influence.

Harrison's letter to *Rugby World and Post* drew an interesting response from the World Freedom in Sport organisation's chairman, Tommie Campbell of Dublin, who indicated that many within Rugby Union were dissatisfied with their attitudes. He wrote: "The Dinosaur Democracy existing within the Halls of Power cannot go on.

Being in close touch with many top players and their minders, I know there will be a violent shattering of these imperfect ideals in the not too distant future."[79]

Harrison's efforts also drew a response from the *Yorkshire Post*'s Rugby Union correspondent Bill Bridge. Writing in the January 1986 edition of *Rugby News* he described the "long and occasionally dirty fight to retain Union's standing in the face of an all-out attack from the British Amateur Rugby League Association." He accused BARLA, and Maurice Oldroyd in particular, of severely misrepresenting the Union position in the media, concluding that "the battle is being lost at the moment by fair means or foul."[80]

Roger Stott M.P. was unimpressed by such Union propaganda and followed up his early-day motion and parliamentary question with a letter to the Sports Minister, Richard Tracey M.P., pointing out that the public expenditure on Union recently identified "is no longer tenable given the fact that they practise this discrimination against amateur Rugby League". Stott asked the Minister whether he was satisfied that the terms of reference under which the Sports Council operated - "Sport for all" - were being observed in the true sense by the RFU. "It is my contention that you can come to no other conclusion than that the RFU and its attitude towards amateur Rugby League is outwith that concept and, accordingly, unless and until they change their rules they should be provided with no further taxpayers' money," he wrote.[81]

The battleground was joined early in the New Year of 1986 by another force. Following confirmation by the Welsh Rugby Union that Steve Ford was banned for life for breaking the amateurism regulations through his contact with Leeds RLFC, the Rugby Football League entered the fray, generating "Rugby at War" headlines in the national press.[82]

The Rugby Football League secretary at the time, David Oxley, indicated that the Ford affair would be discussed by the Rugby League Council, the governing body of professional Rugby League clubs. He stated that: "The Rugby Union's attitude can no longer be tolerated." Until that point the RFL, he said, had kept out of discussions with the RFU, taking the view that it was better for BARLA to provide the contact between the two sports. The treatment of Ford, however, had prompted their involvement. "For a governing body of sport in Britain to say their members can play alongside any professional sportsmen so long as they are not Rugby League players is totally unacceptable discrimination," he added.[83]

Much of the public debate around the Ford affair concentrated on whether, as a trialist with a professional Rugby League side, he was in fact in breach of the amateurism regulations. The Leeds RLFC football chairman, Harry Jepson, insisted that Ford, who had returned to Wales after the trial matches, did not receive a signing on fee or any match fee. "The only money he received from Leeds was for legitimate expenses", Jepson claimed. "In no way did he infringe his amateur status. The Rugby Union also allows their players expenses."[84]

Ford himself confirmed: "Without doubt the claims of 30 to 40 (Welsh) Union players doing what I did up north each season are true," and Oxley was reported to be both considering court action and threatening to release names of others in the Welsh Union side who had played League trials.[85] The *Daily Express* implored him not to take this latter course of action. "To expose them would be to sink to the lowest depths ... the depths plumbed by the Welsh RU in their attitude to Steve Ford."[86] In addition to the public debate over Ford, Ray Mordt, who had recently signed for Wigan from

Union in South Africa, fuelled the row with claims of receiving payment in the "amateur" code.[87]

Against this battery of assaults there were few defences offered by Union other than a reference to their rule book. The Welsh RU secretary, Ray Williams, made clear that the IRB regulations stated clearly that anyone playing in a trial for a professional club would lose their amateur status.[88] Writing in the paper which had named Ford as a Leeds "signing" on 8 October the previous year, the *Yorkshire Evening Post*'s Union writer, Tony Simpson, wondered what all the fuss was about. "The bye-laws may be asinine to those who do not cherish amateur principles so dearly, but their implementation should not bring such a shocked response from those who ought to know better."[89]

Political muscle

The involvement of the Rugby Football League in the aftermath of the Steve Ford affair obviously strengthened the political muscle of those engaged in the battle. David Oxley was a respected figure in British sport and had long-standing connections with senior figures in both main political parties. The treatment of Ford resulted in the RFL receiving offers of help from politicians, the legal profession and other sports bodies,[90] but they were circumspect as to the way they intended to take things forward.

The Welsh RU were certain that their legal position on Ford could not be challenged and while, following a Rugby League Council meeting on 8 January 1986, the RFL announced a proposal to seek legal advice, the main thrust of their challenge appeared to be directed towards pressurising the Central Council for Physical Recreation (CCPR) and the Sports Council into action. *The Guardian*'s Paul Fitzpatrick wrote that the League felt "they must construct a watertight case before deciding their best method of attack. They think this is a once and for all opportunity to put an end to Union discrimination, but are aware that a false step could rebound on them."[91]

The RFL faced greater difficulties than BARLA in establishing whether a legal challenge might be mounted. As Ray Williams had indicated, the Union rules were quite clear on professional trials and, as Ford had gone back to Wales with the declared intention of returning to Union, a legal action in his name was presumably out of the question. Instead, there were suggestions that the treatment of Ford could possibly be pursued as a human rights issue.[92]

BARLA continued to pressurise the Sports Council with a letter from Maurice Oldroyd to John Wheatley, their director-general, on 15 January 1986, saying that, understandably, both their organisations were "receiving strong criticism from many quarters". Oldroyd pressed for the Sports Council to put the RFU/BARLA issue on the agenda for their February meeting, in view of the IRB's likely consideration of the "amateurism" issue at their April meeting. Pointing to 13 years of patient dialogue with Union, Oldroyd concluded: "Sadly their intransigence leaves BARLA helpless on the subject..."[93]

Oldroyd's call to Wheatley was supported within the Sports Council itself with a resolution from its Yorkshire and Humberside regional council in Leeds, pressing the parent body to consider sanctions against Union before their International Board meeting in April. The regional body's vice-chairman, the then deputy leader of South Yorkshire Metropolitan County Council, John Cornwell, reminded his national colleagues that they had thought it necessary to telegraph the RFU five years earlier over the position and, despite the efforts of BARLA, they were still no further forward.[94] Wheatley's response indicated that the full Sports Council would fully consider the matter at their meeting in March 1986.[95]

The selection of Naas Botha for the South African RU party to play matches later in the year in Britain strongly reinforced the view that Union's regulations were anti-league rather than anti-professionalism. The former American Football professional was included in an international squad chosen to play matches in April at both Cardiff and Twickenham in celebration of the IRB's centenary.

Such apparent inconsistencies were usually ignored as Union officials continued to point to the "lies" and "inaccuracies" being peddled about their attitude to Rugby League. In an article in the *Yorkshire Post*, the Yorkshire RFU secretary, Roy Manock, claimed: "Rugby Union welcomes amateur Rugby League players" but reiterated Air Commodore Weighell's reasons for objecting to a complete free gangway. He concluded by drawing attention to the unique sporting quality shared by both League and Union: "The respect of the authority of the referee - which is missing in many sports."[96]

One referee who was less than happy with the Yorkshire RFU's respect for his authority saw fit to respond to Manock's article, outlining his own experiences. David Shaw, like myself, had found himself on the wrong side of Sandal RUFC's enforcement of Union regulations. Writing in the *Yorkshire Post*, he said that he had been fixture secretary for the junior section at Sandal and a member of the Wakefield Rugby League Referees' Society. He had been summoned before Mr Manock's Yorkshire Rugby Union's disciplinary committee - "sitting with the players who had been sent off for foul play' - after his photograph had appeared in a local newspaper refereeing the Ossett Trinity versus Eastmoor amateur Rugby League match. This type of action against those involved in League was, he claimed, commonplace and, "as a result of such intimidation many players naturally become too scared to try the amateur League game because they know they will be 'excommunicated' by their so-called friends for their crime."[97]

There was now some concern as to whether Twickenham were simply enacting IRB regulations, as they implied in their attitudes towards Rugby League. In a memorandum to John Wheatley on 29 January 1986, the Yorkshire and Humberside Council secretary, Cyril Villiers, queried whether the way forward was, as had been assumed, persuading the RFU to recommend an amendment to the IRB's rules. He noted that on 26 June 1981 Air Commodore Weighell had advised BARLA that, the IRB, at its meeting in March of that year, had changed their regulation to allow free movement between the two codes, with no restrictions. Villiers pointed out however that in accordance with an IRB bye-law, allowing constituent bodies to vary the laws according to local needs, the RFU had themselves at their 1981 AGM introduced the "ceased to be so involved" provision. He concluded: "I think you will note from this, therefore, that in fact the RFU's attempt to blame everything on the International Board is far from the truth and that they themselves are the guilty party."[98]

It is doubtful whether the Sports Minister, Richard Tracey, was aware of this point when he framed his reply to Roger Stott on 31 January. His answer indicated that the disbursement of grants to the RFU and its clubs was not, in the Sports Council's opinion of, at variance with the financial memorandum governing its activities. Tracey failed to answer Stott's question regarding his own opinion on the position but said that he understood "that officers of the Council do not believe that applying financial pressure to the RFU would be an effective or proper course of action for them to take at this stage".[99]

Tracey's letter confirmed that the Sports Council would be considering the dispute at its March meeting. But before that took place, the Council's chairman, John Smith, outlined proposals to meet both BARLA and the RFU separately. His public comments at the time evidenced more than a little sympathy with the Rugby League cause. "The situation is bringing sport into disrepute," he told the *Daily Telegraph*. "We may fail in our attempts, but it is incumbent upon us to try to get the RFU to change its position. The historic absurdity is that RFU rules specifically bar their players from taking part in amateur Rugby League games even though they can participate in any other sport [amateur or professional] of their choice."[100]

The battle in Wales

Smith's comments as a "neutral" key player perhaps indicated that some progress was being made in BARLA's lengthy campaign for justice. The RFL's involvement following the Steve Ford affair had ensured that the grievance over discrimination against League was the subject of detailed debate on the sports pages and there were even indications of a possible shift in position in Union circles. The BBC Wales's, *Week In, Week Out* television programme, looking at the Ford case on 18 February 1986, carried an interview with the WRU secretary, Ray Williams, in which he indicated that his organisation was calling for a total review of IRFU regulations on "amateurism". "My feeling of the situation relating to the amateur regulation is that the laws are not in tune with the kind of society in which we are now living; as a committee we have for some time been trying to get some of these regulations changed," he said.[101]

Williams was perhaps faced with more practical difficulties in administering the regulations than his Twickenham counterpart. In the same BBC programme, the Morley and Leeds South Labour M.P., Merlyn Rees, spoke of a list of between 200 to 300 names of past and present Welsh Union players who had been involved in professional Rugby League. "Should Rugby League go to court on behalf of the banned Cardiff wing, Steve Ford, and a top barrister has said they have a good case, the list will be subpoenaed and the names read out," he alleged.[102] "Some of these names are in high places in the Welsh Rugby Union who found themselves in the same position as Steve Ford, except that Ford got banned. The Rugby League authorities have no intention of releasing their names, but if the affair came to court they would have no choice. Officials of the WRU could end up in court having to defend these accusations and being drummed out of Rugby Union."[103]

Rees became a key player in the parliamentary battle for free movement between the codes. As a Welshman with Union roots, he had come north to succeed the former Labour leader, Hugh Gaitskell, as the M.P. for South Leeds after Gaitskell had died in 1963, at a time when Hunslet Rugby League club, in his new constituency, were riding high. He grew to love League and to understand the deep feelings of injustice over the game's treatment by Union. In view of his knowledge of both codes he probably realised the likely dangers of a strategy of "naming names". During the subsequent vigorous parliamentary campaign on rugby discrimination in the 1990s those involved recognised that such an approach could have the effect of turning Union people sympathetic to League against the cause.

While Rees's comments were exercising minds in Wales, his colleague, Roger Stott, had been making use of the resources of the House of Commons library following Richard Tracey's rather disappointing reply in late January. His enquiries raised serious questions about the assurance Tracey had received over the criteria for Sports Council funding as he studied the details of the library's copy of the council's financial memorandum. In particular, clause 8 caught his eye, stating that: "It shall be a condition of capital grant that the recipient will repay the amount of the grant or will surrender a proportion of any relevant enhanced property or land value, whichever is the greater, if, within an acceptable time, the facility ceases to be used by the recipient for the purpose for which grant was given *or if membership ceases to be open to all*" [my emphasis].[104]

Stott wrote to the Sports Council chairman, John Smith, on 24 February 1986, quoting Tracey's reply and drawing his attention to the apparently contradictory information contained in clause 8. Referring to the parliamentary answer indicating capital grants to the RFU of £321,727, he pointed out that by their refusal to allow a free gangway with League, such funding was "in direct contravention of the Sports Council's memorandum."[105]

Stott's covering note to Maurice Oldroyd, with a copy of the letter to Smith, indicated his belief in the significance of this development. "I think we may have got them by the balls," he wrote. The reply from Smith was more formal. He was meeting with the RFU and BARLA and the contents of his letter had been "duly noted".[106]

While Smith was discussing matters in London, representatives of the Welsh Amateur Rugby League were meeting Ray Williams of the Welsh RU in Cardiff. Their discussions on 11 March 1986 concerned the Union's regulation 3.8 (which prevented playing both codes even as an amateur). WARLA's chairman, Phil Melling, the vice-chairman, Clive Millman, and the secretary-treasurer, Danny Sheehy, were interested to learn that the WRU were not only against the regulation but also predicting its removal within the next 12 months. Williams confirmed Cyril Villiers's view that following the removal of restrictions on amateur Rugby League players it was only upon the insistence of the RFU that the offending regulation had remained.[107]

Millman's subsequent letter to BARLA, advising them of the result of the meeting, reflected the generally positive outcome, suggesting there was "a real chance of success at the forthcoming IRB meeting".[108] He urged BARLA to send a statement of its case to the International Board members of all the Unions involved in the hope that they might back any proposal for change from the WRU.

Millman's assessment of the prospect of radical change at the IRB meeting held in April proved somewhat optimistic. While the amateurism question was the subject of considerable debate at the International Rugby Board Centenary Congress, preceding the annual Board meeting, the end result seems to have emphasised the difference in approach between the various members as opposed to any real consensus as to the way forward.[109] There were obvious differences in interpretation of existing IRB regulations on, for example, the payment of allowances for touring players. Of these differences, one Union correspondent asked the question: "When do reasonable subsistence payments become broken-time payments?" Just over 90 years after 1895, he was recalling the reason for the split by the Northern Union - "broken-time" payments for players who had to miss work to play.[110]

While the Board's deliberations were overshadowed by concerns over the tour of South Africa by an unofficial (and usually recognised as "professional") New Zealand Cavaliers side, it did find time to propose some limited steps to relax the rigid restrictions on financial payments to some people involved in Union. After controversy over earnings from books written by former internationals Bill Beaumont, Fran Cotton and Gareth Edwards, the Board agreed that once a player had retired he could freely comment in books, on radio or television and still be involved in coaching or administration.

Although Clive Millman's predictions were a little premature, Ray Williams's suggestion of significant change within the year was to prove spot on. Despite the lack of any obvious progress at the IRB, a few days later the RFU announced that it would be proposing to the 1987 meeting that players should be free to play amateur Rugby League while still members of Rugby Union clubs.[111] The announcement made on 1 May was no magnanimous gesture to the workers on Labour Day. It was a simple acceptance of the fact that, using Stott's terminology, their opponents had indeed "got them by the balls".

There was no apology, admission of guilt, formal statement acknowledging the lengthy, patient pressure from the likes of BARLA - "vindicated for all their efforts", according to Ray French,[112] or mention of Freedom in Rugby's contribution. There was even no word of thanks to John Smith at the Sports Council for his role as honest broker. Just a statement outlining the RFU's intentions and no more. It was a recalcitrance that was to be repeated in an even more spectacular fashion in less than a decade.

Top:
Shaun Edwards with Ian McCartney M.P.
(Photo: Courtesy Ian McCartney M.P.)

Right:
Stuart Evans
(Photo: Courtesy Alex Service)

4: Kick Off 7.00p.m.

On the ground floor of the Palace of Westminster, in one of the oldest parts of the building, near Westminster Hall, are the Cloisters, a quadrangle of corridors which used to house the desks of probably 30 or more members of parliament of either party. Off this corridor immediately adjacent to the hall is a small room in which Oliver Cromwell, reputedly, signed the death warrant of Charles I in 1649. Its significance in recent political history is that it was in that same small room that the idea of a Parliamentary Rugby League Group was born.

During my first few years in the Commons I had a desk in the corridor nearest to "King Charles's room" along with a number of other Labour MPs who, like me, were also serving in their first Parliament. The room off the corridor was occupied by four Scottish MPs. They were Jimmy Hood and Jimmy Wray, two working class Glaswegians, Frank Doran, a solicitor representing an Aberdeen seat, and Ian McCartney, another Glaswegian, representing the Lancashire constituency of Makerfield. I vaguely knew McCartney, through political connections, before he entered Parliament in 1987 and soon struck up a close friendship with him. I had met his father, who until that election had been the M.P. for Clydebank, on many occasions while in the company of my predecessor as Wakefield M.P., Walter Harrison. As a second generation M.P., McCartney Junior had a flying start on procedures but, more importantly, he knew how to work the informal networks that influence the real decisions at Westminster.

Away from socialist politics McCartney had one overriding obsession - Wigan Rugby League club. A former seaman turned Labour Party organiser he had arrived in Wigan to be agent to the town's M.P., Roger Stott, at a time when the Pie Eaters were struggling in the Second Division. He was taken to Central Park where he was immediately converted to Rugby League and he has supported Wigan ever since.

McCartney's work with Stott had brought him into close contact with the debate around a number of the "political" issues relating to League, in particular, of course its relationship with Rugby Union. So he was well aware of exactly where League stood in terms of the establishment divide.

Discussions in the Cloisters moved on to the wider stage of the Commons Strangers bar which, at that time, used to be an almost exclusive haunt of northern and Scottish Labour MPs. Part of the life of an M.P. is being around the House of Commons waiting to vote or for a political debate. Debates usually finish at 10p.m., but can go on much later and even through the night.

Along with McCartney and Stott, many others regularly contributed to nightly debates that frequently ended up with a discussion on Rugby League. Among those regulars were Laurie Cunliffe, M.P. for Leigh, a supporter of that town's team, and Eric Martlew, M.P. for Carlisle, who, along with his wife Elsie, was a stalwart supporter of the now defunct Border Raiders over the years. There was Kevin MacNamara, then Labour's spokesman on Northern Ireland and a Hull Kingston Rovers supporter, Doug Hoyle, then M.P. for Warrington and now a member of the House of Lords, a Wire fan and also father of Lindsay Hoyle, the then chairman of Chorley RLFC and later himself a Labour M.P. Tony Lloyd, M.P. for Stretford, was a regular at Salford and Alice

Mahon, the M.P. for Halifax, along with her husband, Tony, has supported their local Halifax side through thick and thin.

McCartney and I were still very much 'new boys' at this stage but it was apparent to both of us that beyond the realms of the Strangers Bar there was a considerable amount of interest and enthusiasm for the 13-a-side code within the Palace of Westminster. McCartney deserves great credit for originally floating the idea of a Parliamentary Rugby League Group in late 1987 and energetically doing much of the groundwork that led to its subsequent launch. He and I had a clear agenda on so many of the issues that could be addressed by an organised and active lobby within parliament. I would never forget my own personal experiences, nor those of many of my friends, of being treated as a sporting leper because of an association with Rugby League. While this aspect had not touched McCartney personally, I knew that with his own particular background he didn't need me to lecture him on what were, essentially, social-class issues.

The prejudice which we perceived against our sport went far beyond the "amateurism" regulations of the Rugby Football Union. It extended to attitudes towards the game in the media and deeply held beliefs in the higher echelons of Government and Civil Service that Rugby League was, somehow, not a legitimate sport. I would like to make it clear at this point, and it would be wrong not to do so, that I have come across similar attitudes in people belonging to my own party. It is only since I became a Member of Parliament that I have come to realise how many people have been (and in some areas still are) brought up to genuinely believe that playing League is, more or less, on a par with some sort of criminal activity. McCartney had a deeply held belief that we could, and should, do something about this and I, for one, certainly needed no convincing that he was right.

He set about writing to every M.P. who had a professional League team in, or near, their constituency and invited them to indicate if they would be interested in the formation of a Parliamentary Rugby League Group. Inevitably, given the concentration of the game in the north, the initial membership was drawn primarily from the four counties where the vast majority of the teams are based. And, with the north\south divide still very much in evidence, it was also very heavily biased towards the Labour Party. As so many of Rugby League's battles are against attitudes very firmly entrenched within the British class system, it was always going to be something of a challenge to ensure that our lobby was genuinely an All-Party affair. It wasn't until some years later that I came to realise that within the post-Thatcher Tory Party there were some elements with a considerable distaste for the way in which the tentacles of the old school tie brigade stretch way beyond what is immediately obvious.

At a fairly early stage we managed to recruit to the cause a small number of Tory MPs with Rugby League interests in their constituencies. Interestingly, in addition, we were also joined by the former Sports Minister, Neil MacFarlane, who was later knighted and retired from Parliament at the 1992 election. MacFarlane was, like some of his successors, converted to the cause of Rugby League during his time as Sports Minister. He had also become a firm friend of the secretary-general of the Rugby Football League, David Oxley. His early involvement with the group gave us more clout in the dealings we were to have with government ministers and officials in later years.

From the Conservative side of the House of Lords we gained the interest and commitment of a former Government chief whip, Lord David Swinton, the husband of the disability activist Lady Masham. Lord Swinton's family were pre-nationalisation colliery owners in Featherstone and he had been a patron of Featherstone Rovers for many years. He was later to become a vice-chairman of the group along with the then Labour M.P. for Pontefract and Castleford, Geoff Lofthouse, who had originally worked at the Swinton family's pit in Featherstone. Lord Swinton was joined by his Tory colleague Lord Lucas of Chilworth, the only person I have ever met who maintains that he was converted to Rugby League by former Rugby League television commentator and personality Eddie Waring! Apparently he met Eddie during the production of *Jeux Sans Frontieres*, the European version of the television team game *It's a Knockout*, was invited by him to a game and was immediately converted.

Committee Room 20, on the upper floor of the Commons, overlooking the Thames, was a regular venue for meetings during the first period of my membership of the Health Select Committee. At 7.00p.m. on the evening of Wednesday 10 February 1988 it was full for the inaugural meeting of the All-Party Parliamentary Rugby League Group. Twenty-five MPs, one peer and several visitors were welcomed by Ian McCartney. He introduced the Rugby Football League's Maurice Lindsay, then its president, Bob Ashby, its chairman and its secretary-general David Oxley, and from BARLA Maurice Oldroyd and Jackie Reid.

I had what, in retrospect, I now recognise as the privilege of proposing the motion of formal inauguration. I recall speaking of my playing days, a lifetime supporting Trinity and of concerns about various challenges facing the game. Speaking from a completely different personal and political perspective, the Tory Neil MacFarlane M.P., seconded the motion, which was unanimously agreed.

McCartney took the chair, MacFarlane was elected as one vice-chairman and Geoff Lofthouse the other. I was elected secretary and Laurie Cunliffe the treasurer. David Oxley and Maurice Oldroyd addressed the group from their respective positions. After a few cracks about the Commons joining the ranks of televised spectator sport (by having recently voted for televising proceedings) Oxley identified a range of issues that needed to be addressed. As well as ground safety and VAT he referred specifically to concerns regarding relations with Twickenham and the Welsh Rugby Union. He mentioned as well the RFL's relations with BARLA, which sadly were soon to deteriorate quite markedly.

Oldroyd skirted round this point, speaking of the positive achievements of BARLA in the promotion of Rugby League and highlighting the significance of the forthcoming centenary in 1995.

So much of the group's subsequent agenda for action was touched on at that first meeting. The late Bob Cryer and also Geoff Lofthouse flagged up the very real problems facing professional clubs following the Safety at Sports Grounds legislation, which outlined new safety standards for sports grounds. The fact that Rugby League had no equivalent of the Football Trust to fund ground improvements was noted as an area that had to be addressed.

Several members picked up Oxley's point on the issue of relations with Rugby Union and the development of the game in schools and media coverage were also highlighted as issues with which the group should concern itself.

Both McCartney and I were delighted with the success of the first meeting which had clearly established in a formal way the considerable interest in Rugby League that already existed within Parliament and had also framed a tentative but soon to become a very firm agenda of the areas we had to attack.

Among the most annoying put-downs of the game of Rugby League is the one that compares the international expansion of the 13-a-side game with that of Rugby Union. I have lost track of the times I have heard Union supporters in the media imply that it is hard to take seriously a game played only in three northern counties of England and a handful of other countries. Leaving aside the fact that such comparisons are singularly ill-informed, the limited spread of Rugby League world-wide is in itself to some extent testimony to the effectiveness of the Union establishment's efforts at blotting out participation in League.

In *A People's Game*, Geoffrey Moorhouse describes the way the Victorians were great originators of organised sport such as rugby, which was subsequently planted in other countries "by British imperialism".[113] It is clear that Rugby Union's spread to various parts of the globe was very largely the result of its being played within the British armed forces. It was not until I became an M.P. that I was made aware that the playing of League was not allowed in the armed forces. Union, rather than League, had taken off through a British forces' policy that refused over the years to permit the 13-a-side code to be played by British services personnel. During national service days, when young men had to do two years in the forces, many Rugby League professionals, including Alex Murphy, found themselves playing Rugby Union, another curious example of Rugby Union's interpretation of their "amateurism" rules. Often they would be playing against non-forces teams.

The armed forces

The 1980s saw increased agitation within the armed forces by servicemen who contested this ban and wished to play amateur Rugby League. The Parliamentary Rugby League Group became involved during 1989 following representations from BARLA. We were fortunate in having as one of our members Merlyn Rees, himself a former Secretary of State for Defence, and he was happy to pursue the matter. With his appreciation of both codes he found the forces' attitude to League quite intolerable.

The chairman of the Combined Services Sports Board, in response to BARLA's representations, had indicated during February 1989 that the non-recognition of Rugby League stemmed from the Treasury's refusal to sanction any increase in the number of what were termed "fully recognised" service sports. In a subsequent letter on 4 October 1990 the chairman of the RAF Sports Board, Air Vice-Marshal D.P. Crwys-Williams, advised BARLA's national development officer, Tom O'Donovan, that "there is at present insufficient general groundswell of interest throughout the services to justify us seeking Treasury approval for official recognition."

Lord Rees took up this point with the Defence Secretary, George Younger M.P., in a letter on 23 June 1989, suggesting that he did not suppose the Treasury had "a great knowledge of Rugby League". With this in mind he pointed to the playing of amateur Rugby League in parts of Britain other than the north, drawing attention in particular to the game's expansion in higher education, the civil service and the police. "The slight on Rugby League must be removed," he argued.

The junior Defence Minister, Michael Neubert - "Bilko" to his Commons colleagues because of his marked resemblance to the television character - undertook to make enquiries into the possibility of including Rugby League in the list of sports recognised by the RAF Sports Board.

By November 1989 Lord Rees had been told that "insufficient support existed within the RAF to warrant consideration of official recognition and funding for Rugby League football". According to the Parliamentary Under-Secretary of State for the Armed Forces, the Earl of Arran: "in RAF Support Command there were only 30 amateur Rugby League players altogether and in RAF(G) 12 people who had played Rugby League and a further two who had said that they would play if the sport were available to them. Within Strike Command half the stations reported no interest at all and the remaining stations each had one or two players who were actively involved outside the RAF. The exception to this was at RAF Coningsby where a senior aircraftsman had, on his own initiative, organised an unofficial RAF Rugby League Association and representative team."[114]

The information contained in the minister's letter completely contradicted firm information in O'Donovan's possession of extensive interest in Rugby League within the RAF and, while McCartney and I were readily prepared to see conspiracy theories when it came to relations between Union and League, we had now been joined on the forces issue by a former Secretary of State for Defence. Merlyn Rees was becoming more and more convinced that perhaps ministers were not being told the full story.

Following representations from Tom O'Donovan during the spring of 1990, Merlyn Rees told the Ministry of Defence of BARLA's belief that the RAF's trawl of interest in Rugby League had seriously underestimated the degree of interest. But the Earl of Arran replied that he was confident that they had "an accurate view of the general level of interest in the game".[115]

Shortly after Easter that year, Lord Rees and I met O'Donovan and a representative of the unofficial RAF Rugby League Association. In the Strangers' Bar of the Commons, the RAF man told us that he had the names of nearly 70 personnel interested in Rugby League at his own base alone. Eight camps had been represented at a meeting to discuss the formation of an RAF Rugby League team and there would be little difficulty in forming two divisions of teams straightaway. Not only had little effort been made to establish interest in the sport but there was clear evidence of positive attempts being made to discourage it.

O'Donovan made the valid point that substantial recruitment to the armed forces took place in areas of high unemployment in the north, precisely the same areas that often played Rugby League. Armed with detailed documentation to substantiate the pro-League RAF officer's claims, O'Donovan said: "We are being asked to believe that vast numbers of armed forces recruits, born and raised in Rugby League areas, suddenly forget the sport when they join up." And he produced, as well, recruitment material that stressed very strongly to such recruits that sporting opportunities would be endless once they were members of the army, navy or airforce.

Ministry of Defence

Merlyn Rees promised to make personal representations to Defence Ministry contacts to put to them our concern over what appeared to be a deliberate block on recognition of Rugby League. I fired off a series of written questions to the Ministry, following on from O'Donovan's point about recruitment from Rugby League areas, specifically asking about the number of recruits from Yorkshire, Lancashire, Cumbria and Cheshire for each year since 1987. The Armed Forces Minister, Archie Hamilton, replied on 8 May 1990 that nearly 22,000 people had joined from these areas since 1987. These numbers would be added to many thousands of serving personnel from the same areas and we were being asked to believe that few, if any, had an interest in Rugby League. When we saw these figures, McCartney and I were more than ever convinced that those from within the forces who were telling us of positive efforts to prevent the playing of Rugby League were telling us the truth.

Rees's badgering of the ministry continued over the summer that year, with the Earl of Arran again claiming "there is currently insufficient interest in Rugby League in the services to justify its inclusion as a recognised sport."[116]

As the year passed, O'Donovan was involved in direct dialogue with Ministry officials but our group meeting in the new year of 1991 learned of a distinct lack of progress. We began to enquire as to the cost to the tax payer of sporting activity within the armed forces. For example, the playing of Rugby Union in the Navy alone was found to cost the tax payer £30,000 a year.

Such chunks of assistance for Union from the public purse were among many we established during the period when Rugby Union officials constantly claimed their game was a net contributor to the public purse and independent of subsidy.

The Sports Minister, Robert Atkins, was given a detailed file outlining our concerns following his attendance at one of our Parliamentary Group meetings. He agreed to pursue the matter himself with the Defence Ministry but we had little confidence that he seriously supported our concerns. Despite representing a Lancashire constituency he was a typical Tory import from the south of England, whose only sporting connection - on his own admission - was an interest in cricket.

With continuing resistance to all our attempts to get fair treatment for Rugby League in the forces, the Parliamentary Group was incensed to learn immediately prior to the summer recess that year that, according to an advertisement in the July edition of the *Rugby World and Post*, the Royal Navy were seeking to appoint a Rugby Union youth development officer, the full costs of which were to be met by the Defence Vote (i.e. Ministry of Defence budget).

We subsequently resolved to seek a meeting with the Armed Forces Minister to set out in detail our belief that the extent of interest in Rugby League was deliberately being suppressed and that the allocation of funding solely to Rugby Union was profoundly unfair.

We met the Minister concerned, Archie Hamilton, in his office in the Ministry of Defence building in Whitehall on 5 March 1992. We took a sizeable delegation, deliberately choosing as its leader Merlyn Rees.

The Tory M.P. for Keighley, Gary Waller, and I were joined on the delegation by Maurice Oldroyd and Tom O'Donovan from BARLA. The latter two had arrived separately and it was apparent that their personal relationship by then was quite cool. It was not long after this that O'Donovan moved as Development Officer to the Rugby League, one of a number of factors that were to sour relationships between the two governing bodies.

McCartney was due to join us for the meeting at the Ministry of Defence but we were sitting down in the room of the Armed Forces Minister before he arrived. The minister introduced some officials, including one high-ranking naval officer with responsibility for sport, and we were given some tea. Merlyn Rees was outlining the background to our concerns when McCartney arrived, red faced and breathless, and sat himself down at the opposite end of the settee occupied by Hamilton.

After Rees had finished, O'Donovan made an impressive contribution outlining long-standing concerns over the denial of sporting opportunities to service personnel wishing to participate in League. As well as making clear that it was profoundly unfair to deny the rights and interests of forces recruits from League areas, he broadened the argument to include the significance of the armed forces' ban in terms of preventing the spread of Rugby League internationally. Rugby Union was a world-wide game for one reason only - it had been spread through the British armed forces whose personnel were not allowed to play League.

Following supportive noises from others in the League delegation, Hamilton passed over to the senior naval officer for an outline of the government's position. The fellow was Union to his roots and could scarcely disguise his utter contempt for our cause. He had an air of disinterest that implied that all of us - including the former Secretary of State for Defence - were totally wasting his time.

I exchanged glances with McCartney during this performance to see him looking even redder in the face than he had been when he first arrived. As our naval friend continued, arguing that there was no evidence of interest in League in the forces, McCartney was perched on the edge of his seat, visibly shaking with anger. After Hamilton restated the officer's point about lack of interest, McCartney exploded at the other end of the settee.

It was the first time I had heard the word "fucking" used at a ministerial meeting. They are usually polite and fairly sedate affairs with tea and biscuits but, from this point onwards the gloves were off. McCartney reeled off a series of bases where we knew of significant interest in Rugby League and said: "What's more, we can name names if necessary. They should stop giving excuses and accept that the denial of Rugby League was down to the old school tie brigade and nothing else."

Hamilton was clearly shocked at McCartney's outburst and felt it necessary to become more defensive of the status quo. McCartney accused the minister of talking "crap" and the two continued to have a sharp, highly personalised exchange from either end of the ministerial settee.

It struck me, while they were battling it out, that what was being fought out on that settee was a microcosm of a century of class struggle. At one end was five foot two inches of north-country working-class - at the other, six foot five inches of southern ex-Guards Tory, each hating everything the other stood for. But if it had gone beyond the verbals that day, despite the size difference, I would have put my money firmly on the bantam Scot.

It was some time before anyone else could get a word in but, as the settee contenders paused for breath, our naval friend, clearly reeling from his "lack of interest" line being vigorously rebuffed, threw in the difficulties inherent in recognising additional sporting activities. "The Armed Forces Sports Board has, for financial reasons, an upper limit of recognised sports. If Rugby League were to be recognised it would mean another sport having to be removed," he said.

Having tabled a number of parliamentary questions which had revealed the details of this approved list, I was ready for this one. I pointed out to him that there were sports on this list that most people had never heard of. I had tested some of them out on researchers in the House of Commons library and they had been forced to consult dictionaries to establish exactly what these sports were.

I could not prove there was no interest in some of these other activities in the armed forces but I had a damned good idea in view of the geographical recruitment data we had obtained through parliamentary questions that among the thousands recruited from the north of England there would be a fair few with a Rugby League background. "Well, it's essentially the cost factor," retorted our naval friend. "Recognising other activities would involve a significant increase in equipment costs, over and above the existing sports budget, which is why the Sports Board has recognised lists of specified sports."

I was ready for this one as well. "But you already have the changing rooms and rugby pitches, you already have the rugby balls, boots, jerseys, shorts and even jock straps for playing Rugby Union. How is it going to cost you more money when all you need for the sport is there already?" I argued. "All that is different is the rules."

McCartney reinforced the point that we were getting some pretty weak excuses and that the real reason for their stance was nothing other than blatant prejudice against Rugby League. Hamilton intervened again to counter this point with a question to his naval officer about the insurance position of service personnel wishing to play League. Having lost hands down on his previous two arguments, our naval friend was relieved to be allowed to develop a further area of alleged difficulty. But O'Donovan and Oldroyd retorted straightaway that BARLA's own scheme could adequately cover the insurance requirements of the armed forces.

The hour-long meeting ended with Hamilton agreeing to review the position in the light of our comments. Merlyn Rees, somewhat taken aback by the heat of the exchanges, thanked the minister and we made our way back to the Commons.

As I left the minister's anteroom to go into the corridor, I noticed that McCartney had the naval officer pinned against the wall and was laying into him verbally for all he was worth. He explained afterwards that he had told this chap that with the expected election of a Labour government very shortly he would personally ensure his transfer to a domestic post in Aldershot Mess. Sadly Labour narrowly lost the May 1992 General Election and our naval friend's career survived.

The meeting with Hamilton and in particular his officials' comments made those of us present all the more determined to fight our corner. Not long after the ministerial meeting we were incensed to learn that station orders at at least three RAF bases had contained reference to Tom O'Donovan's activities in seeking out players interested in the game. One base had in the orders advised the service personnel to have nothing to do with him.

I had the chance to pose an oral question to Hamilton on 2 June 1992 and raised this development with him and the fact that we also knew that organisers of a forthcoming Rugby League competition at RAF Marham had been refused permission to use that base's pitches. Hamilton said that he "had no idea why facilities should have been debarred or such notices put up" and he agreed to investigate both events.[117]

My question got extensive coverage on national radio as a fairly novel and, for some, a less serious aspect of defence issues receiving parliamentary consideration. For the Parliamentary Rugby League Group it was one of an increasing number of media reports that helped to build up public interest in our fight on rugby discrimination. Almost without fail, every report of our activities in the press, television or radio brought in more evidence of discrimination and more information that could be used in our activities.

Hamilton subsequently informed me that security matters had resulted in the posting of orders concerning O'Donovan and the cancellation of the RAF Marham competition. McCartney pursued the issues further in correspondence himself with Hamilton, also raising with him a threat by the Combined Services Sports Board to cancel a planned meeting with BARLA in the event of representatives of the Parliamentary Rugby League Group also being present. By now we were well aware that senior service personnel were extremely sensitive about our activities and particularly jumpy that the likes of McCartney might be turning up at meetings.

Hamilton assured McCartney that the threatened cancellation occurred because a "misunderstanding may have arisen as a result of the Services' need to comply with well- established regulations governing visits by Members of Parliament to MOD establishments."[118] Neither myself, McCartney nor the Parliamentary Group were totally convinced by the minister's explanation and O'Donovan was particularly amused that as a former mayor of Kirklees who had had meetings with the Queen, Princess Anne and numerous government ministers, he should now apparently be deemed a security threat.

Nevertheless there were by then some signs that we were making slow progress with increasing evidence of what O'Donovan referred to as "ruffled feathers".

Meeting the Rugby Football Union

The Parliamentary Rugby League Group finally met face-to-face with Rugby Union officials on Wednesday 21 April 1993. I met Dudley Wood and Bob Rogers in the Central Lobby of the Palace of Westminster some 15 minutes before the start of our meeting at 6.00p.m. Wood was a tall figure, probably in his early sixties, whose ears indicated lengthy service in the second row. Rogers was the younger man, with an obvious military air. He had an athletic build and I suspect he too had probably played a fair bit of rugby in the past.

I took Wood and Rogers for a beer in the Strangers' Bar before the meeting and we exchanged polite pleasantries. Shortly before 6.00p.m. we went two floors up in the lift to Room 10 on the Committee Floor of the Commons, overlooking the Thames.

Room 10 is one of the largest rooms on the Committee corridor and has a raised platform area for the chair and officials and banks of seats and desks facing each other for government and opposition in a similar format to the Commons' Chamber. McCartney was giving an impression of Ronnie Corbett perched in a huge chair at the centre of the platform and along with myself and the other group officers, Wood and Rogers sat down to face a substantial audience of MPs and Peers.

Looking round the room that night, while I was grateful that there was a good turnout, I was concerned that among the audience were a number of Tories who were not actually members of the group. I feared that the RFU position might have some political support and that our invitation to Wood and Rogers - published on the weekly *All-Party Parliamentary Whipping Notice* sent to all MPs and Peers outlining business for the forthcoming week - might have had some unforeseen consequences.

Wood and Rogers had indicated earlier that they would have to leave before 7.00p.m. to attend another function and, in view of this, the meeting agreed to take the speakers first and deal with minutes, correspondence and other business after they had gone. In view of the Ministry of Defence episode, I was a bit concerned that McCartney might set the tone of the meeting by losing his rag in the chair very early on, but on this occasion he was at his statesman-like best. In introducing Wood and Rogers he sketched out the background to our concerns, mentioning the armed forces issue, and "shamateurism" and the recent banning of players such as Steve Pilgrim, with League connections. Pilgrim, the Wasps' full-back, had been banned for 12 months by Twickenham that year after a trial with Leeds RLFC for which he had not been paid.

Wood did nearly all the talking on behalf of the RFU. He explained briefly the nature of his role as secretary of the RFU and said that Rogers was chairman of the RFU's Amateurism Committee.

"We have no quarrel at all with Rugby League and have traditionally had a very close relationship with BARLA. And David Oxley has been a good personal friend of mine for many years, although I have not had the chance to meet his successor," he said. He described the structure of the Rugby Union game and spoke of the role of their 56-member International Board.

He said the game was self-financing and a net contributor to the Exchequer. "The amateurism principle is in our view the key to this success and we are therefore very keen to protect this aspect of the game. Amateurism could not be sustained if professionals were involved in the sport," he added.

He made it clear that the International Board rules stated that if a player takes part in a trial for a professional club he would lose his amateur status automatically. "It is the clear view of the RFU that Steve Pilgrim was aware of this fact when he went for a trial with Leeds RLFC," he claimed.

He went on to say that "Rugby Union is a game for those in employment, pursuing their own careers". He conceded however that there had been some movement on allowing players to receive payments for undertaking commercial activity away from the game which arose directly from their involvement in the sport. "Rugby Union is a Freemasonry, which opens doors," he informed the meeting.

Wood concluded by saying that while a number of other Rugby Unions had "different interpretations" of the amateurism principle, he was absolutely certain that no payments of any kind were taking place in English Rugby Union.

I noticed Wood begin to turn pink as he was subsequently forced to answer a range of hostile questions. It struck me that it was perhaps the first time he had ever had to face such a critical audience on the issue of the relationship with Rugby League and he was soon, very obviously, quite uncomfortable. Doug Hoyle, Stan Orme, the late Derek Enright, Neil Gerrard and McCartney from the chair threw various allegations of "shamateurism" at him, none of which, Wood replied, were within the purview of the English Rugby Football Union.

Tory M.P. "professionalised"

I described the experience of many in my era of exclusion from Union and was quickly followed by an surprising ally. One of the "unexpected" Tories present at the meeting was Michael Jopling, the veteran former Government Chief Whip and Member for Westmoreland. He stood up to make what I was sure would be a contribution in defence of the RFU. Instead, to the astonishment of all present, he vividly recalled an experience over 30 years earlier. "When I was prospective Parliamentary Conservative Candidate for Wakefield in the 1959 election, along with my Labour opponent, I was invited to kick off a Rugby League match between Wakefield Trinity and Hunslet. We tossed a coin. I kicked off the first half and the Labour candidate the second. Following the match I found that I was deemed to have 'professionalised' myself by taking part," he told us. I remembered this event because it was the first General Election campaign I was old enough to be really aware of. Jopling was the unsuccessful opponent of the M.P. Arthur Creech-Jones and I recall the kick-off arrangements he described.

Jopling went on to say how ridiculous such a situation was then and how sad he was that such stupidity was still occurring nowadays. Wood had no answer to Jopling's intervention. Even the extreme right-wing Tory, John Carlisle, who had defended South Africa's apartheid regime to the end, also found it impossible to wholeheartedly endorse Wood's position. He said it was "time for change". Wood's face was nearly purple when he left with Rogers. As they left, McCartney put the boot in further by presenting them both with Parliamentary Rugby League Group ties and expressing the hope that they would be worn at Twickenham.

The All-Party Parliamentary Rugby League Group take to the pitch. The match was to raise funds for a Yorkshire under-16 team to tour South Africa.

Top: The parliamentarians with their opponents.
Middle: Lord Lofthouse used his speaker's skills to referee the match.
Bottom: Gerry Sutcliffe M.P., Jeff Ennis M.P., Lord Dominic Addington, David Hinchliffe M.P. and Derek Wyatt M.P. (a former England Rugby Union international). (Photos: Steve Wells)

5: The National Lottery Bill

The proposal by the Conservative government to set up a National Lottery had long caused debate in particular among Labour MPs. There was a general view that the government would grasp any opportunity to develop alternative sources of public funding; indeed it was thought that future lottery funding would not be confined to sport and the arts, but be funnelled into more essential areas of provision in lieu of government funding. And among those colleagues representing seats in the north-west in particular, there were real fears that a lottery would totally undermine the Liverpool-based pools companies, which provided a large number of jobs in an area of exceptionally high unemployment.

I shared this broad view of opposition to the legislation although recognising, like most Labour colleagues, that it was unlikely to be defeated. There was huge media pressure for the lottery and many on the Labour side became progressively more shaky about seriously opposing what was increasingly being presented as a huge pot of gold within the grasp of all our constituents.

I had no personal qualms about voting against the measure from the word go, in line with a long-standing opposition to gambling probably passed down from my parents. But while I intended to back those opposing the measure, I recognised early on that the Bill might provide a useful opportunity to debate, in a sporting context, the merits of various organisations that could gain a great deal from this new source of funding.

As I indicated earlier, there had, over many years, been occasional grumbles among northern Labour authorities about the receipt of public funding by Rugby Union clubs who continued to apply discriminatory rules against Rugby League players.

Despite the establishment of a so called "free gangway" between the codes for amateur players, Union rules continued to outlaw former professional Rugby League players in a way which, in my view, raised serious questions about their right to receive public funding via local authorities, the Sports Council or for that matter a future National Lottery. Hundreds of players who perhaps only played professional Rugby League for a couple of seasons were banned for life from Rugby Union.

I was struck by the lessons of the previous political steps taken during the 1980s which had established an end to discrimination against amateur Rugby League players. In conjunction with Paul Fitzpatrick of *The Guardian*, and Maurice Oldroyd of BARLA, the Wigan M.P., Roger Stott, had eventually brought about a change in the attitude of Rugby Union through threatening their Sports Council funding.

The National Lottery Bill seemed too good an opportunity to miss in terms of raising the on-going discrimination against former professional Rugby League players by the Union establishment, whose traditional discretion over boot money was to our certain knowledge increasingly going by the board. For example, Scott Gibbs's book, *Getting Physical*, confirmed that he was being paid £60 win bonuses by Neath in the early 1990s, as an "amateur".[119] McCartney supported the idea of an amendment to the National Lottery Bill and shortly after its second reading I was upstairs with the parliamentary clerks, seeking advice about the most appropriate wording. These clerks (who, despite the title are highly skilled employees of parliament) advise MPs on procedures in relation to Government Bills and also assist MPs to produce their own

Private Member's Bills. They came up with a suggested form of wording which, it was thought, might offer the chance of a debate at Bill's Report Stage.

Our concerns had been briefly flagged up while the National Lottery Bill was in committee by Ian Davidson, a Union playing Scottish Labour M.P., who sympathised with Rugby League's concerns. But we had been anxious to limit debate in Committee to ensure the possibility of full consideration being given to the Bill when it returned to the Commons later, and Davidson respected our views. He understood that the selection of specific amendments at report stage is unlikely if the Committee's Chair and the Speaker consider a matter has had a good airing in Committee.

I showed McCartney the proposed amendment which was geared to blocking lottery funding to discriminatory bodies or organisations. He put his name to it and we also got Gary Waller to support it from the Tory side. I was saddened, however, to be approached a day or so later by Labour's Shadow Sports Minister, Tom Pendry, who told me in passing in the Members' Lobby that the amendment was unlikely to be selected for debate. I gained the impression then that Pendry had no real feel for what was essentially a fairly clear cut social-class issue.

McCartney and I discussed our concerns with Geoff Lofthouse, by then a Deputy Speaker who, while officially neutral in terms of his role in considering the selection of amendments for debate, was 101 per cent behind what we were trying to achieve. At 8.15a.m. the following morning - the first day of the Bill's report stage - McCartney and I were sitting with Lofthouse in Madam Speaker's office, overlooking the Commons terrace and the Thames. "Well, lovey, what can we do for you?" Betty Boothroyd asked and we explained the background to our concerns. We learned later that day that our amendment had been selected for debate.

During the morning I had paid my usual visit to the Commons library to look at the papers and later go through my constituency mail. In giving thought to what I would say in the debate later in the day, I could not believe my luck in coming across a piece in *The Times* of that morning, headed "RFU Finds Breaches of Amateurism Rife". According to the article: "the amateur ethos of Rugby Union, the sacred element of the heart of its structure has been found to be permeated with abuse in breach of the sport's rules, a Rugby Football Union report has concluded."[120]

Here we had a report emanating from the very same Rugby Football Union whose senior officials had assured a parliamentary meeting, only the previous week, that while, yes, there may be problems in other Unions, there was absolutely no evidence of financial benefits to amateur players involved with English clubs. But the report apparently gave a very different message. According to the article, English players were receiving monies and inducements in a variety of ways in direct contravention of the amateurism regulations. "They arise through excessive expenses, cars, after-dinner speaking, fictitious employment, cash playing-bonuses, clothing, fictitious expenses, housing and mortgage support, writing rugby articles, appearance money, overseas trips, free or subsidised accommodation, car passenger expenses, fictitious appearances, sponsorship, holidays and family support," it suggested.[121]

The Times report indicated that the document - with the title *Inducements to Move, Incentives to Stay and other Illegal Payments* - was circulating among senior English Rugby Union clubs. I was certain that the article could not have arisen as a result of an official statement from Twickenham because it completely undermined everything Wood and Rogers had said to us during the previous week. In defending the Union position against League, in response to a whole host of questions, they had repeatedly denied any knowledge of "professionalism" in English Rugby Union.

I was sure the contents of the report must have been leaked to the press from sources at one of the top RU clubs. I had had a number of conversations by then with various people in some of the senior English clubs and was well aware of the particular concerns about various inducements on offer to persuade talented players to move. Jim Kilfoyle, then coach of Wakefield RUFC and brother of Peter Kilfoyle, the Labour M.P. for Liverpool Walton, had told me of the difficulties facing clubs such as Wakefield in holding on to quality players and continuing to toe the amateurism line. He and others had made me very much aware of the serious concerns of clubs, especially in the north, about the means by which their best players were being drawn, in particular, to the more fashionable and wealthy outfits in the south. This simmering resentment was the most likely reason for the report ending up in the public arena.

I asked the research staff in the House of Commons library if they could obtain a full copy of the report from Twickenham. I was delighted when the RFU naively obliged in time for the evening debate. While the report did not, as I had hoped, name individual clubs concerned with these malpractices, it did tell us of the make-up of the working party. Its chairman was none other than the same R. A. G. Rogers who had solidly supported Dudley Wood's assertion that the RFU in England was "whiter than white" on the question of amateurism.

Our amendment was listed some way down the Speaker's selection list and was eventually reached somewhere around 11.30p.m. that night. Because of concerns about opposition to the Bill, the government MPs were on a three-line whip and McCartney and I took particular pleasure in almost single-handedly keeping the Tory ranks detained in the House until past 1.00 in the morning. I heard subsequently that there was near outrage among some of the Tories when word got to the smoking room and bars that they were missing their sleep because of a debate about Rugby League! But as word spread there was a gradual filling of the government benches while I spoke, as Tory MPs came to listen to the debate out of curiosity.

When I got up to speak I had a splitting headache, which miraculously cleared as I began to get up steam. When you are on your feet in the Commons you know, intuitively, whether you are on to a winner or not and that night I was in exactly the right frame of mind. I was on completely familiar ground and knew that our argument was fundamentally right and just.

Most of the Labour members had departed some hours earlier and only a handful of Opposition MPs were present, but during one intervention in my speech, I learned that at least one M.P., 200 miles away, was very much with us in spirit.

McCartney passed to me a pink telephone message form, handed to him by one of the doorkeepers. It was from Roger Stott at home in Wigan, watching the debate on satellite television. It said: "You're doing a magnificent job. Keep it up. I'm watching you." Stott told me later he saw me read the message and grin broadly.

After Gary Waller had made a telling contribution in support of the amendment from the government benches, and I had made the point that the vast majority of Rugby League is played by amateurs, not professionals, the professional game is a small part of Rugby League and it annoys many who have an interest in the game to hear it called a professional sport, McCartney rose to give the speech of his life. At heart he's always been essentially a class warrior, proud of his roots and bloody angry at the cant and hypocrisy of the Union ranks. The statesmanlike constraint he had demonstrated chairing the recent group meeting with Wood and Rogers, from the RFU, was nowhere in sight. He latched onto the contents of the Rugby Football Union's Amateurism Committee Report and as good as said that these two gentlemen had been lying when they had spoken to our group. McCartney was so heated that the Deputy Speaker, Michael Morris, pulled him up on at least two occasions.

Some days later, I was approached during a division in the chamber, by a Tory M.P., whose identity I didn't know. "David, I heard you speak on Rugby League during the National Lottery Bill and was astonished at what you described. I had absolutely no idea of the situation. Can we meet and talk about it?"

It was Iain Sproat, the Tory M.P. for Harwich, who had just been appointed Minister for Sport by John Major. Sproat had been M.P. for Aberdeen South, between 1970 and 1983, and a Junior Trade Minister in the early Thatcher years. He had resurfaced in the 1992 intake of new MPs representing his English constituency and, as a former editor of *Cricketers Who's Who* was obviously, from the cricket-loving Major's point of view, tailor-made for the sports job. As a southern Scot, educated at Winchester, the University of Aix-en-Provence and Magdalen College, Oxford, he did not immediately impress me as a likely key player in rugby's class struggle, certainly not from League's side of the fence. He was the latest in a long line of sports ministers with little knowledge of, or apparent interest in, our game.

The Parliamentary Rugby League Group had jogged along with Colin Moynihan as Sports Minister in the early days. He came to the occasional match and meetings of our Group, made the right noises, but was essentially a boxing and rowing man. As I indicated earlier, Robert Atkins, the M.P. for South Ribble, who later took the job, despite representing a Lancashire seat, was a cricketing southerner, with no interest at all in our Rugby League concerns.

David Mellor's appointment at the new Department of National Heritage in 1992 seemed at first more hopeful. I recall him enthusing over his first Rugby League match when I met him while breakfasting in the tea-room and I believe he was genuinely impressed by what he'd seen at the previous weekend's Wembley final. But when he spoke at a Parliamentary Rugby League Group meeting later that summer, he seemed confused and uncertain. The reason soon became clear when, two days later, he resigned from the cabinet after the exposure of an extra-marital affair.

The affable Robert Key, M.P. for Salisbury, handled the Sports brief while the Lottery Bill was in the House, but he was essentially a "rugger" man by background and untouched by all this fuss about discrimination from a few obscure northerners. I had no reason to believe Sproat would be any different from the rest.

By that time I had been in parliament long enough to know that 99 per cent of contributions in parliamentary debates are delivered, recorded in Hansard and immediately forgotten about. It was therefore a somewhat novel experience to learn from Sproat that someone had actually listened to what I had said and, more important, was prepared to try to do something about the problem I had described.

Sproat subsequently embarrassed me on a number of occasions by referring to the manner of his conversion to our cause that night. He spelt it out in detail on one occasion in my constituency during 1995. "In the spring of two years ago, I, then a backbencher, wandered into the chamber one evening at about 11 o'clock. It was yet another debate on the about-to-be-set-up National Lottery. This was not a subject in which I was then specially instructed. I was just about to leave the chamber, when I overheard one Tory M.P. say to another that the next bit of the debate (a proposed Amendment to the Lottery Bill) was to be about the Lottery and rugby football. As I was once a keen player of Rugby Union, and am now a keen follower, having been brought up in the Borders of Scotland, I decided to stay and listen. The amendment was proposed by David Hinchliffe. The rugby of which he spoke was Rugby League, not Union. David made a speech of logic and passion. I was riveted. I listened intently. He spoke of the slights, stupidities and snobbery, which, as he saw it, the practitioners of Union had inflicted on League. It was a brilliant speech and, although I did not agree with every word, it made a deep impression on me."[122] Although none of us realised it at the time, the efforts of McCartney, Waller, Lofthouse and myself at the Report Stage of that Bill were to prove something of a watershed in the parliamentary struggle over Rugby football.

Rugby League people meeting in Parliament: Lord Lofthouse, Billy Thompson, Ian McCartney M.P., representative from Stones Bitter, Iain Sproat M.P. (Sports Minister), Lord Brookes, Sir Rodney Walker, Maurice Lindsay, the late Roy Waudby, David Hinchliffe M.P. in 1995. (Photo: Varley Picture Agency)

BARLA Dinner: Sir Rodney Walker front row one from right, Lord Lofthouse and David Hinchliffe M.P. in second row, and Maurice Oldroyd in centre of the third row, behind Sir Rodney Walker. (Photo: Gerald Webster / *Rugby Leaguer*)

6: Payments in the Valleys

One of the benefits of being an M.P. is the dialogue you have every week with colleagues representing all parts of the United Kingdom whenever the House is sitting. In the late 1980s, the core membership of the Parliamentary Rugby League Group naturally attracted comments from other MPs about our game and in particular its relationship with Rugby Union played in areas outside the northern counties. A passing remark from other MPs in the Commons corridor would frequently relate to the Saturday match then televised on BBC's *Grandstand* and I have always been encouraged to note the amount of interest in the game from MPs representing non-Rugby League areas.

Sometimes the most unlikely of individuals have turned out to have associations with the game. Sitting in the queue for gallery tickets for some constituents one day, I had a conversation with Ken Maginnis, the Ulster Unionist M.P. for Fermanagh & South Tyrone and found out that he had once played a trial with Bradford Northern. While McCartney and I were Shadow Health Ministers and slogging it out with the Tory Minister of State, Brian Mawhinney, we found out that he too was a Rugby League fanatic. I discovered that my Tory "pair", John Townend, the M.P. for Yorkshire East, had a grandfather who had played, uniquely, for both Hull FC and Hull KR on the same day.

I learned as well some interesting lessons about social class and the perceptions of different sports in different parts of Britain. I recall a conversation during my time in the Cloisters with Tommy Graham, Labour M.P. for Renfrewshire West, who also had a desk in the same area. I made some remark about the results of an international in the Five Nations Championship involving the Scottish Rugby Union side. He looked at me completely blank, then subsequently explained that in most of Scotland, with the exception perhaps of the Borders, Rugby Union was the exclusive preserve of the non-state schools and played only by an upper class elite. His comments offered a fascinating insight into some of the reasons League has faced difficulties getting a toe-hold north of the border.

Scotland and Wales

Richard Holt, in his *Sport and the British - A Modern History*, has suggested that Scotland wanted to go even further than England in the enforcement of strict amateurism, with the Union game beginning as the preserve of the "elite" Edinburgh schools. "Although it spread to the farming towns of the Borders with great success, it remained an exclusive game self-consciously distinct from Association football", he wrote. "By placing great stress on strict amateurism the large class of industrial workers in central Scotland would be discouraged from taking part."[123]

The class attitudes underpinning the Scottish Union's approach were epitomised in the reported comments some years ago of their international referee, Crawford Findlay. In their history of Welsh Rugby Union, *Fields of Praise*, Dai Smith and Gareth Williams comment on him: "Mr Findlay did not seem to appreciate the finer points of the Welsh game nor, perhaps, its structure for he had informed the school teacher Rhys Gabe at a dinner in 1903 'that he was surprised that Wales selected miners, steelworkers and policemen for their international teams and suggested that these players should join the Northern Union'."[124]

I had always felt particular disappointment that League had not taken off in Wales, and especially in the industrial valleys in the south of that country. The conditions that prevailed in the industrial north in late Victorian times were replicated in South Wales and top Union players faced similar pressures to those in Yorkshire and Lancashire when required to "break time" for matches.

The "amateurism" issue came to a head with the Arthur Gould affair in the 1890s, when Wales's top amateur player was given a remunerative testimonial and was declared a professional by the RFU. English clubs were instructed not to play against him. In protest, Wales withdrew from the International Board. But the RFU realised that, two years after 1895, to have lost the Welsh clubs from Union as well as large parts of the north would have been a devastating blow to their game. As Tony Collins and John Coyle outlined in *Tries in the Valleys*: "But when it came to Wales, the RFU were prepared to compromise. A Welsh split would have been a massive blow to it and a huge boost for the Northern Union."[125] They also outline that the Welsh Football Union's leadership were not prepared to break away, and were loyal to the British state and Empire. Also, following their famous victory against the All Blacks in 1905, Rugby Union became an important part of the growing Welsh national identity.[126]

The Northern Union game did take off in Wales before the First World War, with up to six clubs competing against the northern clubs. The transport and communication difficulties of those early years, combined with administrative weaknesses in these clubs resulted in them all collapsing by 1912. Also, the best Welsh players who wanted to play Northern Union still went north, where the established Northern Union clubs could offer them more lucrative financial deals.

Welsh Rugby historian Gareth Williams has written extensively of what he termed "blindside remuneration" in Welsh Rugby Union, saying that before the First World War, "In many parts of South Wales there is no doubt that the term 'reasonable expenses' was interpreted generously, so that they virtually constituted broken-time payment".[127] Writing on amateurism in sport in Wales then, he concluded on Rugby Union that: "... the game's administrators were prepared to tolerate the over-generous payment of expenses to working-class players. What they would *not* consent to was the professionalising of the game and therefore proletarianising of the game..."[128]

As Phil Melling's wonderful book about Dai Davies, *Man of Amman*, shows, lucrative expenses were the norm in Welsh Rugby Union. In the 1920s, before going north to play League for Broughton Rangers Dai was on £3 a week as an amateur from Neath, whatever the team's result. At Broughton, losing money was only £1.50, so some weeks he could be worse off as a professional.[129]

In my contact with Welsh Labour MPs who follow rugby, on many occasions I have referred to the Welsh "betrayal" at the time of the great split. Their response to such banter has not been to echo the Southern English Tory line about the "amateur ethos" but rather to attack Rugby League for "stealing" their best players. With the decline of Welsh Rugby Union over the past decade or more, League had increasingly become the whipping boy for their teams' failures. Interestingly, in contrasting their decline with the England Rugby Union team's success, none of them appeared to consider the fact that England were also deprived of much greater talent, to be found playing Rugby League in the north.

The parliamentary campaign for Rugby League was fortunate to have a small number of Welsh activists and sympathisers from very early days. Merlyn Rees, who moved to the Lords in 1992, had been a valiant campaigner for a more honourable relationship between the two codes of rugby. Alan Rogers the Labour M.P. for the Rhondda, combined the role of being president of Treorchy RUFC with championing the cause of Rugby League as well. It was, I am sure, entirely coincidental that as the debate about financial inducements to players in Wales became increasingly public during the 1990s, the Treorchy club seemed to get rather a lot of mentions.

The Labour peer, Lord Brookes of Tremorfa, was equally active in fighting Union discrimination against League in Wales. As the leader of a major local authority in the area, he had struggled hard to ensure that fledgling League clubs were able to obtain playing facilities and financial support in the late 1980s and early 1990s. Through him and other activists in South Wales, we came across numerous examples of discrimination against Rugby League players in South Wales in particular.

Lord Brookes and Doug Hoyle M.P. were active in exposing the lengths to which the Welsh Rugby Union went to unsuccessfully prevent an amateur Rugby League Sevens tournament being held at the Swansea Uplands Rugby Union ground on 10 August 1991. Brookes said he was "quite appalled at the tone and content" of a circular letter sent by the WRU with a warning about player participation in the tournament. In a letter to Hoyle, Brookes said of the WRU that "it could well be that they are using Rugby League as a whipping boy for all that is wrong in Rugby Union".[130]

Sometimes the actions of the Union hierarchy bordered on the downright petty. The banning of former Welsh Rugby Union captain Jonathan Davies from the commentary box at Cardiff Arms Park in early 1989, not long after he had switched to Rugby League and signed for Widnes, resulted in our tabling a parliamentary motion of condemnation which attracted substantial Welsh support.

Shortly after his exclusion from the Arms Park the Welsh Rugby Football Union stepped in to stop Davies's Widnes team playing a Welsh Select Rugby Union side to raise money for the Towyn Flood Appeal. The idea had been to play one half of the match under League rules and the other under Union rules. With the success of the Widnes side at the time the match had generated huge spectator interest. After its cancellation we tabled another parliamentary motion deploring the Welsh RFU's objection to this match because of their attitude to Rugby League.

Such actions contrasted quite markedly with the increasing evidence coming to light in the early 1990s of professionalism within Welsh Rugby Union. While what we were increasingly hearing from very reliable sources came as no surprise, what was surprising was the frequency with which we were learning of quite detailed examples.

The simple fact was that throughout its history Welsh Rugby Union had contained elements of scarcely concealed professionalism which made their actions against the players who had gone to Rugby League, and against all attempts to develop Rugby League in Wales, the more difficult to stomach. Geoffrey Moorhouse, in *A People's Game*, points out that even before the great split of 1895, the Welsh were turning a blind eye to breaches of the amateurism regulations. Citing the case of the Swansea brothers, Evan and David James, who had moved north to play rugby and had been deemed "professionals", he quotes the reported comments on the affair by the Swansea representative at the Welsh Rugby Union's AGM in 1893. He had apparently declared that "the professional rules in existence were not only 'totally unnecessary' but also unsuitable to the game as being played in Wales. They have been consistently broken by the majority of Welsh clubs and have never been enforced."[131]

I had spoken in the past to professional Rugby League players who had played alongside Welsh Rugby Union signings as far back as the 1950s and 1960s and been made aware of the rewards available then at club level. My colleague Kim Howells, the Labour M.P. for Pontypridd, a useful Rugby Union player in his time, played briefly for Wakefield Trinity but told me he earned far more in Rugby Union than ever he got in League.

I can write about this now with Howells' consent, but was sworn to secrecy for many years. Just as Ken Maginnis had been warned that his awful secret would, if discovered, result in him being banned from Irish Rugby Union clubs, Howell has been aware that until very recently public knowledge of his activities in the north could have had serious repercussions for his political career.

The private, personal "professionalism" secrets of individual Welsh players, however, were nothing compared with the Welsh Rugby Union's inactivity on the issue of payments apparently made to Welsh international players involved in the unofficial 1989 Centenary Tour of South Africa. The report into the affair, drawn up by the senior Welsh RFU official, Vernon Pugh, alleged, according to press reports, that individual players had received substantial cash sums for their participation.

The report stated: "Had we been deciding this issue on the balance of probabilities then, from the evidence we heard, we would have found that most (and quite possibly all) of the players were handsomely rewarded for going to South Africa. By that we mean they received money, and not just the incidental benefits. At least one of the players received at least £30,000 and others as much or broadly comparable figures".[132]

Such payments were clearly in breach of International Rugby Union Board rules and those of the Welsh RFU. The reluctance of either body to act on the contents of this report provided yet another example of the remarkable contrast between the official Union attitude towards blatant breaches of the "amateurism" regulations within their own game and player involvement in Rugby League.

Stuart Evans

The Welsh situation was finally brought to a head as a consequence of the grievances borne by one former Rugby Union player over his treatment. Peter Hain, who had been elected as M.P. for Neath in a 1991 bye-election, approached me not long after his entry into Parliament expressing interest in the growing political battle over the discrimination issue. He had a long-standing antagonistic relationship with Twickenham over his key role in the "Stop the Seventies Tour" campaign against the representatives of the South African apartheid regime, the Rugby Union Springboks playing in Britain. But our discussions concerned Rugby Union's "sporting apartheid", as Hain told me of a constituent in Neath by the name of Stuart Evans who was fighting a battle with the Welsh Rugby Football Union for reinstatement following a period in professional Rugby League with St Helens. Evans' situation sounded particularly interesting as, according to Hain, he was in the process of mounting a legal challenge to the Welsh RFU and Union's IRB over his treatment.

I spoke to Evans at Hain's request and subsequently also had contact with Evans's lawyers regarding his proposed legal action which by that time was at a fairly advanced stage of preparation. Although I had talked to other ex-Rugby League players who were considering mounting legal actions over being debarred from returning to Union, what particularly interested me about Evans's case was the fact that the core of his legal argument was not just about discrimination but more specifically restraint of trade. He intended to allege that the Welsh RFU and the IRB were, through their rules, preventing him earning his living by refusing him permission to return to playing Union. In discussing his situation with me it was clear that he could prove conclusively that Rugby Union clubs in Wales were already paying good money to players and that the International Board ban on his return was restraining his trade as a player.

Evans's case was to prove of immense importance in pushing forward the debate on the discrimination issue within Wales in particular and increases the pressure on Rugby Union to move towards professionalism in that country. While I harboured some doubts about Evans's ability to prove the restraint of trade allegation, his lawyers convinced me that, by using subpoenas if necessary, they could produce clear evidence of payments at club level. They would, if necessary, require players and club officials to come to court and be subject under oath to cross examination to establish beyond doubt that professionalism was already widespread within Welsh Rugby Union. Stephen Jones, a leading Rugby Union writer said in 1993 in his book *Endless Winter*, that particularly in Wales, there had always been payments to players and that win bonuses existed throughout Welsh senior club rugby.[133]

I had by that time little doubt that Evans's claims of professionalism in his home country were true. The Welsh media had taken a close interest in the Parliamentary Rugby League Group's activities on the discrimination issue and as a consequence McCartney and I had been involved in a substantial number of Cardiff-based TV and radio programmes which had examined "professionalism". I had taken part in one TV documentary which had featured a Welsh player claiming he had seen payments made to players in the presence of a Welsh Rugby Union official.

However, I was concerned that Evans would not necessarily have the stamina and wherewithal to mount what inevitably would be a tricky and very expensive action. But Hain, who had looked at Evans's case in great detail, seemed optimistic of success and had no doubts about his constituent's determination. I also got the impression from our conversations that he believed Evans was not short of a bob or two as a result of his Rugby League signing-on fee and business activities as a pub owner in South Wales.

Hain was aware from our discussions about Evans that Sports Minister Iain Sproat was quite sympathetic to our arguments on discrimination and he made arrangements to take his constituent to meet the minister, asking me to join them at the meeting. I arranged to meet Evans in Hain's office in the Norman Shaw North Building at the end of Whitehall with the intention of going over the main points we were to raise.

We briefly discussed his League experience and the fact that I had seen him play for St Helens on a number of occasions, including his one appearance at Wembley in the Challenge Cup Final defeat by Wigan in 1989. His remarks about the current attitude of the Welsh Rugby Union and the International Board confirmed Hain's opinion that he was determined to fight the issue all the way. As we walked down Whitehall to the Trafalgar Square offices of the Department of National Heritage, Evans and a playing colleague who had accompanied him from Wales, described in detail some of the arrangements for paying players in Union there. It was a good deal more refined than the old 'boot money' with, in some instances, envelopes given to players containing cheques that could be cashed behind the clubhouse bar.

Sproat and his officials gave us a very sympathetic hearing and were clearly impressed by Evans's articulate and reasoned presentation. I thought it was helpful for the minister to be made aware that concerns about Union hypocrisy were not simply confined to the M62 corridor. And Sproat learned at first hand about "shamateurism" in Union from a player with direct personal experience of the practices.

In view of the increasing importance the WRU's Vernon Pugh was to play in the international debate in Union over amateurism, Evans's role in bringing matters to a head in Wales was by no means insignificant.

7: The taxman cometh

Rightly or wrongly, Steve Smith, the former Sale and England Rugby Union scrum-half, has attributed to him a statement that became increasingly quoted as our parliamentary campaign on "shamateurism" developed. He is reputed to have said some years ago that the only difference between Union and League at the top level is the fact that League players pay income tax. What may have been a half-serious crack at a rugby dinner began to take on a more serious mantle when the Parliamentary Rugby League Group considered its tactics towards Union discrimination against League as we entered the new decade of the 1990s.

From the formation of the group in 1988 it became our practice to meet both the Rugby Football League and BARLA prior to the start of each Parliamentary session to discuss in some detail the issues that those administering the game thought should be considered by Members of Parliament and Peers. We frequently examined the increasing concerns over football related crowd problems and the implications for Rugby League. We looked at the consequences of government legislation on safety at sports grounds and pondered over various steps that might be taken to counter the resistance to the development of Rugby League in areas such as the armed forces.

The ban on the return to Union of players who had opted for professional Rugby League was an issue raised at that stage more regularly by the parliamentary group than either the Rugby Football League or BARLA. It had come as something of a surprise to me to realise, as I got to know those administering professional Rugby League at the top level during this period, that the Union ban was largely accepted as inevitable. It was a simple fact of life and other issues required more attention.

BARLA had won their own particular battle to establish a free gangway for amateur Rugby League players during the 1980s and obviously saw the question of banning former rugby professionals from Union as a matter for those running the professional arm of the game.

I was surprised, at this particular time at least, that the Rugby Football League was not more active on opposing such discriminatory practices, bearing in mind that the prejudices underpinning them were manifested much more widely than simply in terms of their impact on individual players. They permeated a whole range of other areas that the Parliamentary Group found itself having to address. From the armed forces ban to the treatment of Rugby League by the BBC, the bottom line was that League was essentially a third-rate game, living a parasitic existence on the back of the "pure" form of rugby.

The secretary-general of the RFL at that time, David Oxley, himself came from a Rugby Union background. Educated at Oxford University, he could talk to Rugby Union officials at Twickenham on their own terms and he prided himself on his relations with the Union fraternity. He was towards the end of his tenure at the Rugby Football League when the Parliamentary Group was formed and his relaxed attitude to the Union ban must have had a bearing on the marked lack of effort made by League to challenge it.

I had always viewed Oxley's reign at the head of the RFL in a fairly positive light. Along with David Howes, then the game's public relations officer, he contributed significantly to turning around the fortunes of the game in the 1970s and 1980s and, in the light of this, it had come as something of a surprise that Union's position had not been more vigorously challenged through the parliamentary process or by legal means.

It came as even more of a surprise to find that during its early days, the Parliamentary Group was not encouraged to give this matter a high priority. During one meeting with BARLA and the Rugby Football League during the late summer of 1989, held at the birthplace of the League code - the George Hotel in Huddersfield - I put forward the possibility of tabling some parliamentary questions on the income tax arrangements for Rugby Union players. Bob Ashby, then chairman of the Rugby Football League, was adamant that this was not the right way forward. Coming from a very different background to Oxley, and as a former amateur Rugby League player like myself, I expected him to be more sympathetic to tackling this issue. But, if he was, he certainly did not see the income tax question as a tactic to be adopted.

But history has proved he was wrong, because of all the tactics adopted in the discrimination fight in Parliament, the income tax question was to become arguably the most important and effective.

Despite Ashby's reservations, on our return to Parliament some weeks later, I tabled a question to the Chancellor of the Exchequer specifically asking what income tax was received on fees paid to Rugby Union players in the previous financial year. Peter Lilley, then a Treasury Minister, told me in an answer on 25 October 1989 that it was not possible to identify from the information available about income tax receipts the amount paid by Rugby Union players.

Some days later I rephrased my question, asking if the Chancellor of the Exchequer would specify the information which was available about income tax paid by Rugby Union players in respect of relevant earnings. Lilley again replied, on 3 November 1989, referring me back to his earlier answer and stating that no such information was available. We were clearly being blocked on this issue in both our formal and informal enquiries and it was some time after the next general election in 1992 that further efforts were made to press the government on the income tax question.

We were spurred into action again in early 1993 by the treatment handed out by the Rugby Football Union to Steve Pilgrim. The Parliamentary Group tabled a motion contrasting his suspension with the lack of action taken on the Pugh Report's allegations of huge payments to players on the 1989 South African tour. The motion argued that Pilgrim's treatment breached both basic sporting principles and civil rights. Noting that extensive public subsidies were received by Rugby Union through government departments, the Sports Council and the Foundation for Sport and the Arts, we called upon the newly established National Heritage Select Committee "to investigate whether the granting of such public subsidies is appropriate in the light of the Rugby Union's blatantly discriminatory practices."

While the latter call was a long shot at that stage, it was a useful marker in terms of the direction which was to be eventually taken. It was significant as well that with the support of a number of other Labour MPs representing Welsh constituencies, Peter Hain tabled a supportive amendment to the motion also drawing attention to the "unfair and hypocritical treatment" of Stuart Evans.

On 15 February 1993 I asked the Chancellor of the Exchequer what arrangements he made for the taxation of income or benefits arising from the playing of Rugby Union football. Stephen Dorrell's answer in his capacity as Financial Secretary to the Treasury caused considerable amusement to those of us aware of the extent of "shamateurism" being increasingly referred to in the media around that time. He told me that under Rugby Union rules "players are forbidden to receive payment for playing. If they were to do so, they would be taxed in the same way as other professional sportsmen and women."

Three days later, Dorrell answered another question from me as to the steps the Inland Revenue took to ascertain the taxable income or benefits received by Rugby Union players as a result of their sporting activities. He told me again that the Inland Revenue ascertained such taxable income in the same way as sums received by other sports people but added on this occasion that amounts shown on a player's tax return were taken into account in calculating any tax due. He added: "As with any other tax payer, if there is any information, either in the tax return or received from other sources which suggests that income may have been omitted, the Inland Revenue makes appropriate enquiries."

While Dorrell was somewhat more forthcoming than Lilley had been on the issue, I still felt that we were being messed around in terms of our perfectly reasonable enquiries and I told Dorrell as much when I saw him on the floor of the House during a division a couple of days later. I knew him reasonably well from our dealings on health issues in his previous role as a junior Health Minister and told him to give me a straight answer to a straight question. He knew full well that I was after confirmation of tax payments on earnings by Union players to prove an important point but he told me he could not oblige. Such information, even though I was not asking for names of individual players, was confidential to the Inland Revenue.

But despite these difficulties we were by this time beginning to build up a useful head of steam on the income tax issue and the wider discrimination question. Peter Hain's active involvement with the Stuart Evans case gave an added dimension to the cause and alerted outsiders to the fact that the issue was not simply the parochial concern of a handful of obscure embittered northerners.

"Hypocrisy of shamateurism"

Hain asked an excellent oral parliamentary question to the Sports Minster, Robert Key, about Evans's case on 22 March 1993. He pointed out the contrasting interpretation of International Board rules in Australia and France and spoke of the "hypocrisy of shamateurism". Referring to the likely humiliation of the Rugby Union authorities if Evans took his case to the European Court, he urged the Government to "press for changes in the rules so that Rugby League players can play Rugby Union and the oppressive and anachronistic bans may be ended."

Key's answer set out the official position that it was for the rugby authorities to set and employ their own regulations and for players to decide which code they wished to play by and ensure they were fully acquainted with the appropriate regulations. He went on to state that only the courts could determine whether there had been a breach of the law but then, interestingly, went on to note that "the chairman of the Sports Council, Sir Peter Yarranton, had expressed his concern over the current situation."

Yarranton's significance on this issue was not simply his role with the Sports Council but more importantly the fact that, as Key pointed out, he was a former Union international and the immediate past-president of the Rugby Football Union. We had asked him to address a meeting of the Parliamentary Group in 1992 after he was widely reported as having made derogatory remarks about Rugby League at the launch of Rothmans' *1992 Rugby Union Yearbook*. Yarranton strongly rejected the press interpretation of his remarks and to be fair, after our meeting, he did on a number of occasions make representations to the RFU about their discriminatory practices.

I followed Hain's question that day with another one to Key about the Pilgrim affair, drawing attention to the fact that by then 130 MPs had signed the Early Day Motion, indicating their support. Outlining the basic facts concerning Pilgrim's treatment, I drew attention to the receipt of public funding by the Rugby Union and evidence of payments for playing Union. When I ended by saying: "There are people in the Chamber now who have been paid for playing Rugby Union football," a rich Welsh accent in the general direction of Kim Howells further along the Labour benches said: "Thanks, Dave". Key maintained that this latter point "is a matter for dispute" but made it clear that he accepted "the tone" of my remarks. "I too am disappointed about that particular [Pilgrim's] case," he added.

Shortly after my dialogue with Dorrell, McCartney drew up a detailed letter to the Inland Revenue including in it a series of examples where it appeared that a number of Rugby Union clubs and the Unions themselves in Britain were in breach of their own amateurism regulations. The press reported that the Parliamentary Group had presented a "dossier of evidence" on payments to the Inland Revenue and both McCartney and I found ourselves under considerable pressure for quite a time to supply this "dossier" to certain national newspapers. We refused to do so because the so-called "dossier" contained not a great deal more than press cuttings concerning allegations of payments and the RFU's internal report on *Inducements to Play*.

We did occasionally have put to us allegations concerning payments to certain prominent players but took the decision not to raise these with the Inland Revenue for fairly obvious reasons. Essentially we were arguing that there was nothing wrong in being paid to play rugby and it would have been ridiculous for us to give the impression of pillorying players allegedly in receipt of payments. We knew as well from certain Welsh MPs sympathetic to our cause that a number of prominent Union players were also privately sympathetic to our campaign and watching developments with close interest. It was essential that we did not alienate those within Rugby Union - especially in Wales - who were themselves agitating for reform. To name names, as we were constantly urged to do by the press, could have proved totally counterproductive.

On 17 May 1993 I asked the Chancellor of the Exchequer in a written question what assessment the Inland Revenue had made of *Inducements to Play*. Dorrell indicated that the Inland Revenue was aware of the RFU report. "It is making enquiries to establish whether any players have received taxable income of benefits which they have not declared. It will take appropriate action when its enquiries are complete," he added.

At the meeting of the Parliamentary Rugby League Group on 16 June 1993, McCartney reported that he had been advised that the Inland Revenue were looking in detail at the "shamateurism" issue in response to the Group's representations. He had been phoned by an official working at their Special Investigation Branch who had expressed gratitude for the Group's letter. Privately, prior to the meeting, McCartney told me that the person who had phoned him said they had for some time been looking for grounds to mount an investigation into practices at certain Union clubs. McCartney got the clear impression from this conversation that they had been leaned on to steer clear of the affair by individuals at a very high level. The message we got was that this level was political and thus the pressure on the Treasury through parliamentary questions had been extremely important from the Inland Revenue's point of view.

By the late summer of 1993 it was becoming clear that our efforts were having some effect, in South Wales at least. Lord Brookes of Tremorfa sent me a copy of the front page of the *South Wales Echo* of 3 September which had a headline "Tax Probe on Rugby Perks". It reported that "three top Welsh rugby clubs are under investigation by the tax man", and went on to detail allegations of a first-division club offering a £10,000 transfer fee for a player, a Welsh international being offered a package worth £20,000 and another club giving a player a £10,000 per year package, including payments of £180 per week.[134]

The article alleged that the main incentives to players were jobs and cars while most clubs also offered bonus payments. "A typical bonus structure would be £40 per man for the first win, £60 for a second win in a row, £80 for a third and £80 for each subsequent consecutive victory. Bigger clubs would pay £60, £80 and £100."[135] When Parliament resumed in October, one Welsh M.P. told me we had "caused bloody havoc" in South Wales by raising the tax issue. "People are running around like headless chickens," he said. At our Group meeting on 20 October McCartney reported that he had been informed that the Inland Revenue's Solihull Special Office had made significant progress in their examination of taxation issues relating to payments to Union players. They had offered to meet representatives of the Group to discuss the issue in the new year.

By the beginning of the 1993-94 parliamentary session the Rugby League Group's activities finally provoked a handful of Union-supporting MPs and Peers to establish a Parliamentary Rugby Union Group. Leading lights in the initiative were Roy Hughes, the Labour M.P. for Newport, and Sir Peter Fry, a Tory M.P. representing Wellingborough. I did not know Fry but Hughes had not infrequently had a go at me in the tea-room over the "theft" of Welsh talent by Rugby League clubs. I had a similar banter with other Welsh Labour MPs but I was conscious that with Hughes it was a little more serious. Seven MPs and one Peer attended the inaugural meeting of the Union Group and I am certain that the speaker that night, Dudley Wood, was not exactly delighted that two of the seven MPs present - Laurie Cunliffe and myself - were officers of the Parliamentary Rugby League Group.

Following the Christmas recess, I asked a number of written questions to the Minister at the Department of Social Security regarding National Insurance contributions in respect of Rugby Union players in the hope that a different Department, with officials not alerted to my motivation, might finally confirm that payments were being made. William Hague, the DSS minister concerned, failed to oblige, which is probably just as well for him, bearing in mind his appointment as Secretary of State for Wales very soon afterwards.

When we finally got confirmation from the Inland Revenue of the extent of payments and rewards in Union, it came in a form we could not at that stage use publicly. Our contact at the Inland Revenue's Solihull Special Office met with Gary Waller, McCartney and myself during the spring of 1994. He was obviously somewhat circumspect in what he was prepared to tell us, and, as we had expected, was not willing to name individual clubs. But he made it absolutely clear that, at the top level, Union was "at least as professional as Rugby League" - and that professionalism was by no means confined only to Wales.

Cross-code challenge: Wigan RLFC versus Bath RUFC
at Maine Road, Manchester. (Photo: Mike Haddon)

Wigan RLFC with the 1996 Rugby Union Middlesex Sevens trophy
(Photo: Gerald Webster)

8: The Sports (Discrimination) Bill

The idea came to me during the Easter recess in 1994. I was away with the family for a few days in our caravan on a site in Wensleydale when it struck me that if the Union discrimination against League players was not illegal then we would have to try and make it so.

I had previously introduced a number of Private Members' measures under the Ten-Minute-Rule procedure. The Parliamentary Labour Party has a procedure whereby the Deputy Chief Whip, at that time Don Dixon, co-ordinated applications for these bills by Labour MPs.

I spoke to him and he made the quite reasonable point that there were others on the Labour benches who had not yet introduced any bills, were anxious to have the opportunity and whose names were on his "waiting list". I did not go into detail about the purpose of the Bill because Dixon, coming from soccer-obsessed Geordie country, was not likely to be particularly enthusiastic in its support.

With a Ten-Minute-Rule Bill out of the question and the Government obviously unwilling to introduce legislation on the issue, I had two other options - introducing the measure as a Ballot Bill or bringing it in from behind the Speaker's Chair at the start of formal business in the Commons. If a Ballot Bill has cross-party support and an MP is fortunate enough to win the ballot, he or she has a good chance of getting it on to the statute book.

I had entered the ballot unsuccessfully each year since coming into Parliament and discounted this method because the chances of winning were exceedingly thin. In any event I would have an eight-month wait for the next opportunity. My only option really was to bring it in from behind the Speaker's Chair. This approach did not allow any speeches in support but merely a reading of the Bill's title and setting of the date for its second reading. Then the bill would be included in a list of similar measures at the end of business on a Friday.

Ninety-nine per cent of such bills were blocked by cries of "object" from the Government whips and subsequently hit the dust. But this did not matter. I knew I had no chance of gaining a second reading because I was certain it would be opposed once its purpose was known. Nevertheless, in making its purpose known it would be possible to ensure that far more people were made aware of the discrimination issue. The sole achievement of most Private Members' measures was, as I was well aware, the publicising of grievances and concerns.

Shortly after Parliament had resumed for the summer term I ventured upstairs into the office of the Clerks of Public Bills to seek their advice on the possibility of a bill being drafted to address the practices of the Rugby Union authorities. These clerks are responsible for administering the procedures whereby what are usually government bills make their way through parliament from first publication to becoming a statute. They serve as clerks to the standing committees of those bills which have gained a Second Reading and advise the chairs of such committees on detailed procedural points. In addition, as I had discovered through introducing previous bills, they were usually more than happy to help individual MPs prepare their own Private Members' Bills on particular issues.

I was especially fortunate that day to be met in their office by a clerk who had more idea than most of the background to the measure I wanted to introduce and its central purpose. Paul Silk, the clerk who took responsibility for helping me with the drafting of the bill was not only a Welsh Rugby Union fan but also vice-chairman of Blaneau RUFC. He saw the funny side of this particular assignment but, despite his background could not have been more helpful in terms of his advice and support with the bill. I suspect he was one of a growing number of Welshmen within the Palace of Westminster embarrassed by the growing evidence of "shamateurism" in the valleys and struck by the utter hypocrisy of the official Union attitude to League.

By the following week, Silk had produced the first draft of the Sports (Discrimination) Bill and I was able to have a detailed discussion about its possible introduction when, on 27 April, with McCartney, I met Maurice Lindsay and Harry Gration of the Rugby Football League. They were in London prior to giving evidence the next day to the National Heritage Select Committee Inquiry on sports broadcasting.

All three reacted positively to the idea of the Bill, the general consensus being that it was something which should have been tried a good deal earlier. Lindsay agreed to take the draft bill back to the RFL headquarters to discuss with their Board and Council prior to consideration being given to an appropriate time for its introduction.

I joined McCartney, Lindsay and Gration that night for a meal in the Churchill Room at the Lords' end of the Palace of Westminster. During the meal, Iain Sproat came to our table to tell us that the Ministry of Defence had that day announced, through a parliamentary answer, that Rugby League was to be accorded full recognition within the armed forces. It had been a long hard battle but we seemed at long last to be making some headway. The wonderful progress the game has made in the forces since then bears out that it had been an issue worth pursuing.

The trauma of party leader John Smith's sudden death a couple of weeks later meant that Labour MPs obviously had other things on their minds for much of the summer term. Nevertheless, I arranged with the RFL to introduce the bill on Tuesday 21 June following a morning press conference which would set out its purposes. McCartney was to chair the press conference with comments from Lindsay, myself and a player directly affected by the ban. Gration had organised the attendance of Ian Birkby, the former Castleford and Oldham player, who was attempting to get reinstatement in Union with the Wilmslow club in the Cheshire area where he was now living. The choice of Birkby to contribute at that conference and at other presentations on this issue was a masterstroke by the Rugby League. We could not have had a more articulate and presentable player to front the argument and he emerged without doubt as the star of the show that day.

The press conference was held in the largest of the siderooms off Westminster Hall and we were delighted with the turnout of TV crews and the national press. McCartney set out the background and we heard a number of messages of support for the bill including one phoned in that morning from Colin Welland articulating the depth of his anger about the current position. I set out the specific purpose of the bill before handing over to Lindsay who outlined the RFL's strong support for the measure and the extent of concern over the hypocrisy of the Union position.

But we were merely the warm-up acts because it was Birkby who gripped the audience by doing no more than outlining his own treatment by the Rugby Football Union. He summed it all up in one sentence that was carried in various national newspapers and on TV. "Since I finished playing Rugby League, apartheid has ended, the Iron Curtain has come down and the Israelis have given up the Gaza Strip to the

Palestinians but I still can't play Rugby Union on a Saturday afternoon." His honesty and sincerity struck a chord with so many at that press conference who were obviously quite astonished that such attitudes still prevailed. After Birkby's contribution a number of other members of the Parliamentary Rugby League Group voiced their support for the measure with Alan Rogers indicating its particular relevance to the situation in Wales. The Bill's introduction featured on the lunchtime national news.

Formal first reading

Its formal first reading entailed me hovering behind the Speaker's Chair after Prime Minister's Questions that day and standing alongside the Clerk at the Table of the House while he read out the title of the Bill. The Speaker then asked: "Second Reading what day?" I responded, "Friday, 1 July", and that was that. For what it was worth, the show was on the road although, in accordance with the usual experience of Private Members' Bills, I did not expect the road to go very far.

Following Iain Sproat's sympathetic response to representations on the discrimination issue and other matters of concern to Rugby League, I had written to him before the formal launch of the bill asking about the Government's likely position on the measure. Specifically, I asked him whether I could expect any support (publicly or privately) from Government sources. His response referred me to his own attempts in meetings with both the RFU and RFL to encourage the two bodies to engage in a constructive dialogue. He said that both governing bodies were responsible for their own rules and regulations "and it would be wrong for Government actively to intervene in their affairs or to favour the rules operated by one body at the expense of another."

Second reading

His message left me in no doubt as to the Government's intentions towards the bill. Accordingly, when Friday, 1 July, came, I was doing constituency work in Wakefield. I had briefed the Labour Whips to formally move the bill's second reading but expected to learn the following week that it had been blocked by a cry of "object" from the Government benches.

But shortly after 3.00p.m. that afternoon I took an urgent phone call from Alan Meale, the MP for Mansfield and a Labour Whip. "Your Bill's got a second reading," he said. "It was unopposed this afternoon." My immediate reaction was one of complete amazement and disbelief. Meale was a member of the Parliamentary Rugby League Group from the days of the Mansfield Marksmen team in his constituency and he had continued to take a close interest in the discrimination issue. He knew the purpose of my Bill and was therefore as surprised as I was that it had gone through on the nod. "You'll need to get a committee together to do the committee stage. It's your responsibility as the bill's author," he added.

When I returned to London the following week my first port of call was the Public Bill Office to seek advice on the procedural arrangements for the committee stage. I sought the clerks' opinions on why, in view of the Government's clearly stated opposition, the measure had gained a second reading. Had the Government Whip on duty that day blundered or had Sproat privately indicated he had no objection to a second reading as a means of bringing increased pressure to bear on the Union establishment? One of the clerks suggested a third possible option - conspiracy to cock-up - in view of Sproat's sympathies.

The committee

Paul Silk advised me that I would have to await a Wednesday morning slot in the particular Standing Committee dealing with Private Members' Bills. This might take a week or two but the Committee of Selection required my nominations for the membership of the Committee at its meeting in two days' time. The make-up of the committee had to be eight Conservative members, plus the Government Whip, six Labour and one from the minority parties.

I spoke to McCartney later that day regarding the committee's make-up. We both agreed it was important to draw members from areas other than traditional Rugby League country. In addition to McCartney and myself we added Peter Hain and John Owen-Jones, a Union-supporting Labour Whip from Cardiff. Kate Hoey, a London Labour MP and former Olympic hurdler, also agreed to join. She had been to several meetings of the Rugby League Group and fully understood our concerns. Tom Pendry, the Shadow Sports Minister, made up the Labour six.

I asked Liz Lynne, the Liberal Democrat MP for Rochdale, to represent the minority parties and she readily agreed. She had been a member of the Rugby League Group since taking over from Cyril Smith in that constituency in 1992.

The Tory nine were more difficult and I was also conscious of the need to balance out the bill's supporters and sponsors with other MPs who would offer some defence of Union for the rest of us to break down. Gary Waller and Elizabeth Peacock, the Tory MP for Batley and Spen, were both active in the Parliamentary Rugby League Group and were obvious candidates in support of the measure. Bob Spink, the Tory MP for Castle Point in Essex, also agreed to serve. Originating from Keighley, he had become a member of the Group on entering Parliament in 1992 and fully supported the bill.

I asked Sebastian Coe, the Tory MP for Falmouth and a former Olympic champion, if he would be willing to serve. He had earlier made clear to both McCartney and me that he sympathised with our efforts but his recent appointment as a Parliamentary Private Secretary to a minister restricted his freedom. Nevertheless he undertook to seek out some Tory volunteers and, with his help, we added Stephen Day and Nick Hawkins, the Tory MPs for Cheadle and Blackpool South respectively. I recruited Terry Dicks, the MP for Hayes and Harlington, who, although sitting on the Conservative benches, had a reputation for outspoken criticism of upper class elites. He had made clear his sympathy for our efforts with the Twickenham authorities over a long period of time.

I also persuaded Graham Riddick, the Tory MP for Colne Valley, to join us, knowing that he was one of the few MPs who would be prepared to stand up and defend the Union position. Unfortunately, we were to be deprived of his contribution when his involvement in the "cash for questions" row became public on the day the committee eventually met.

The Tory Whips Office nominated Giles Brandreth, the MP for Chester and a former TV presenter and, with the addition of Sproat as the minister responsible we had our full complement, with the exception of the neutral chair who was subsequently appointed from the all-party Chairman's Panel.

Within the limited time constraints I had thought long and hard about the make-up of the committee, particularly in terms of the inclusion of Union opponents. Politically, I did not want to have the embarrassment of Labour MPs fronting the defence of the Union position and I had therefore deliberately not invited Roy Hughes, who was behind the establishment of the Parliamentary Rugby Union Group.

I did not know at the time that Hughes was actually a member of the Chairman's Panel of senior MPs from which the Chairs of Standing Committees are selected. I found out when Paul Silk told me that Hughes had been nominated to chair the standing committee on my bill at a sitting to be held on Wednesday, 13 July at 10.30a.m. It was ironic that the Chairman's Panel had nominated to chair the committee the MP who was probably its most virulent opponent in both the Commons and the Lords.

I discussed with Silk procedural arrangements for the committee. When a Private Member's Bill reaches its committee stage the member concerned acts in exactly the same way as a minister would with government legislation. I was required to introduce the measure, move any amendments necessary to tidy up the bill and respond to questions raised about its purpose and specific provisions,

In most instances, when a Private Member's Bill reaches committee stage, the MP concerned is supported and advised by those organisations - often charities or pressure groups - advancing the case for a change in the law. I had raised this point with Maurice Lindsay of the RFL some time earlier, before the bill had made such spectacular progress. Through him I discovered that Neil Tunnicliffe, a Rugby Football League official, had been in dialogue for some time with the London-based lawyers Frere, Cholmely, Bischoff over the legal position of former League players who faced a ban on their return to Union. Tunnicliffe put me in touch with one of their solicitors, Simon Levine, who agreed to sit in on the committee, acting in a similar advisory capacity to myself as civil servants do to ministers.

Levine was not just a very competent lawyer. He originated from Hull, watching Rugby League at the Boulevard (Hull FC's ground) as a boy and he had a deep personal commitment to fighting the rugby discrimination issue. Like myself, he had found that the experience of exile in the south of England, witnessing first-hand attitudes to Rugby League, had reinforced his anger over practices that Rugby Union had got away with for far too long.

The media coverage following the bill's introduction in the House was usefully raising the temperature outside Parliament over Rugby Union discrimination. I was asked to write articles about the purpose of the measure in national newspapers and, along with McCartney, did numerous television and radio interviews, especially for the Welsh media, outlining our aims.

I began to receive letters from people telling me of their own bitter experiences of Union hypocrisy, some from pre-war years, long before I was born. I was astonished at the number of letters I received from the south of England offering strong support for the Sports (Discrimination) Bill. One such writer, from Kent, told me he had played for Stroud RUFC's second XV against the Leyhill Prison team in the mid-1960s. Their opponents' team included a well-known killer serving his time in that prison. "So a convicted killer can play Union but not someone who has had half a game for Batley," he wrote.

Some newspapers even determined to campaign actively for change in the Union-League relationship, drumming up support for the Sports (Discrimination) Bill. I was delighted when the traditionally conservative *Yorkshire Post* launched a "Tackling Rugby's Sham" campaign aimed at exposing Union hypocrisy on the professionalism question. Their senior reporter, Roger Cross, had over several years taken frequent digs at the nonsensical Union position in his regular light-hearted column on that paper's Saturday sports page. Cross, like myself, had grown up in Wakefield during Trinity's greatest era but he had also actively followed Union and was privy to much inside information on "shamateurism" which he took pleasure in bringing to my attention. His success in persuading a paper with the status and politics of the *Yorkshire Post* to support the parliamentary battle was, I am sure, a significant factor in the pressure for change. Sadly, Cross died suddenly shortly before the end of 1994 and was never to witness the profound changes of the following year.

I began to receive letters from Australia and New Zealand, including cuttings of press reports about the bill in papers in those two countries. And arising from this coverage on the other side of the world many of those writing from abroad also sent me useful information both about alleged payments to Union players outside Britain and the pressure to drop barriers to the return of former Union players who had played professional Rugby League.

Of particular significance was the case of Brett Papworth, a former Australian Rugby Union international, who signed for the Eastern Suburbs professional Rugby League club in 1987. Papworth's League career had been hit by numerous injuries and he decided to go back to Union. However, his return was blocked after the IRB refused two applications by the Australian RFU for his reinstatement.

Like Stuart Evans, he was affected by the application of Regulation 7 of the IRB rules but, unlike Evans, Papworth had the support of the Australian RFU. The Australian RFU had pressed for changes to the regulations in 1991 after legal advice had been received to the effect that, as they stood, the regulations were unenforceable. A further legal opinion in October 1992 had confirmed the need to ensure that the reinstatement of former professionals was not totally impossible as a means of reducing the risk of legal proceedings.

Papworth was supported in his personal battle by another former Wallabies player, Tony Melrose, who had also returned to Union after playing with Easts. Melrose had only been granted permission to resume playing Union after threatening legal action and Papworth subsequently challenged the New South Wales Rugby Union in court in April 1994. Shortly before his appearance in the Supreme Court on 15 April the issue was settled in Papworth's favour and he returned to playing Union.

The Union magazine, *Rugby World* magazine subsequently made clear its belief that any legal action taken against Regulation 7 could not be defended. "What will happen if some current [Union] players are subpoenaed and questioned under oath about whether they have received any money from playing rugby? I don't think it would be pretty," the writer said.[136]

Only a few weeks later the New Zealand Rugby Union was to consider the application for the reinstatement of Brett Iti, the former Bradford Northern half-back. Following their receipt of three separate legal opinions they came to the conclusion that it would be unreasonable restraint of trade to prevent his return to Rugby Union. The New Zealand press reported the NZRFU chairman, Eddie Tonks, as saying: "Looking at the Australian experience with Brett Papworth and Tony Melrose, trying to ban Iti would probably be unenforceable in a court of law." [137]

Both McCartney and I were disappointed that what had seemed to us to be a fairly high quality debate in the standing committee received minimal coverage in the national media on the following day. Perhaps we had failed to alert sufficiently the parliamentary press lobby to the significance of the bill, concentrating instead on the sports writers. National newspaper editors assume, not unreasonably, that anything worthy of note in parliament will be covered by their parliamentary correspondents. Sports correspondents do not always write about off-the-field events, however important they may be to their particular sport.

Nevertheless, over the coming weeks an increasing number of serious articles began to appear in the national media concerning the bill, most of which were supportive of our aims. These obviously had the effect of stimulating activity by Rugby Union. I had been made aware when the bill was in committee that the RFU were represented in the public gallery and after the committee stage it was increasingly apparent that the Union authorities had finally woken up to the fact that we meant business.

New clauses and amendments

When I met Paul Silk to discuss arrangements for the report stage and third reading which was to be held on the Friday following the standing committee I discovered that a substantial number of new clauses and amendments had been tabled by Sir Peter Fry for consideration. These would, subject to the Speaker's selection, be debated on the floor of the House with votes, if necessary, on 5 July.

Fry's new clauses proposed a number of changes to the bill including the prevention of its application "to any rule-making body of a sport which forbids payments to those who take part other than for legitimate or authorised expenses". More specifically Fry listed four sports to which the subsequent Act would not apply, adding boxing, Gaelic Football and hurling to Rugby Union football, presumably to drum up Scottish and Irish opposition. He proposed another new clause which specifically exempted from the subsequent Act any association which was bound by the rules of an international body in the way the home Unions were subject to the IRB.

While these new clauses clearly had the intention of completely wrecking the bill, three others concerning the starting date for the measure were more conciliatory, reflecting what increasingly came over to me in conversation with Fry as his personal resignation to the fact that internal change within Rugby Union was by now inevitable. He proposed that the Act should not come into force "until the rule-making body of any sport whose rules are affected would be able to make representations, within one year of the passing of this Act, to the appropriate Secretary of State". He proposed that the Act should not come into force until the responsible Secretary of State was satisfied that its implementation "would have no adverse effect upon any sport in the United Kingdom" and until a date specified by the Secretary of State.

The contents of Fry's amendments indicated that they had been drafted in something of a rush. Included in them was a proposal to remove from the bill the provision for the taking of civil proceedings by plaintiffs who believed they were victims of discrimination by a particular association. He proposed instead that such individuals may "make representations to the Secretary of State for permission to take civil proceedings against the ruling body concerned; but such permission may not be reasonably refused provided that the action will not cause excessive havoc to the sport concerned". Where it was deemed that "excessive havoc" would not be caused, Fry generously suggested that the civil proceedings would "entitle any successful claimant to damages not exceeding £10".

I saw little difficulty in arguing against any of Fry's proposals but was more concerned that there would be insufficient time to deal with them all on the day. In such circumstances, even if a bill is reached, the chair can reasonably refuse to allow a vote if there are outstanding new clauses and amendments.

I spoke to a number of the bill's sponsors regarding the tactics for the report stage and all of them shared my view that, even without Fry's new clauses and amendments, we would be lucky to be allowed more than a few minutes time towards the end of the Friday business.

After speaking to both Geoff Lofthouse and Paul Silk I established that it was possible to defer consideration of the bill until after the summer recess. It was clear to me that even if there had been time to debate Fry's concerns on the Friday, the bill had virtually no chance of completing its Lords' stages before the end of the parliamentary session. Accordingly I decided that the best tactic was to move the bill's report stage to 21 October, which was the last day in that parliamentary session that private members' bills could be considered. The key factor from the point of view of the bill's sponsors was that this kept it alive for three more months and maintained pressure on the Union authorities to review their attitudes towards Rugby League.

As a consequence of this decision most of the bill's sponsors and supporters had long departed when it was finally reached in the Commons at nearly 2.20p.m. on the afternoon of Friday 15 July. There was no need for their presence and we were wise to have agreed to defer the measure. After petitions concerning the Abbey Wood sorting office and dog dirt in Yeovil, the House dealt with the final stages of the Merchant Shipping (Salvage and Pollution) Bill, the Inshore Fishing (Scotland) Bill [Lords], a statement on disability, the Marriage Bill and the Sale of Goods (Amendment) Bill [Lords]. My bill was listed immediately before the Energy Conservation Bill, a measure I would have been embarrassed to block through a discussion on rugby.

Iain Sproat was present in the chamber as the minister responsible for dealing with the Bill on the Government's behalf. I explained to him my tactic and apologised for wasting his time and that of his civil servants. He fully understood the position.

I did not offer a similar explanation to Fry who protested loudly about his amendments after I had formally deferred the bill's consideration to 21 October. He was told he was out of order by the Deputy speaker, Dame Janet Fookes.

Open professionalism

The England Rugby Union team's experiences on the June 1994 tour of South Africa generated even more argument about "amateurism". Even prior to their visit some papers were alleging that the England players were envious of the open professionalism apparent in South African Rugby Union, with Natal's players being on £800 a man according to one report.[138]

The extent of the movement that was rapidly building up was signified when the *Sunday Times* Rugby Union correspondent, Stephen Jones, was forced to concede the shambles that was becoming increasingly apparent. He wrote at the end of the South African visit: "Some scenes from England's tour were instructive. At one function Ian Beer, president of the [English] RFU, castigated South African rugby for swinging towards professionalism, and fiercely recommended the amateurism espoused by his own Union. There was a short pause while every South African in the room aged forty and under asked their sage elders to tell them about amateurism."[139]

I was having a short holiday with my family near Whitby in early August when the BBC's *World at One* radio programme asked me to do a studio interview down the line from Middlesbrough, along with Jonathan Davies, over new allegations concerning "shamateurism" in Wales. The national media had gained a preview of an interview with Scott Gibbs to be published in the September edition of *Rugby World* in which the former Welsh Union international, who had signed for St Helens RLFC earlier in the year, had given detailed information about payments within Rugby Union.

Alongside his allegations concerning the receipt of win bonuses, monthly payments and lump sums to join clubs, the magazine included a quote from Brian Hanlon, the Bristol RU coach, which indicated that such practices were not confined to Gibbs's Wales. "It's just a sham at the moment and the English are one of the worst. As a coach I am sick of it. All I hear is 'what's in it for me?' The game is going professional ... There is a hypocritical situation".[140]

Attacks on the Bill

In the *Sunday Times* on 11 September 1994 Stephen Jones broke new ground in an article about my Bill with, in my opinion, a somewhat desperate suggestion that "amateurism" was no longer the issue. Despite absolutely no changes in the International Board's regulations relating to this question and no change in their interpretation in Britain by the home Rugby Unions, Jones wrote that the game had a new position which was "severely practical". Attributing this to the efforts of Vernon Pugh, the chair of both the Welsh and International Rugby Boards, Jones wrote: "Restrictions on players trying to return to Union will remain not as a defence of long-lost amateurism, but as a protection of assets. The ban is seen as Union's only weapon, a disincentive for players to move to League."[141]

As I was subsequently to discover, nobody had seen fit to tell Dudley Wood of this apparent change which, according to Jones, meant that "Hinchliffe has been fighting the wrong battle on the wrong pitch". The Sports (Discrimination) Bill, he suggested, is "history before its third reading".[142]

Far from being angered by Jones's attack on the bill's sponsors and myself, I regarded his obvious wriggling as the clearest evidence yet that Union was now on the run. On the few occasions in this long battle that our spirits had flagged, McCartney and I would turn to his articles and go back to the struggle with renewed vigour. In this latest article and others he had peddled the line of Rugby League being parasitic, conveniently ignoring the existence of amateur Rugby League as the source of recruitment of well over 90 per cent of professional Rugby League players. He was not alone in completely ignoring the existence of BARLA and the amateur ranks. The southern based media almost in its entirety consistently referred to Rugby League as the "professional game".

As we returned for the short spill-over parliamentary session in October and the Sports (Discrimination) Bill's report stage and third reading, Gavin Hastings, the Scottish Rugby Union captain, helpfully raised the temperature again with references to widespread breaches of amateurism in his autobiography, *High Balls and Happy Hours*. Extensive press coverage was given to his allegation that "there is blatant abuse all over the world ..." He was reported as claiming that: "There are now underhand payments, not only in South Africa, but in Australia, New Zealand, England, Wales and Ireland."[143]

But despite increasingly authoritative allegations about breaches of amateurism, the home Unions continued to view my bill with alarm and stepped up their active opposition as Parliament resumed. I had been told during the recess that the Union authorities had taken on a lobbying company to help block the Bill and Dudley Wood had on 29 September circulated every MP with a copy of a letter he had written to Iain Sproat strongly opposing the measure.

Iain Sproat had taken up the Union's position on "amateurism" in an earlier letter on 9 September to Dennis Easby, the President of the RFU. Wood's reply, riddled with derogatory remarks about Rugby League, suggested that my motivation in introducing the bill was "to restore the ailing fortunes of his preferred sport by opening the door to the best Rugby Union players, who might be tempted by cash offers if they could readily return to Rugby Union." Wood referred to the proceedings of the committee stage of the bill saying: "Much play was made during the debate of the allegation that Rugby Union is no longer an amateur sport." Echoing Jones's line, he argued: "This may be a matter of definition but the RFU complies totally with the regulations relating to amateurism established by the IRB."[144]

Wood's letter came over as arrogant to a number of the MPs who spoke or wrote to me about it and one, Elliott Morley, the Labour MP for Glanford and Scunthorpe, actually wrote back to Wood saying that his letter had moved him from a position of neutrality on my bill to positive support for it.

As the date of the report stage grew nearer it was interesting that, despite the bill having absolutely no chance of making further progress, the various Rugby Union authorities seemed to have a very different idea. I was particularly disappointed to receive on 20 October a hand-written note stating, "As a matter of courtesy I should tell you that if nobody else does I aim to 'object' on Friday on behalf of the Welsh Rugby Union". It was from Donald Anderson, a respected Welsh colleague, who was Labour MP for Swansea East.

Anderson told me some time later that the WRU were concerned that I had not discussed the measure with them, despite the previous dialogue with Wood which had stemmed from an original approach to the International Board. Knowing Anderson, I had expected him, like several other Welsh Labour MPs, to support the principle underpinning the bill and I was saddened that he was prepared to do the WRU's bidding in this way. However, it is worth recording that over a year later, during the 1995 RL Centenary World Cup, Anderson came up to me, having seen his first live Rugby League match when Wales played the Western Samoans in Swansea: "What a marvellous game," he said. "It was so much easier for me when I knew only one side of the story."

I don't know whether it was Anderson or others who finally sealed the bill's fate by shouting "object" on 21 October. I had known in July that further progress in the 1993-

94 parliamentary session was impossible and did not hang around for the formal proceedings that afternoon.

The start of the 1994-95 Parliamentary session saw us wrestling to maintain the momentum which we had built up, through the remarkable progress of the Sports (Discrimination) Bill. It was obvious that things were moving almost by the day. Reports alleging professionalism in Union were appearing so often that I could no longer keep tabs on them for the group's files. Stuart Evans had phoned me, alerting the Group to the fact that he was about to serve writs on the Welsh Rugby Union and the IRB.

Maurice Lindsay and Harry Gration spoke at the first group meeting after the recess on the proposals contained in their *Framing the Future* document on the restructuring of Rugby League. McCartney and I had a meal with them in the Churchill Room after the meeting, where we were joined by London Broncos' manager, Robbie Moore.

We discussed rumours that were circulating regarding the immense frustration, in Wales in particular, over the continued farce of "amateurism". Several Welsh Labour MPs told me of the increasing difficulties facing Rugby Union clubs in their country as a result of the Inland Revenue investigations. There were even suggestions that serious consideration was being given by some to completely changing codes.

I told Lindsay that I believed we were on the verge of developments, possibly as significant as those of 1895, and he agreed. He then told us of two developments that made such predictions seem even more possible. He had had a phone call from Vernon Pugh, asking for a meeting in the strictest privacy. Pugh's role was central to the future of the "amateurism" regulations in Union. He was charged with bringing forward a report on the "amateurism" question to a meeting of their International Board, scheduled for March 1995. Apparently, a date had been fixed for the meeting but Pugh had, for some reason, cancelled it at the last minute.

As if that was not enough, Lindsay went on to tell us of another development. He had been summoned to another top secret meeting, on this occasion in France. The actual agenda was vague, but when he got there he found himself in the same room as Jacques Fouroux, the former French Rugby Union coach and the man at the centre of the proposals for a professional Rugby Union competition to take place after the 1995 Union World Cup, it was rumoured.

"Fouroux's plans are not for a Union competition, they are for League," Lindsay said. Such an idea from such an individual and in France, where Rugby League had struggled in recent years, was yet more evidence that someone at the heart of the 15-a-side code also saw the possibility of quite remarkable changes being on the horizon.

Privately, in the Strangers' Bar before the meal, I had tackled Gration about something Trevor Gibbons, of *Open Rugby* magazine, had told me about during the previous week. He said that the Rugby Football League had been on the verge of landing a huge sponsorship deal with a major national bank until it was scuppered at the very last minute, following the alleged intervention of a right-wing pressure group. Gibbons was as aware as I was of the politics of this organisation and had gathered from a conversation he had had with Lindsay that at the heart of the matter were Rugby Union interests and specific concerns about my bill.

Gration gave me the impression, without specifically saying so, that he thought Lindsay had been a little indiscreet in giving Gibbons this information. I was well aware of some of the tensions at the Rugby Football League between Gration and his boss, and several Leeds-based journalists had told me they were certain Gration's departure was only a matter of time, which proved to be the case. What Gibbons had told me was confirmed by Gration, who was certain that concern over my bill was at the bottom of it. Such an intervention left me spitting blood. I was livid that the tentacles of the Rugby Union hierarchy could block a crucially important sponsorship deal that would have started Rugby League on the long road away from its dependence on the tobacco industry for sponsorship.

It was my view, and McCartney's, that we should not let them get away with it. There were many ways of raising the issue under privilege in Parliament and a particularly good opportunity the following week, when I had an oral question on Rugby League and Rugby Union to be answered by Iain Sproat. Gration promised to talk to Lindsay about it, and came back the following week with the request that I should not pursue the matter. The RFL feared that blowing Union out of the water on this one might have a detrimental effect on other sponsorship negotiations.

Instead, I directed my question to the issue of Mike Catt, the Bath and England player, who had gone on the record in a newspaper stating he had earned money for playing Rugby Union in South Africa. But immediately prior to Question Time, without giving him the details, I told Sproat of my anger that Union interference in League now extended to the blocking of sponsorship deals.

We included Catt's comments in yet another parliamentary motion condemning the RFU following their banning of the Cambridge University Union player, Adrian Spencer. Spencer was accused of having played Rugby League as an amateur with London Crusaders - the Broncos predecessors - but this had only come to light after his appearance in the Rugby Union Varsity Match at Twickenham earlier that year. With Spencer being a young university student, the motion was widely supported by other MPs, angered at yet another example of Union hypocrisy.

I spent the autumn of 1994 and the early part of 1995 in dialogue and correspondence with various lawyers over the revision of the Sports (Discrimination) Bill to take account of the objections received from both the Sports Council and the Central Council for Physical Recreation. I had met representatives of both bodies, who had assured me of their support for a future measure that addressed rugby discrimination specifically and did not impact upon other sports.

Several of the bill's opponents, during the previous parliamentary session, had stressed the possibility of the bill impacting upon other sports. Michael Jopling, who supported the Bill in principle, had declined to act as a sponsor because of his concern over its possible impact on motor cycle racing where he was personally involved.

Simon Levine suggested that the bill should be redrafted in terms which applied specifically to the dispute between the RFU and RFL over the amateurism bye-laws. He proposed also that it should be made more specific in terms of remedies which could be obtained for contravention of its sections.

Paul Silk in the Public Bill Office subsequently came up with a draft that targeted Rugby Union but did not, as far as we were aware, affect any other activity. I circulated the revised measure to the Sports Council and Central Council for Physical Recreation to ensure that they were both fully on board, knowing as well that it was a good bet they would in turn draw the measure to the attention of their Rugby Union contacts.

The possible meeting between Vernon Pugh and Maurice Lindsay became public knowledge through press reports during early January 1995. Both McCartney and I had respected the confidentiality of the information Lindsay had given us during the autumn about Pugh's approach and had not even told fellow members of the Parliamentary Rugby League Group.

Lindsay subsequently made clear to me that it was Union sources that gave this information to the press in early 1995 and not unnaturally, once the proposed meeting was public knowledge, there was considerable speculation about the likely agenda. Steve Bale, *The Independent*'s rugby correspondent at that time, played down the idea that the two bodies were snuggling up together to come up with the idea of one code. "Pugh has a more specific motivation," he wrote, "to head off the Sports (Discrimination) Bill being brought before Parliament by Dave Hinchliffe MP". Bale quoted Pugh as saying that the meeting was "simply opening a basis for dialogue with not much more to it than the ability to talk to them about some issues that are common to both of us. The one that has concerned me is the Sports (Discrimination) Bill. If we were to end up with Parliament imposing a free gangway between League and Union, I believe it would be a dreadfully retrograde step for us."[145]

Pugh's comments about the bill - implying as he did that it was primarily this measure that had brought talks between Union and League after a century apart - justified all the efforts I and others had put in since its conception last Easter. It also justified Iain Sproat's behind-the-scenes diplomacy and support for change which had entailed him treading a political tightrope as far as many of his Conservative colleagues were concerned.

While I accepted that it was highly unlikely that the revised Bill would again get as far as its committee stage, the Rugby League Parliamentary Group took the view that its introduction once again would keep up the pressure on Pugh and his colleagues. On this occasion we determined to introduce it in the House of Lords as well to broaden the support for the measure within Parliament. I anticipated that the Lords might turn up a few ennobled dinosaurs prepared to give the measure more stick than it got in the Commons, but I was wrong. By then - with one honourable exception - even the dinosaurs had departed.

Cartoonist Steve Spencer's view of Wigan's triumph in the
1996 Rugby Union Middlesex Sevens at Twickenham

9: Defending the undefinable

It was lunchtime on Thursday 26 January 1995 when I strolled into the Members' tea-room. Joe Ashton, the Labour MP for Bassetlaw, called me over to his table. "I bet I can make you laugh," he said. "We're gonna do an inquiry into Rugby Union and Rugby League. It'll only be a short'un, sometime before Easter."

He was referring to the fact that during the morning, at a private meeting, the National Heritage Select Committee, of which he was a member, had agreed to take evidence from various parties and produce a report of its conclusions that would be made available to the Government department responsible to Parliament.

This was an important breakthrough and the culmination of a lot of effort from the Parliamentary Group's point of view. Joe Ashton was primarily a football man, heavily involved with Sheffield Wednesday, but over recent months he had become interested in the grievances we were expressing, especially on the "amateurism" question.

He had been present in the Chamber when I and others had questioned Iain Sproat. I had spoken to Joe and Roy Hattersley together, shortly before Christmas, regarding Adrian Spencer's case. They had supported the parliamentary motion condemning the Union stance without hesitation.

The National Heritage Committee's chairman was Gerald Kaufman, the Labour MP for Manchester Gorton, and I met him later that afternoon in a corridor. I had bent his ear on the discrimination question during the previous summer while I was on a parliamentary visit to America, looking at health care, in a party which he led. He had been heavily lobbied by others, including McCartney and Lofthouse, but I still remained to be convinced that, despite originating from Leeds, he really understood what we were aggrieved about.

Nevertheless, he had grasped that it was an issue of some importance to northern Labour MPs in particular, and had been willing to accede to pressure for an inquiry, including from some within his own committee.

The decision that day was a reminder of how important the debate on the National Lottery Bill had been. John Maxton, the Labour MP for Glasgow Cathcart, and grandson of the legendary Labour figure, Jimmy Maxton, had intervened in my speech in what I thought was a rather hostile way but he had since been won over to our point of view. Despite a Union background he understood the hypocrisy of their stance and had made his views clear as a member of the National Heritage Select Committee.

Roland Boyes, the Labour MP for Washington, had also recently joined the Committee and his background, originating from near Huddersfield, watching Huddersfield RLFC and previously playing Union, lent weight to such an inquiry. Sadly he was diagnosed as suffering from Alzheimer's Disease shortly after evidence sessions began and, as a consequence, the only member with Rugby League connections took absolutely no part in the drawing up of the report.

I was personally surprised that the decision to mount this Inquiry was barely covered in the media, perhaps because it was clearly a victory for Rugby League. On behalf of the Parliamentary Group, I issued a statement making the best of its significance from our point of view. I urged people to submit detailed written evidence to the committee clerk and drafted a detailed submission from the Parliamentary Group which, after minor amendments were made at our February meeting, was forwarded to the committee, providing the basis for much of their subsequent questioning. It told me something about the subservience of League - or its complacency in terms of fighting discrimination - that the only evidence submitted from my home town of Wakefield came from a Wakefield Rugby Union supporter anxious to stave off any possibility of Union being refused lottery funding. The Select Committee should have had letters from every Rugby League club, professional and amateur, throughout the land. The fact that it did not could not be put down to the clubs being unaware of the Inquiry. Both BARLA and the Rugby Football League knew immediately and so did the Rugby League press. I could see why Union had got away with it so easily for 99 years.

The organisation of the evidence sessions was entirely a matter for the Select Committee members. They acceded to suggestions from a number of members of the Parliamentary Rugby League Group that Ian Birkby should speak from the point of view of those barred from Union because of past involvement in League. Other than agreeing to our view that the Inland Revenue should be called, the remaining witnesses who were examined were chosen by the committee itself. Representatives of Wigan RLFC and Bath RUFC were invited, presumably because they were then deemed to be the top clubs in either code. Officials of BARLA, the RFL and the RFU were summoned, along with Armed Forces representatives responsible for the organisation of sport in the services.

The first evidence session took place on the committee floor of the House on Thursday 2 March 1995 and began with an examination of Ian Birkby's evidence. His earlier written memorandum to the inquiry had outlined how he was debarred from playing Union because, prior to a professional Rugby League career, he had played a handful of games of Union at the age of 17. He had not played League for seven years. His submission ended with: "My final plea is, as a 33-year-old scrum-half, please take action quickly. I do not have many years left before the big guys start to catch me."[146]

Birkby's oral contribution was an effective mixture of reasoned argument and humour. Those of us who sat through the session on the public benches were unanimously of the opinion that he had won over the committee members with an articulate account of his own circumstances, which neatly summed up the complete nonsense of the situation for members unfamiliar with the two codes' relations. Birkby's contribution got excellent coverage on national television that night, drawing further public attention to the indefensible position of the Rugby Union authorities.

His appearance was followed with oral evidence from Jack Robinson, the Wigan RLFC chairman, and Joe Lydon, the Wigan assistant coach and former Wigan and Great Britain player. Much of their session related to specific questions about earnings in professional Rugby League and relations with Rugby Union. Lydon talked of payments in Union which had come to his knowledge through contacts with players in Union. "I know of one player... whose expenses to travel from his home to his playing club would only be equalled out if he had travelled via Bahrain," he said.[147]

That morning's evidence session concluded with a series of questions to Major J.W. Quinn, the Bath RUFC secretary, mainly around the disposal of their £2 million per annum gate income. Joe Ashton established from his questions that Bath charged £7 ground admission and £3 stand transfer to an average 8,000 home spectators. They paid their players 20p per mile travelling expenses, no compensation for loss of earnings and employed just six people plus cleaners. Ashton had calculated that these arrangements must leave a substantial surplus but was unable to establish from his witness where these additional resources went. Everyone, including Quinn, knew exactly what he was getting at. But the Bath secretary was more forthcoming in his answers to questions about Birkby's dilemma. "There is one way out: if he is young enough he could join the army and then he could play Rugby Union," he suggested.[148]

The second evidence session was for some reason put back a week and took place on 16 March, two days after Union's IRB announced, following a week-long meeting in Bristol, that former Rugby League professionals would be allowed back into Union after a three year stand-down period. Despite the length of the meeting they determined to defer further consideration of the professionalism question, to be addressed by a specific working party of the IRB, to a special meeting in August in Paris.

The media in general described this development as a great concession to our cause and were surprised at my reaction on behalf of the Parliamentary Group that frankly nothing had changed. The comments of the Rugby Union correspondent of the *Independent* were typical. He wrote of the decision: "Although this lowers one of Rugby Union's few defences against Rugby League and so was quite a momentous change, it was not enough for David Hinchliffe, the MP who has been pursuing Rugby Union for its 'bigoted discrimination'. Although no Union has yet imprisoned anyone for going north, the Member for Wakefield has worked out that 'the proposed sentence roughly equates' with that for gross indecency or grievous bodily harm'."[149] The *Yorkshire Post* put my comments in context and had their sports page lead saying: "Union fudge leaves Hinchliffe furious".[150]

I was bloody livid with the IRB's cheek, but also angry with myself when I read in the press the following day that in making comments hurriedly to the Press Association on the day of the announcement, I had failed to spot something of obvious significance. Press speculation prior to the announcement had suggested that there would be a two year "sentence" on former League professionals. So why had they gone for three? I had suspected they would go for the maximum possible and ought to have realised that in setting any specific period they would obviously take account of the implications of Stuart Evans's legal action. Until I read the *Western Mail* on the following morning, it had not struck me that he had served a three-year gap and could be reinstated in Union straightaway. He had faxed his request for reinstatement to the WRU and therefore the crucially important legal action for restraint of trade was dead and buried.

Evans had been convinced that he could prove that the WRU and the IRB were preventing him from earning a living through their ban. He told the press he did not intend signing himself away to any club just yet and said: "They all know where I am, and I'll wait to see what they have to say to me before I decide who to play for."[151]

Evans's reinstatement got Rugby Union out of a particularly difficult corner and obviously they were well aware that by getting him back on board they had immobilised one particularly important weapon in Rugby League's armoury. But we knew we had them in serious difficulties on the income tax issue and were delighted that the Select Committee had acceded to the Rugby League Parliamentary Group's request that they take oral evidence from the Inland Revenue.

The evidence session with the Inland Revenue witnesses was the first item at the committee's meeting on 16 March. Unfortunately their witnesses - Eugene McGivern and Roger Allen of the Personal Tax division and John Gribbon of the Business Profits division - did not include the officer who informed McCartney, Waller and me of the outcome of their Union investigations. These three were obviously intent on being a good deal more circumspect about the rewards received by Union players. Spectators in the committee's public seats were forced to admire their skilled failure to give any real insight into whether Union players paid income tax or not.

Kaufman obviously saw their reluctance to be more forthcoming as something of a challenge and pressed them very strongly after it was established that Union players could claim tax allowances against expenses incurred in the "amateur" game. "They only get tax relief... if the activities which give rise to the expenses produce a profit in their hand," said McGivern. "But if they are getting a profit in their hands, as you say, that profit must mean they are not amateurs," responded Kaufman.[152]

The tax treatment of expenses became central to the questioning in this session. In response to further pressure from Kaufman, McGivern said, "If, for example, the player received a flat rate allowance for expenses of £1,000 - and may I ask you not to read anything into these examples, because I am giving them off the cuff - and the expenses that the player incurred amounted to, say, £300 or £400 a year, then there is clearly a profit element in the payment the individual has received. We would contend for tax on that". He continued: "If the individual were paid money in respect of loss of earnings, we would equally contend that that was profit and was taxable. If the individual were in receipt of other payments at the club, for example, signing on fees, or loyalty bonuses, or payments to remain with the club, or whatever, we would contend that they represented taxable emoluments."[153]

McGivern continued with other examples of benefits for which Kaufman cryptically thanked him. "That is very helpful, Mr McGivern, because although I do not ask you to comment on this, you have clearly not plucked these examples out of the air. I would take it that they all must exist here or there or somewhere for you to have been so easily able to think of them," he concluded.[154]

The supplementary memorandum submitted by the Inland Revenue to the inquiry confirmed their inability to establish how much income tax is paid by Rugby Union and Rugby League. "To collect this information from our network of local offices would involve disproportionate cost", it stated. And in response to the committee's interest in whether there were Union clubs paying National Insurance contributions on behalf of their players, he replied: "The Inland Revenue regret they are unable to supply this information because of the tax and National Insurance rules which protect the confidentiality of tax payers' and contributors' affairs."[155]

While I was disappointed that the Inland Revenue evidence had not been more clear cut, it was obvious that Kaufman felt that McGivern's answers indicated that some Union players were clearly in receipt of taxable payments. Indeed the subsequent Committee report indicated that the rest of the membership shared his view.

The subsequent evidence from the Rugby Football League punctured the myth in my opinion peddled by Stephen Jones and some other Union writers that League is parasitic in terms of its relationship with Union. Appearing alongside Maurice Lindsay and Tom O'Donovan from the RFL, Neil Tunnicliffe, their project co-ordinator, informed the committee that of the 2,393 players signed by professional Rugby League clubs over the previous 10 years, only 8.1 per cent had come from Union.

Maurice Oldroyd and Billy Gill from BARLA were the concluding witnesses that morning, Oldroyd reinforced League's independence in terms of player recruitment. Citing the current Great Britain squad, he said: "... as many as 15 of the 17 players would have gravitated from the amateur [Rugby League] game and the other two, such as Martin Offiah and Alan Tait, have probably come from the Rugby Union game. We are proud to serve the professional game with players."[156]

"Breaches of Amateurism Rife"

Two days before the final evidence session of the Select Committee Inquiry, I spotted a small article in the sports pages of *The Times* of 21 March 1995, entitled "Union Finds Breaches of Amateurism Rife". The article related to the completion of the report of the IRB's amateurism working-party, which was due to be considered over the summer by the full Board. I asked the Commons library to obtain, urgently, from the International Board's office in Bristol, a full copy of the report. I didn't know whether it was a public document but, if it was, the brief piece in *The Times* had indicated it would be worth examining.

By late afternoon a letter on the message board in the central lobby informed me that a faxed copy of the report had arrived in the library and was awaiting collection. I picked it up immediately and at the first opportunity, later in the evening, sat down to study it. I couldn't believe my luck. The working-party's conclusions on Union's "amateurism" could have been written by the Parliamentary Rugby League Group.

Chaired by Vernon Pugh, the working-party membership of Bernard Lapasset, F.H. McCleod and Rob Fisher, according to the report's preface, all recognised that breaches of the amateurism regulations were "wholesale". Pugh's opening remarks flagged up the fact that "it may also be necessary to seek legal advice on some aspects, particularly the ability to continue to restrict free movement between Union and League if the amateur principle is more openly eroded or ended."[157]

The report's introduction detailed the background to the so-called "amateurism" principle and referred to the divisions in the sport over reimbursement for lost wages "...in 1893, when the clubs of the RFU disagreed as to its acceptability". Interestingly, the introduction went on to state, "As to why it was considered that the question of compensation for bone fide loss of time was thought to be contrary to '... the true interest of the game and its spirit' is not made clear in the surviving documentation of that time." While not subscribing to the social class analysis of the Great Divide, the report conceded that the amateur principle "... did reflect a social ethic and attitude which also had a place in other sports, albeit in a modified form." The past distinction in cricket between gentlemen (amateurs) and players (professionals) was referred to, with the report suggesting that the gentleman was generally accorded "an enhanced social status".[158]

In the context of today, the working-party stated: "If Rugby Union were to be first introduced as a sport in the latter part of the 20th century, then it is highly unlikely that defining participation such that those who could not, or would not, regularly lose time, wages, or suffer blighted careers without compensation, could be disadvantaged from active participation at the highest level, would be considered socially unacceptable and divisive. It is not easily defensible as a social or moral ethic judged by the standards of today." This refreshing admission was followed by the qualification: "That, of course, is not to deny its historic pedigree and a relevance to a time when the social order and inequalities were the more manifest."[159]

The report's main body outlined the conclusions of the working-party members' investigations. It said that: "The nature and extent of the breaches of the current regulations have been found to be most concerning", and went on to give a detailed outline of the current situation. It claimed: "Many, and in some countries, most, of the senior club coaches are paid", and that: "Players, to a greater or lesser extent, receive payment for playing in many countries". According to the working-party: "Few if any of the major Unions are free of some form or other of payment to players or coaches." In terms of the public perception they concluded that the attitude of Union was regarded as "anachronistic".[160]

The working-party examined a series of alternatives open to the IRB in its future deliberations, including an option to "Lift the Veil - A Paid Game". Detailing the increased pressure on top Union players in terms of the commitment required and the growth in commercial involvement in the game, it suggested: "In such circumstances it may be inevitable that a game that is currently professional in so many respects will inevitably become openly so in due course."[161]

It would be putting it mildly to say I was surprised at the frankness of the conclusions of Pugh and his colleagues. While they were saying nothing that had not been common knowledge for years, the fact that the IRB working-party had made such frank admissions concerning the current situation was a refreshing contrast to the previous ostrich-like position of both that board and the Home Unions.

The timing of the report's appearance could not have been better from our point of view. My first concern was to alert Gerald Kaufman to the relevance of this report and its crucial importance in addressing the questions right at the heart of the Select Committee's enquiries. I knocked on the door of Kaufman's office, two floors below mine in the Commons. We were on a three-line whip, and had to be available to vote.

Despite my initial concerns that he might fail to grasp key points central to our grievances, he had by this stage a comprehensive understanding of why we were angry. He recognised a very great injustice and was happy to discuss this latest development.

I underlined key passages in the working-party report. Kaufman shared my view that they were highly significant and undertook to copy the report to the Select Committee's members, prior to the following morning's meeting to hear more evidence. He was as good as his word and by the meeting was proving himself more familiar with the contents and consequences of that report than the Secretary of the RFU.

There was quite a crowd outside committee room 10 on Thursday 3 March for the final evidence session of the Select Committee's Union-League inquiry. While the committee had a private briefing meeting in the committee room, witnesses from the armed forces, there for the first evidence session that day, had gathered outside, along with interested members of the public and a substantial press contingent.

As we talked, I noticed the tall figure of Dudley Wood, Secretary of the Rugby Football Union, coming slowly down the corridor towards us. Our last meeting had been some months earlier when he had addressed the newly established Parliamentary Rugby Union Group, initiated by my old sparring partners Roy Hughes and Sir Peter Fry. Since that time he had been involved in a car accident and looked a lot older and much more frail. I had the distinct feeling that he would have aged a good deal more by the end of that morning.

The forces personnel - four in all - looked somewhat bemused by the experience of being summoned before the Heritage Committee and were obviously in some difficulty responding to members' concerns regarding the alleged discrimination against Rugby League. In response to Kaufman's opening comparison of the numbers playing Union and League in the forces, Major-General Alan Yeoman, CB (retired), the director of the Army Sports Control Board, said: "Rugby League is a very baby sport, for want of a better word. Until four years ago there was no call within the army to have even *one* Rugby League team."[162]

He was pressed by John Maxton who referred to the fact that as a sport Rugby League was now one hundred years old. "Are you saying that during the times of National Service, when large numbers of young men from the north of England were put into the forces and were Rugby League players - some of them professional Rugby League players, because I remember watching them and I have even played rugby with them - are you telling me that those Rugby League players would not rather have played Rugby League?"

"I cannot answer that question," was Yeoman's rather tame reply, which broadly summed up all the evidence given by the Major-General and his colleagues.[163]

Maxton subsequently opened up with questions to Dudley Wood, establishing initially that Wood, in the context of the inquiry's terms of reference, deemed the new three year stand-down period "an enormous step forward". But he was far less positive about the contents of the IRB working party report which Maxton subsequently referred to. The exchange went as follows:[164]

Maxton: "Essentially this report is saying that Rugby Union at the top is not an amateur sport any more, is it not?"

Wood: "You have to define your terms. What is amateur? In this country - and I can only speak for England - we have 375,000 players, say. So far as I am aware, all of them play for love of the game and not for financial reward."

Kaufman quoted the report's own admissions that the Union position on amateurism was seen as hypocritical by many in their own game. Wood restated that the (English) RFU stood by the rules: "Of course certain things are happening in other countries which we do not approve of...but as far as this country is concerned, our players do not receive payment from their Union, or so far as we are aware, from their clubs."

At this point I realised that the Parliamentary Rugby League Group's submission to the Select Committee ought to have included a copy of the RFU's own *Inducements to Play* document which could have formed the basis for useful questions in response to Wood's disclaimers concerning England.

Define amateurism

Kaufman continued with a quote from the working party report that "the term amateurism is now incapable of a constructive or clear explanation..."[165] Wood agreed that the word amateurism was outdated and did not describe the current position. "Amateurism disappeared from Rugby Union football when it was made possible to pay expenses," he said. "Previously to that, of course, everyone financed their own activities ... but that has disappeared at the top level because the money is there and it seems right, if the money is there, that these expenses should be met. That is a very, very different thing from professionalism."

Maxton reminded Wood that payment for loss of earnings was exactly the reason why League broke away in 1895. He said: "... the fact is that the principle on which Rugby League was formed has gone. It has disappeared from Rugby Union, so why do you kick them out for three years?" Wood did not answer this direct question but set out instead the reasons for his opposition to professionalism - insufficient income in the game, and forcing players to choose between rugby and their careers.

After he had referred to "the amateurism of Rugby Union" in another answer, Kaufman pounced again. "You use the word amateurism." Mr Wood replied: "As I say, we have yet to find a word, and if your committee can help, I would be grateful." "I fear we cannot provide you with such a word. Politicians are not used to such circumlocutions," responded Kaufman.

The questioning of Anthony Coombs, the Conservative MP for Wyre Forest, was a good deal more hostile than that of either Kaufman or Maxton. He told Wood that his argument had two flaws: "First of all, you cannot define amateurism, and obviously you regard that as one of the principal bastions which you are seeking to defend by this form of apartheid with Rugby League players. To defend something you cannot even define does seem to be a rather curious way of carrying on. The second point is this: even if one assumes that one can define amateurism, this great Corinthian spirit which somehow imbues Rugby Union players but no-one else, I would have thought if it is so strong then the lure of Rugby League ... would not be very great, and as a result your concerns about the need for having such a rule would really not have been justified."[166]

Coombs had got to the heart of it all with his question which left Wood floundering. "Firstly, as to defining, what I said was we call it amateur and we are trying to keep it as a recreational sport, and we have not found a word to describe what happens when certain regulations and compensations are paid within regulations," he rambled.

Coombs's Tory colleague, Patrick McLoughin, the MP for Derbyshire West, subsequently pressed Wood on what he described as the new three year "cleansing period" for League players returning to Union. In response to both McLoughlin and subsequent questions from Jim Callaghan, the Labour MP for Heywood, Wood confirmed my belief that these recent changes had been more or less forced on the IRB as a consequence of legal advice. "I do not think the International Board, or the Rugby Football Union, wanted to lift the restriction on players who turned professional, but on legal advice they decided it was time they did so," he admitted. Clearly, while the IRB could ignore challenges Down Under, those on the horizon nearer home were not as easily dismissed. The new three-year cleansing period kept Stuart Evans nicely away from the courts.

Kaufman was not briefed on the details of Evans's situation but he was increasingly irritated at Wood's prevarication on the "amateurism principle". They debated the point as follows:[167]

Kaufman: "You have spoken with, what I might say, some emotion about amateurism but according to the report ... any principle of amateurism defined in terms similar to those of 1893 or as commonly understood thereafter, has already been set aside."

Wood: "Yes, I agree with that."

Kaufman: "You agree with that? I become as somebody who is a stranger to these issues - I have to tell you - more and more bewildered as this morning goes on ... You described Rugby Union as a sport in which players are not paid. But they are paid. The Inland Revenue taxes them on their payments. The fact that they are not paid in wage or salary does not mean that they are not paid."

Wood: "We... do not pay players. They derive their income from other sources but we do not pay players."

Kaufman: "I fear, Mr Wood, that I do have to challenge you on that because they are paid emoluments, when they are paid expense allowances (which are taxed because they are larger than expenses incurred), they are being paid. The fact that they are not being paid a wage or a salary, frankly might seem to some people a dodge to preserve the myth of amateurism."

Wood continued to refute Kaufman's central concerns about players profiting from playing, stating that they only received reasonable expenses sanctioned under International Board rules.

Kaufman: "Just because it is not a wage or a salary does not obscure the fact that it is, nevertheless, a payment for participation in sport."

Wood: "Any payment over and above what has actually been expended is excessive and we do not pay."

Kaufman: "The Inland Revenue seems to think that you do pay, because the Inland Revenue does charge tax on a difference which it works out, with that meticulous care for which the Inland Revenue is noted."

Wood: "I find that very hard to believe."

Kaufman: "That is what they have told us."

The most supportive noises, as far as Wood was concerned, came unsurprisingly from Toby Jessel, the musical Tory MP for Twickenham. He reminded the committee of Wood's central point that the distinction between amateur and professional was no longer simple and straightforward.

Wood responded: "Yes, exactly right. That is exactly the situation we are struggling through. For the reasons I have explained we still believe it is worthwhile trying to maintain a position in which we are not a professional sport..."

Conscious of the earnings of Will Carling and others, Kaufman argued: "...what you are telling us is that these players who could get very substantial sums are unwilling victims of predatory commercial interests?"

Wood: "No! I have never found a player receiving cash to be an unwilling victim ... I would just remind you, we have 375,000 active players and a few at the top have learnt how to derive considerable benefit out of the fame they have achieved."

Kaufman: "So that makes it all right?"

Wood: "I do not see that I can possibly have any objection to somebody who does not do any damage to my sport - in fact, is actually a great credit to it - I cannot see any objection to the fact that he has used his ability in a way which does not affect the sport but derives money from it. I cannot see any objection to this."

Kaufman: "So that northern ruffians like Dr Birkby ... are doing damage to your sport because they play Rugby League, and they now have this strange and unconscionable aspiration to play Rugby Union."

Wood: "I was delighted to tell Ian Birkby the other day that he is welcome to play Rugby Union football."

McLoughlin: "But not in competitions."

Wood: "He does not qualify. He is not eligible for competitions in the same way as a lot of other people are not, like overseas players."

Kaufman: "I never thought the day would arrive when I was rendered speechless."

After exchanges with Maxton over allegations that Mike Catt, the Bath and England player had been paid in South Africa - "not true" according to Wood - Michael Fabricant, the Tory MP for Lichfield, became the final committee member to question

Wood. With his reputation for uncritical government support, I expected more along the lines of Jessel but Fabricant began by saying he had "been listening in a somewhat stunned state to most of the evidence which has been given this morning." Outlining Wood's inability to define amateurism alongside the refusal to readmit Rugby League players he said his position was "at the very least ... illogical, and at the very worst ... hypocritical."

After Wood refuted his assertion, Fabricant continued: "How can you define some people as being professional, some people being amateur, when they are all receiving taxable income in one way or another?" Wood replied with reference to the difficulties of describing the retention of the essential principle of the sport "played as a recreation".

Wood agreed with Fabricant's suggestion that at some small soccer clubs individuals were playing as a recreation and yet still receiving an income from their activities. Michael Fabricant continued to challenge him:

Fabricant: "Is this not directly comparable with Rugby League and the smaller clubs there, where no Rugby League player is able to derive sufficient income just by being a Rugby League player... Yet you would say you are going to operate this system of apartheid and immediately brand these people... saying they will never be allowed back in the sport."

Wood: "This has changed, as you have heard already. That is no longer the case."

Fabricant: "Three years?"

Coombs: "They have gone into quarantine."

Kaufman: "Mr Wood, you said you did not want them back. That is what you said."

Wood: "The Rugby Union was not supportive of that change, but we accept the change has been made."

Maxton: "You did not vote for it."

In brief final exchanges with Kaufman a tired looking Wood concluded: "We have tried very, very hard to maintain amateur regulations in accordance with the International Board provisions for many years, and it is because of what has been happening in other parts of the world it has become increasingly difficult." After Kaufman thanked him for his contribution, Wood left as the committee concluded its final meeting to hear evidence.

Wood's feelings on that morning's experiences were not particularly apparent from his expression as he departed but soon after he put pen to paper condemning the "hostile attitude" and "sarcastic tone" of some of the Select Committee's members. Wood's subsequent memorandum to the Committee, published as part of their report into the inquiry said it seemed "that minds had already been made up".

10: Amateurism through the looking-glass

It was during the week after Wood's appearance as top of the bill that I came across another Stephen Jones invective which seemed very timely. Browsing through publications in a shop in Wakefield specialising in remnants I came across his book *Endless Winter* which includes two chapters which, in the main, attack Rugby League, rather out of context in a book analysing the changes Rugby Union was undergoing in 1993. Among other allegations he accuses Rugby League of providing bogus figures to show that it was second only to football as the best supported team game in Britain.

Although Rugby Union until recently has traditionally been coy about producing attendance figures, when the Rugby Football League made this claim in 1992 I asked the House of Commons library to check it out. They confirmed that *Social Trends 1990-92* did indeed show that while greyhound racing and horse racing were ranked second and third to football in terms of spectator attendances in 1990-91, Rugby League (on the basis of League matches only) came fourth with Rugby Union and Test and County cricket fifth and sixth respectively.

Jones went on to attack those who had protested about the RFU's treatment of Steve Pilgrim: "People spoke, with just a tinge of pomposity, of appeals to various courts of human rights. David Hinchliffe MP is the secretary of something called the Parliamentary Rugby League Group. He asked that Gerald Kaufman, chairman of the Commons National Heritage Select Committee, should act against the RFU. The prospect of Mr Kaufman arriving at Twickenham would almost certainly have won Pilgrim an immediate reprieve if only Kaufman promised not to stay too long. However, the Parliamentary Rugby League Group turned out to have as much practical clout as the United Nations."[168]

I copied this paragraph to Kaufman while he and his Committee were considering the outcome of the Union-League inquiry. "Maybe he'll like me better when he's read our report," was the cryptic comment on his note in return.

Jones had continued his assault on the response to the Pilgrim affair by suggesting: "Others demanded that all the vast government subsidies that Union enjoyed should be cut off. A swingeing step, too, had it not been for the fact that Union receives not a penny from anyone and is entirely self-financing."[169] As the Department of National Heritage evidence to the Select Committee showed, the Rugby Football Union in England alone received £118,320 from the Sports Council in 1992-93 and £219,196 in 1993-94. The various Home Unions were receiving millions from the Sports and Arts Foundation at the time Jones was writing his book and have received many millions more since the advent of the National Lottery. However, I anticipated that the balance was likely to be redressed in the not too distant future.

Some Rugby Union writers, such as Ian Malin or Eddie Butler, have a more balanced view of Rugby League, but in my opinion Stephen Jones has often been the most outspoken of the Rugby Union writers when commenting on Rugby League, although he recently claimed that it was a "popular misconception" that he didn't like the game.[170]

Strangely, in an odd sort of way, I was by then almost grateful for Jones' occasional outbursts. While others in the Union camp dressed up their feelings with blather about the "special ethos" of their game, Jones's pieces often contained no such camouflage and *The Sunday Times* was happy to oblige by publishing his thoughts. For example, in

May 2000, he wrote an article questioning whether enticing Jason Robinson to switch codes to Rugby Union was worthwhile, based on his opinion that he had not been a success during a short-term contract at Bath in 1996. A perceptive letter to *League Express* from Phil Stockton pointed out that in *The Times* and *The Sunday Times* it was only Stephen Jones who had regarded Robinson as a failure and quoted other Union writers' positive comments on his spell at Bath.[171]

The redrafting of the Sports (Discrimination) Bill had been completed by early April 1995 and I had arranged with the Earl of Swinton, the Conservative peer, to reintroduce it at the same time in the Commons and the Lords on the 19th of the month to coincide with the publication of the National Heritage Committee's report. We were convinced that the report would strongly attack the Union position and believed the political climate would be even more favourable to the measure as a result.

The unearthing of Vernon Pugh's report to Union's IRB prior to Dudley Wood's appearance at the last evidence session of the Inquiry had put the final seal on the certainty of a report which could potentially give a huge push to the process of change. The report had effectively been a self-declaration of hypocrisy by Rugby Union. From our point of view it was all going so smoothly. **Then it happened.**

Super League

I had been aware from press reports of a dialogue among Rugby League club officials regarding 'Super League' proposals that seemed, from what I had read, to be progressing some of the ideas contained in Maurice Lindsay's *Framing the Future* document, circulated some time earlier as the basis for discussion about the direction of Rugby League. But when, on the Thursday of the week before Easter, it became apparent that Rupert Murdoch's News Corporation was involved, McCartney was on the phone to me immediately. He was deeply disturbed that Rugby League had become involved with someone whose newspapers were in our opinion so often blatantly anti-Labour and, as he put it, "anti-working-class".

I shared his serious worries over Murdoch and pondered over what might be the implications for what had traditionally been seen as a working class game. But the Murdoch owned Sky TV's record in projecting the game on television had been good and some positives might arise in terms of packaging and presenting what we both believed to be the best sporting product in the world. Two days later, however, our worst fears were to prove well founded.

The phone rang at my home on Saturday afternoon. BBC Radio Leeds wanted me to go live on to their sports programme to comment on Super League proposals agreed that day. Murdoch's News Corporation were pumping £77 million into a deal for a European Super League, to be played during the summer months, involving 14 clubs, including two in France and one in London. The club chairmen had agreed the deal that day in Wigan, naming the fourteen clubs which included several mergers. My team, Wakefield Trinity, along with Featherstone Rovers and Castleford would merge under the title of Calder!

I told the woman who had phoned me that I simply did not believe what she was telling me and she agreed to fax me the Press Association's story to prove it was true. My immediate reaction related more the to the suggestion that anyone could seriously propose such a merger. Knowing the area well, with the fierce rivalries between supporters of these three teams, I suggested during the interview that it would perhaps be inadvisable for any of the club chairmen concerned to pass through the centres of Wakefield, Featherstone or Castleford on their journey back from Wigan that Saturday night. While I conceded the need to project the game in a fundamentally different way, I feared that we would be in very real danger of losing so much of what the game meant to local communities in areas such as my own.

From that point onwards my phone was red hot. First to call was Gary Waller, the Tory MP for Keighley, livid that Keighley had been excluded from this new Super League despite the fact that they were certain for promotion from the second division. He was setting off for Pakistan on the following day but felt strongly that the Parliamentary Group should publicly set out its views as soon as possible. He rang McCartney to agree a press release outlining our immediate concerns.

Geoff Lofthouse phoned me in an unprecedented state of anger. How dare they propose to merge his beloved Featherstone Rovers. Trinity supporters, led by a local councillor, the late Richard Clarkson, editor of the club's fanzine, began to ring. The clear view was that we had to fight to retain Trinity at Belle Vue and we agreed to meet at the match the following day to discuss tactics.

It was to be some 12 days before Maurice Lindsay made contact with us to discuss the Parliamentary Group's views. But to his credit Ted Richardson, the Trinity chairman, was on the phone the following morning. "We'd no choice, David - it's too good an offer to turn down," he said. I told him that in his own interests he should put out a statement explaining his views on both the proposed merger and the concept of Super League. I reminded him that at Trinity's last home match the referee had been chased off the field, an almost unprecedented incident for Rugby League which made the national news. On this occasion it might be him that had to depart in a hurry.

By the following day the Super League was national news and virtually the only topic of discussion on local media broadcasts. I arrived at Belle Vue for the match against Widnes to find "No Merger" slogans had been sprayed on doors to the East Stand and a group of supporters handing out hurriedly printed leaflets arguing the case against Super League.

I met Clarkson and a group of supporters for a brief chat on what we could do. We were all totally shell-shocked and no one had a clear idea of the way forward. However, contact had been made with Featherstone and Castleford supporters and a meeting to discuss an anti-merger campaign had been convened for the following week.

The scene at Belle Vue that day resembled a funeral. Small groups of devastated supporters congregated outside, unable to take in what was happening and the enormous sense of loss. I had been going there since the late 1950s but one chap who collared me had been going since 1929. He was scarcely in control of the emotions he felt that day. What made it worse from my point of view was the fact that a number of those I spoke to at the match were convinced that I knew more about the deal than I was letting on. Some seemed to assume that the Parliamentary Group had a key role in running the game and I was being deliberately non-committal.

We won the match that day - a rare win against a Widnes side having as bad a season as we were. It was a victory but I went home feeling there was little to celebrate.

The following day was the start of the Easter parliamentary recess. The phone began ringing before 8.00a.m. with request after request for interviews on the only thing that mattered - Super League. Apart from local and national radio, BBC2 were doing a special television programme in the evening and wanted me in the studio. Yorkshire TV's *Calendar* news programme wanted me live in the studio to interview Maurice Lindsay. They told me that I knew more about Rugby League than their presenter, Richard Whiteley - a back-handed compliment if ever there was one!

I apologised to them all for sticking to our family's plan to go to Wensleydale in our touring caravan. I had desperately needed a break before the events of the previous two days and even more so now.

Hawes is a fine place to unwind but it was impossible to get away from an issue that somehow gripped the nation in a way Rugby League had never done before. On the morning after our arrival, walking down the Hawes main street, I met a Trinity supporter who told me of the coverage Super League and specifically the proposed demise of Wakefield Trinity had had on Radio 4 that morning. I felt that could have been up Mount Everest, but someone would have been talking to me about Super League there.

Parliament resumed after the Easter break on 18 April 1995 and that day must rank as one of the worst of my life. I had returned from Hawes to a Bank Holiday weekend of constant calls concerning Super League and the future of Trinity who had suffered a club record 87-0 defeat at the hands of Castleford. The cumulative effect was what seemed like a blackout at the despatch box when I rose to ask a question from the Labour front bench that afternoon. I had to apologise to the Speaker and leave the Chamber, and one press report the following day deemed me to have been "Super League's first victim".[172]

I was advised to go home and rest, but my return to Wakefield that afternoon had another purpose. The Trinity directors had convened a special shareholders meeting to ratify the proposed merger with Featherstone Rovers and Castleford and the formation of the new "Calder" club. While I and others with small shareholdings argued passionately against the proposal it was clear that the major shareholders who favoured the move would win. We were defeated on a show of hands and I knew that if the individual shareholdings were taken into account then the defeat would be substantial.

To this day I have never understood how so many followers could be so easily persuaded to bring to an end the existence of one of the most famous rugby clubs of either code in the world. To their eternal credit, the followers of Castleford and especially Featherstone Rovers, which was still a members' club at that stage, were to prove more difficult to convince.

The following day saw the formal publication of the National Heritage Select Committee report on Rugby League and Rugby Union. I was back in London on the morning of 19 April and collected a copy of the report prior to its formal publication. Having submitted evidence to the inquiry on behalf of the All Party Parliamentary Rugby League Group, I was delighted with what I saw.

It refuted, on the basis of objective fact, so many of the arguments used by Jones and others in the media establishment to discredit the sport of Rugby League. Its conclusions could not have been more strongly supportive of all our arguments and more condemnatory of the Rugby Union position.

I suspect it was Kaufman's literary bent that resulted in the inclusion of a quote from Lewis Carroll's *Alice Through the Looking-Glass* at the top of the very first page. "When *I* use a word ... it means just what I choose it to mean - neither more nor less," summed up succinctly an issue that the committee saw as being at the heart of their concerns. Even the secretary of the RFU, Dudley Wood, had been unable to define what "amateurism" now meant. But it was the defence of this concept that remained the formal reason for Rugby Union's unwillingness to recognise certain players who had previously played Rugby League.

The committee's conclusions and recommendations wholly justified the Parliamentary Rugby League Group's efforts over the previous seven years. A Select Committee with a majority of southern-based Conservative M.P.s had unanimously found "the attitude of Rugby Union to Rugby League both discriminatory and indefensible", endorsing the use of the word "hypocritical" in summarising the situation. The committee had, in a unanimous report, recommended that "...until the regulations governing Rugby Union are amended to remove the discrimination against Rugby League, no further money from the Sports Council or any other body which distributes public funds either at national or local level should go to the RFU of any of its member clubs."[173] It further proposed that "...no further distribution of National Lottery proceeds should be made to Rugby Union clubs until Rugby League is treated equally with all other sports in Rugby Union's regulations."[174]

The key recommendations could not have been stronger and the icing on the cake was a reference to the disparity in the numbers playing League and Union in the Armed Forces being "highly unsatisfactory".[175] The Committee proposed that "the armed forces should publicise and provide facilities for both codes with equal zeal."[176]

The implications of the proposal to block Union funding was predictably played down by Twickenham in subsequent media reports with Dudley Wood deploring the fact that: "This committee was inspired by the activities of the Rugby League supporters group in the House of Commons."[177] But there was much more obvious concern in Wales with fears that the proposals to build a WRU Superdome, revealed only a fortnight earlier, might be hit by the possible loss of £70 million Millennium Commission funding needed for the £100 million project.[178]

The *Yorkshire Post*, which had vigorously campaigned for changes in the relationship between the two codes, concluded that even though Union was unlikely to suffer any financial penalty because of the committee's report "... the threat of eventual sanctions is clear."[179] Its editorial concluded: "The moral ... must be that, if one wants to organise a socially divisive sport, it is wiser not to accept public money."[180]

If there had been any triumphalism over our success with the committee's conclusions we were in no mood for a celebration with the debate on Murdoch's "take-over" and the merger proposals showing no sign of abating. The irony of League's own position at the time of the National Heritage Committee report was not lost on the *Daily Telegraph*'s Paul Hayward. In a perceptive and well-argued article following the report's publication, he wrote: "On the very day MPs were assaulting the RFU for excluding ex-professionals, our own Rugby Football League were announcing that Great Britain will refuse to play all Australian sides containing players from outside Rupert Murdoch's proposed Europe-based Super League."[181]

Although writing from a strongly pro-union perspective, Hayward made a perfectly reasonable point about League having clearly departed from the moral high ground at an especially inconvenient moment. I felt it necessary to make clear my willingness to amend the Sports (Discrimination) Bill to take account of this development. The bill as it stood dealt with discrimination by another sport but I felt it might be possible to consider redrafting it to outlaw the proposed distinctions in League, although I recognised that contractual law took us into muddier waters.

On the evening of the launch of his committee's report, Gerald Kaufman addressed a packed meeting of the Parliamentary Rugby League Group and outlined the way in which he had personally moved from a position of disinterested neutrality on the Union-League issue to full appreciation of the anger of League supporters, as the Inquiry had progressed. Inevitably the Group's delight at the outcome of the inquiry was tempered by the Super League developments about which there was intense cross party concern. It was established that Labour's Trade and Industry Spokesman, Jack Cunningham, had already asked for the media ownership aspects to be referred to the Monopolies and Mergers Commission and the Group agreed to press for a full parliamentary debate at the earliest opportunity.

Traditions of the game

On the following morning, 20 April - 12 days after the Super League decision was made public - I received a phone call from Maurice Lindsay who had just got off a plane at Heathrow on his return from Australia. He was clearly aware from press reports that the Super League proposals had gone down like a lead balloon with most of the Parliamentary Group and we had an exchange over the complete lack of communication on the most important development in the game in 100 years. Having sweated long and hard on a range of fronts, with some progress on the Armed Forces issue and the Select Committee report, I felt that basic courtesy would have merited a letter, fax or phone call before then, particularly bearing in mind that those MPs with constituencies affected by merger proposals had been inundated with representations from angry supporters.

Lindsay's explanation was that the Rugby Football League had had no option but to bite the bullet. There had been no time for dialogue and consultation with the offer on the table for only a limited period. I made him aware that I had learned that morning that I had been granted a debate on the Rugby League developments for the following week and he agreed to meet representatives of the Parliamentary Group before the debate, while the Rugby League International Board were meeting in London.

He lectured me - not for the first time or the last - on the "traditions" of the game being no guarantee of a future. My emotional attachment to Wakefield Trinity was understandable but hard-headed decisions had to be made to ensure there was such a future for our sport.

The emotions of all Trinity supporters were to be tested to the full that Sunday when, on 23 April 1995, our team played what we believed could be their last ever match. It was against an old enemy - Leeds - who won 30-14. I sat in my usual place in the stand next to Neil Fox, whose marvellous rugby career I had followed from his teenage debut for Trinity. I wondered what was going through his head that day as arguably the most famous player in the club's long and distinguished history.

As a supporter from childhood, through adolescence and into middle age, I made no bones about what Lindsay termed an "emotional" attachment. Perhaps he could never understand that when a team dies, a dream dies. For the lifelong follower, a part of their person is gone forever. My lasting memory of that day is of seeing an old chap who had sold club programmes for many years quietly weeping on the edge of the field at the end of the match.

As Trinity supporters assembled outside the team's dressing room and exchanged applause with the players, Sir Rodney Walker, the club's former chairman and at the time the chairman of the Rugby Football League, emerged from the clubhouse to face the verbal anger of a number of the fans present. His appearance was either one of great bravado or incredible foolishness as many supporters clearly bracketed him with Maurice Lindsay in the conclusion of the Murdoch deal.

Simon Kelner, in *To Jerusalem and Back*, his book on the advent of Super League, recorded what happened later that day behind the scenes in the Trinity dressing-room. He quoted the recollections of Stuart Farrar, the club's football chairman: "After the last game of the season I went into the dressing room to talk to the players ... I started to thank them for everything they had done, but I just broke down. Some of the players, particularly those who had been around for many years, were also in tears. It was a very emotional time."[182]

I moved from this incredible mix of great anger and profound sadness to do what was probably the most difficult television interview of my life back in the east stand. BBC2 chose to film at Belle Vue that day in preparation for a programme called *A League Apart - A Hundred Years of Rugby League* to be shown later in the year to celebrate the centenary of Rugby League. It was to be fronted by Michael Parkinson. I had just watched what was likely to be the last match my team would ever play but could make no mention of my feelings that day because the programme was not to be transmitted for some four months. The producers were wise to keep off the immediate issues because, by the time it was shown on 5 October, public anger and an additional £10 million from Murdoch had resulted in mergers being off the agenda for the time being at least. Nevertheless, my own anger at what I perceived to be the apparent abandonment of much of Rugby League's history and culture came over fairly clearly in what was subsequently shown in the programme.

On the following day, Monday 24 April 1995, McCartney and I met Maurice Lindsay and Sir Rodney Walker at the Regent Hotel, Marylebone, to raise with them the very serious concerns of MPs and Peers over the way the game had rushed headlong into bed with Murdoch and the consequent moves to mergers and summer rugby. McCartney did most of the talking and set out a range of serious fears over what had happened, evidencing his personal commitment to Rugby League rather than just a narrow parochial concern with the interests of his own team, Wigan, who it might be assumed were likely to continue to progress within the new arrangements. I reinforced his arguments with a number of points about the ditching of traditional Rugby League communities, to be met again with the riposte that tradition did not pay bills. Walker spoke from detailed knowledge of Wakefield Trinity's parlous financial state and Lindsay produced figures for the alleged aggregate current indebtedness of all the professional clubs.

During our meeting the room's telephone rang frequently requiring Lindsay's response to a number of urgent concerns. We subsequently discovered that, by then, the battle with the Australian Rugby League for the contractual loyalty of the game's top players had begun and he was faced with trying to retain some key British players. In assuring McCartney and me that the Murdoch deal had secured the game's well-being for the next five years there was perhaps no real idea of the extent to which resources which should have been invested in League's future were to be thrown away in payments to players and legal costs in a quite disgraceful battle for contractual loyalty with the Australian Rugby League, backed by rival media mogul, Kerry Packer.

At a social function in the same hotel later in the evening for International Board members, McCartney and I spoke to the ARL's Ken Arthurson who was devastated by the developments in Britain. He gave us a brief account of the way the whole affair had broken in Australia and outlined his fears for the future of the game as a consequence of the decisions taken by the RFL.

I had seen Arthurson play for Australia many years earlier and in my brief contact with him on some of his previous visits to Britain had developed a respect for his deep personal commitment to the game. But two days before I was due to open a parliamentary debate on Super League which I knew would be followed with great interest on the other side of the world, I had only the sketchiest idea of the complex battle which had been raging in Australia for some time between Murdoch's News Limited and Packer's Optus Vision over pay-to-view TV rights. Sports coverage was seen as the key to success in this market and with Packer's Channel 9 network having signed a contract to televise Australian Rugby League, including a first option on pay TV rights, Ken Arthurson had become a central figure in this fight.

Mike Colman's book, *Super League - The Inside Story*, describes the efforts that were made to reach a compromise between the two parties before the Super League concept became a reality. Arthurson had been involved on behalf of the ARL in meeting News Limited representatives earlier in the year. According to Colman, when proposals were put forward concerning the ARL's possible backing for Super League, Arthurson, aware of Channel 9's past support for the ARL, remained loyal to Packer.

While, at the time, my parliamentary colleagues and I had no detailed knowledge of Arthurson's relationship with Packer, as we approached the Parliamentary debate on Rugby League, later that week, the key question we were asking, over and above mergers and summer rugby, was whether the RFL was now effectively owned and controlled by News Corporation.

Rugby Union and professionalism

My prediction during the debate that what was happening to Rugby League could impact in an even bigger way on Rugby Union was, on reflection, clearly an underestimate. At the time I knew that there was intense pressure within Australian and New Zealand Rugby Union to move toward some formalised arrangement for professionalism but had not taken account of the impact that Super League would have on Union's position in those countries.

Reports began to emerge of fears of wholesale Rugby League "raids" on the international Union sides of both countries, with suggestions that 12 Wallabies and 19 All Blacks had been targeted for offers.[183] Union officials were said to have responded to the threat by proposing a professional provincial tournament and dialogue had begun with Murdoch over a new competition designed to replace the existing Super Ten arrangements. *The Guardian* suggested: "The ARFU believes it can persuade Murdoch that Union, not League, has genuine international appeal in scores of countries and represents a better commercial investment".[184]

Predictably, Dudley Wood deplored the development, fearing a split between the northern and southern hemispheres. With only a matter of weeks to go before his retirement as secretary of the RFU, he suggested that is was a serious mistake for the Australian RFU to develop a strategy of competition with League in an attempt to survive. "I cannot see northern hemisphere countries, particularly England, Scotland and Ireland, going down that route [into professionalism] ... It's serious and sad that all this has been brought about by Murdoch's latest involvement in Rugby League."[185]

While those advocating the Super League concept were stressing that it was essentially about expanding the game, Wood's perception was that it would lead to contraction. He was quoted on 27 April 1995 as saying: "...the latest Rugby League developments, which will have the effect of shrinking their game, must reduce the number of players they require."[186] He saw the emergence of Super League as the chance to project Union's positives. "We have a marvellous opportunity here to stand up and declare that we are a highly successful global *recreational* [my italics] game and competition does not trouble us."[187]

Whether Wood's reassertion of belief in Union being essentially "recreational" contributed to Will Carling's subsequent reference to the RFU being run by "old farts" is unclear. But as the 1994-95 Union season ended, the profound difference in philosophy and outlook between English Union players and the RFU hierarchy had never been more apparent. Even before Carling's outburst it is difficult to perceive how Wood could continue to dismiss the increasing pressure for some form of professionalism within his own Union. By then it appeared that his own passionate commitment to "amateurism" - somewhat redefined as even he admitted - continued to blind him to the most obvious developments in his own backyard.

Late May 1995 saw the start of the Union World Cup in South Africa, a competition that was very likely to further force the pace of change within Union, in England and elsewhere. Despite Wood's failure to grasp the inevitability of quite significant changes, other observers argued for the need to embrace professionalism in order to ensure Union's future. Writing with, in my opinion, the peculiar arrogance which seems the hallmark of some Union correspondents, David Miller suggested in *The Times* on 24 May 1995 that an intelligent approach to professionalism could ensure what he termed the "superior code's" future. With the Union World Cup in mind, he wrote that: "With its audience of billions as the world's third largest sporting event, a projected £30 million profit plus a base to its playing pyramid around the world that is vastly larger than that of Rugby League, Union is unquestionably the superior code visually as well as numerically." He suggested that it could halt the movement of players to League "if its own professionalism is rationalised in August" (when the Rugby Union International Board was due to meet).[188]

But while arguing for a move towards professionalism as a means of defending Union's "superiority", Miller flagged up his fears that it faced greater challenges than the Murdoch involvement with League: "How long can it be before Union clubs in England are taken over by commercial operators who then pick off the best international players from Wales, Scotland and Ireland, thus jeopardising the international performance of those countries, as in football?"[189]

As the Union World Cup began, in late May 1995, news broke that the RFU were looking after the England players by negotiating a shirt sponsorship deal which would give them around £30,000 each. Commenting on this news, the England hooker Brian

Moore predicted: "Professionalism is not an option, it's a certainty. It might not be on the lines of Rugby League in terms of win bonuses and the like, but it's coming and you'd better get ready."[190]

Moore's view was confirmed only a month later when, on 23 June 1995, the governing Unions of South Africa, New Zealand and Australia announced a £370 million, 10-year deal with Murdoch's News Corporation for the broadcasting rights to a new international competition. With funding now available to pay players for their involvement in the game, *The Times*'s Union correspondent, David Hands, wrote: "Rugby Union, which has been reading the last rites over amateurism for a decade or more, finally committed the corpse to the grave yesterday."[191] Presumably in an effort to deflect similar criticism to that following the Super League announcement, Murdoch himself was quoted as saying: "For the benefit of those who will seek to construe this deal, let me be very clear. News Corporation is not going to run Rugby Union."[192]

The response of Dudley Wood's replacement, Tony Hallett, as secretary elect, was to deem the southern-hemisphere deal a challenge for the RFU: "There will be some members of the RFU who will be very, very dismayed by these events but equally there is a progressive element who will embrace it." Like Wood, he expressed concern at a possible split between the two hemispheres, suggesting that discussion would: "go to the wire". He said: "It is no use saying that this is the end of amateurism, for the simple reason that we passed that point long ago. Amateurism is in a state of *rigor mortis*."[193]

Having faced dealing with its funeral arrangements on behalf of the IRB, Vernon Pugh suggested that Murdoch had done the European Union game "an enormous favour".[194] Pointing to the larger TV audiences in Europe and the possibility of News Corporation televising international championship matches, Pugh was optimistic about what the future held: "With a European League on the horizon, he [Murdoch] has the bait for capturing the best of the world game. If he does that, I can see him dumping Rugby League."[195]

Pugh's upbeat response was hardly surprising. As chairman of the Welsh RU he had faced the impossible task of keeping the lid on an increasing disregard for the "amateurism" rules in his own country and as a lawyer he knew that both the WRU and the International Board had been wide open to legal challenge from excluded former League professionals such as Stuart Evans. His International Board working-party had faced a hopeless task and the Murdoch deal with the southern hemisphere countries gave him a very welcome ladder out of an exceedingly deep hole.

Having been in the front line of critics of the Murdoch deal with Rugby League some weeks earlier, I realised from some of the comments made following the southern-hemisphere Union deal that there had perhaps been more than a little envy among some elements in the Union ranks when the RFL signed up for the Super League money. The Union agreement was perceived by some as putting their code back in the driving seat where it belonged, with the cheerful implication that the demise of Rugby League was once again nigh. Mick Cleary, in *The Observer*, thought it necessary to assert that: "Those who feel that a hybrid sport may emerge from the two codes of Union and League have to factor in that, if it were to come to pass, it would have to be on Union terms for the Union code now holds the trump cards."[196]

At the RFU's annual meeting on 14 July, the outgoing president, Dennis Easby, argued that the eventual consequence of giving Murdoch effective control over both Union and League may be much greater than foreseen. "The contract with Rugby

League injected much needed cash into an ailing game, but at what price?" he asked.[197] His successor, Bill Bishop, warned of the damage inherent in huge sums of money flowing into Union but stated his belief that the term amateurism had become "an anachronism".[198] As the new RFU Secretary, Tony Hallett, made clear, they could not carry on with what he termed "this grey shadowy world of innuendo and hypocrisy".[199]

Hallett was not to know it at the time but, in emerging from those grey shadows Union would, along with League, find itself torn apart as a pawn in the multi-million dollar battle between Murdoch and his Australian media rival Kerry Packer. In his analysis of the background to Super League, Mike Colman describes how, at the start of the battle with the Australian Rugby League, Packer discussed with his advisers ways of blocking Murdoch's plans. One of them, a lawyer called Geoff Levy, originating from South Africa, suggested leaving League alone and going instead for Union "as a TV property".[200] Colman suggests that Levy argued: "Unlike Rugby League, the ostensibly amateur Rugby Union was already an international game with an enormous following. Instead of educating the world about Rugby League as Rupert Murdoch planned, Packer could just take over a slumbering giant without the enormous costs of establishing an infrastructure and chasing an ignorant and perhaps disinterested viewing public."[201]

Reports in the British press on 18 July 1995 suggested that Levy's idea had manifested itself in the form of a new professional Rugby Union circus, with Australia, New Zealand, South Africa, English and Western Samoan players considering contracts.[202] *The Guardian*'s reporter in Sydney wrote that organisers of a global competition, including several well-known Australian and New Zealand players, were "seeking backing from Kerry Packer's businesses, the ESPN pay-television network and the South African Broadcasting Corporation".[203] It was suggested that the new competition was being planned to rival the Murdoch organisation's Super 12, the Southern Hemisphere's provincial Union tournament and the triangular Test series involving Australia, New Zealand and South Africa.[204]

Packer's "World Rugby Corporation" (WRC) as it became known, dispatched the former Australian RU official and Wallaby forward, Ross Turnbull, to Britain during July to recruit players for the professional circus, a development that concentrated the minds of the Home Unions on addressing the demands of their leading internationals. Against a background of reports that the WRC had "stashed away in a London vault, statements of intent from the majority of players in the squads of the leading rugby playing countries in the world with the exception of England",[205] officials confirmed they had had talks on what one official termed "updating and progressing co-operation with the national squad".[206] The players were less reticent in their thoughts on developments, claiming they could not lose. "If the Packer competition takes off players will make hundreds of thousands of pounds. If it does not, it will be because Unions finally grasp the fact that rugby at top level is anything but amateur", suggested one unnamed England player.[207]

The Packer initiative was perhaps the straw that finally broke the amateurism camel's badly decomposed back. Wood's successor, Tony Hallett, spoke of being in a "high stakes game of poker" but made clear his belief that if the consequence of defeating Packer was paying players "then so be it".[208] He indicated that he had seen the contracts on offer and suggested that the RFU would match anything on offer from

Packer. "I was in charge of the £60 million rebuilding of Twickenham. I'd be pretty pissed off if there was no one there to play in it. I'm just not going to let it happen."[209]

As top All Black players were threatened with expulsion from the national team if they joined the Packer circus, the chairman of the RFU "Players' Working Party", Malcolm Phillips, promised his internationals a guaranteed £30,000 plus from the 1995-96 season. And he conceded that regardless of the forthcoming IRB's deliberations "the word 'amateur' is now obsolete".[210]

The Scottish Rugby Union, which had been hoping to wait until after the IRB meeting between 24 and 26 August before finalising its arrangements for rewarding their top players, found themselves having to bring forward discussions on contracts because of the WRC's activities. Fred McLeod, the SRU's senior vice-president and "regulations officer on amateurism", admitted, however, at the end of July 1995 that his Union had been considering the need for contracts before Packer's professional circus.[211]

In early August, with England squad members reportedly unhappy about Phillips's £30,000+ proposals, 120 English players were alleged either to have had, or were likely to receive, Packer contract offers.[212] The possible consequences to Rugby Union clubs in the Courage League spurred Leicester's president, Peter Wheeler, and Harlequins chairman, Roger Looker, to meet other first-division clubs and propose that English clubs should turn professional. "It's no point waiting for the Union to do something. They are all on holiday," said one club official, revealing a clubs-Twickenham divide which was to become considerably wider.[213]

The WRU had by then already drawn up contracts for its leading players worth at least £20,000 a year but they also faced grass roots concerns as their 12 first-division clubs met on 2 August to consider the establishment of a football style premier League in response to frustration over the bulk of television and sponsorship money going to other clubs.

In what *The Guardian* described as "an audacious reversal of roles", the WRC were reported to be approaching former Welsh Union internationals with League clubs. "Rugby Union is now in the position of predator," it suggested. The Welsh Rugby League's team manager, Mike Nicholas, responded by stating that League had always argued for a free gangway between the codes. "Rugby Union has been professional for years, but it has taken Packer for them to face up to it. We would welcome an equal battle because ours is the better sport for both players and spectators."[214]

Less than three weeks before the International Board's Paris meeting, it seemed that Packer's vision was crumbling. Both the South African and Australian Unions signed contractual deals with their leading players, leaving Ross Turnbull to ask: "Whatever happened to honour and integrity?" a question described by *The Observer*'s Eddie Butler as "one of the richer reflections from the world of sport".[215]

In a thoughtful consideration of the implications of Packer's intervention, Butler noted how the WRC's contractual offers had prompted some English First Division Union clubs to offer £25,000 a man to prevent a loss of players. "An English club, for goodness sake, going pro'," he wrote. "Does that mean that for all those years when the likes of Harlequins and Leicester said that Rugby Union clubs could not afford to pay the players, they were telling porky pies?"[216]

As a frequent critic of the boring nature of top-level Rugby Union, Butler reflected as well on the implications of a post-Packer professional era for the style of play on offer. He wondered: "how patient are the punters going to be if first-division rugby, or English grand-slam rugby, continues to be the most monotonous activity since St Cadoc's, Llanllowell, the one-bell church, held a Ringathon?"[217] But, monotonous or not, by 24 August, Packer's intervention had led the RFU to announce that its England squad members would earn at least £40,000 in the 1995-96 season. Interestingly, Tony Hallett claimed this new agreement with the players was "within current International Board regulations".[218] What on earth would Kaufman have made of that one?

Back where he learnt his sport: David Hinchliffe M.P., the Wakefield Trinity Wildcats'
mascot and enthusiastic school students Lawefield Lane Primary School, Wakefield.
(Photo: Ken Wilkinson, West Yorkshire Fire Service Visual Services)

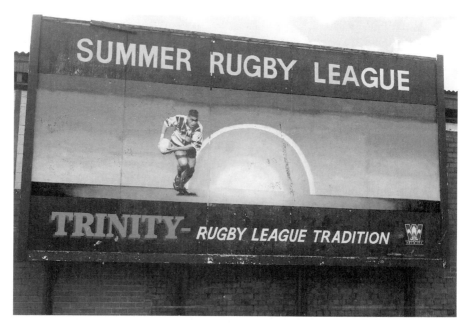

Wakefield Trinity: Modern season, proud tradition
(Photo: Peter Lush)

11: The ironies of 1995

Stand up bingo was not really what I had expected as a key component of celebrating the centenary of Rugby League. But it was infinitely preferable to the performance of the comedian who followed the Rugby League centenary dinner at Huddersfield's McAlpine Stadium on August bank holiday Monday, 1995. It was a rather tacky affair heralding, on reflection, what some would view as a pretty tacky new era for the game.

The night before I was privileged to witness a genuine celebration of the game. Only a few yards from its birthplace in the George Hotel, Huddersfield, the city's famous Town Hall hosted a dramatic and musical tribute to Rugby League which was a moving and truly memorable occasion. Brass bands played, choirs sang and there was an impressive re-enactment of the historic meeting which confirmed the break away from Union, with Dewsbury's representative loudly booed for dithering over the decision.

There was perhaps only one man who could really articulate what it all meant and Colin Welland did it brilliantly. Waxing lyrical about the history, tradition and essential decency of Rugby League, he captured it all in a short speech delivered straight from the heart. It featured, inevitably, wonderful words about his hero Brian Bevan and ended with "Happy Birthday Rugby League".

Others may have dwelt more on the supreme irony that on the very weekend on which League was celebrating its centenary, Union announced that it was turning professional. With his experiences of Union more positive than some, Welland was magnanimous over the fact that they had finally come round to League's approach.

Of course, that was not quite how it was formally presented when the three-day session of Rugby Union's International Board came to an end in Paris on 27 August 1995. Few official explanations for the decision were subsequently reported by Board members and those that were made no reference to acceding to League's long-standing openness on the payments question. Any reference to League, like Ian Robertson's subsequent BBC radio broadcast, raised serious questions about its future.[219] The underlying assumption of Union writers reporting the Paris decision was, as usual, that League was simply a professional offshoot of Union, dependent for its survival on recruiting top name Union players.

Vernon Pugh was quoted as saying: "The decision we took was almost inevitable."[220] A subsequent article in *The Times* quoted extracts from his confidential recommendation to the board which suggested that between March and August 1995: "we have come close to witnessing the game being lost to us."[221] In another marked departure from Dudley Wood's stance at the Select Committee a few months earlier, Pugh told the board: "The game is already a paid game at every level that chooses to, and can afford to, make payments to players."[222]

It was indeed an inevitable conclusion brought about by a range of events, even if the end of "shamateurism" had come somewhat sooner than many, including myself, had expected. Union had lived a lie for years, the sin compounded by exclusive attitudes towards those associated with League who, in most instances, like my own, had been genuinely amateur sportsmen unlike significant numbers in the Union ranks. As an editorial in *The Times* noted: "While amateurism had died formally with the International Board decision, it had already been moribund for some years."[223] Written, I would imagine by someone other than a Union correspondent, the piece analysed the role of amateurism in historically sustaining the British class system: "Given the role played by games in imbuing generations of Britons with qualities of order, morality, tribal loyalty and hardiness, the 'essence' of each sport was prone to acquire a quasi-mythical status", it suggested, "yet the longer a sport kept aloof from changes in society outside the field of play ... the more unconvincing its high priests became in defence of its 'ethos'."[224]

While the passing of "high priests" like Dudley Wood was undoubtedly a factor in the departure from Corinthian ideals, it was clearly a fear of the possibility of Packer or Murdoch establishing control of the sport which had really concentrated minds in Paris. In practical terms, Packer's operation had forced payments into the open within the Home Unions and markedly speeded up the process of change which was already well underway. And the stark realities facing Pugh in his Welsh backyard made him a central figure in grasping the nettle and opting for full-blown professionalism.

It was subsequently claimed that the IRB's decision flew completely in the face of the RFU's chosen stance. Oliver Grievson, a retired bank manager from Selby, and one of Yorkshire's representatives on the RFU, was quoted some months later as bitterly critical of the board and by implication the RFU's representatives at the meeting: "After much debate our representatives (John Jeavons-Fellows and Peter Brook) were sent to the International Board with the clear instruction of keeping Union non-vocational. In the end, the game went totally professional without them even taking a vote."[225] As a strong advocate of a "non-vocational" game at club level, Grievson targeted Pugh for some strong comment: "Vernon Pugh is a QC and a smooth talker. Wales were losing players to Rugby League and their committee was a complete shambles."[226]

But Pugh knew more than most - and in internal reports had made clear - that the previous position (whatever it had been) was unsustainable. Hallett subsequently summed it up very nicely: "In Paris, when the Board members actually emerged and said: 'Well chaps, we've found out the game was professional all along', it was rather like an alcoholic admitting he was one for the first time."[227] What a pity that not even the modernisers - like Pugh or Hallett - could, in the context of this revised history, find it within themselves to express just a little remorse for nearly 100 years spent by the Union authorities in trying to destroy Rugby League.

The IRB's decision in late August was followed by further deliberations in Tokyo on 1 October 1995, when the various Unions met to consider the question of readmitting former League players. While the Board formally decided that no qualifying period was necessary before League players could return, it was left to individual Unions to decide their own arrangements. Predictably, despite the professional status now accorded to England's squad players, Twickenham managed one last flick of amateurism's tail with reports indicating that the RFU favoured a period of requalification. I found it necessary to indicate publicly that any continued restrictions on free movement would be vigorously fought through Parliament.

The Sports (Discrimination) Bill had completed all its stages in the Lords through the efforts of Lord Swinton before the summer recess and I had until then assumed that further efforts in the Commons had been rendered largely redundant by the Paris decision. I was prepared to pick up the measure on Parliament's return later that month but realistically there was no chance of making any further progress during that particular session. I noted that the RFU President, Bill Bishop, had conceded the likelihood of losing any test case on such a restriction,[228] and assumed, correctly as it turned out, that Twickenham would quietly drop the idea once the dust had settled.

Nevertheless, before they did, the former New Zealand Union full-back, John Gallagher, who had played League with Leeds and London Crusaders, had the distinction of being one of the last to be banned by the RFU under the old arrangements, being prevented from playing for Kent in a County Championship match in late November 1995. His treatment was, according to *The Guardian*: "perceived inside and outside Union as further evidence of Twickenham's vindictive bias against Rugby League".[229]

Other former League players returning to Union in England faced lengthy delays in gaining reinstatement. Orrell, who wished to reinstate Nigel Heslop and Martin Street, were reported to be among several leading clubs concerned about the RFU's refusal to lift the ban on former League players. Bob Rogers, its amateurism chairman, pointed to the difficulties dealing with the number of cases involved with some 2,500 clubs and schools, but his excuses were dubbed by the press to be "a massive red herring".[230]

Such minor scuffles were, however, merely an aperitif to the remarkable exchanges during autumn 1995 which followed the publication of the report of the RFU's commission on professionalism. This six-man body had been initiated by the RFU president, Bill Bishop, to consider the challenge of the new era and make recommendations on Union's subsequent structure and organisation in England at the end of the proposed one year moratorium on professionalism.

The results of their two month discussions were, according to the *Yorkshire Post*, "a recipe for as good a row as English rugby can muster".[231] The positions of the various Union camps were so obviously polarised on the key issues arising since the Paris decision that conflict was inevitable. "In the blue corner will be the conservatives, witnessing the destruction of amateurism, and in the multicoloured strobe-lit corner will stand the purveyors of the new style rugby in the professional era. It should be quite a scrap," the paper suggested.[232]

And indeed it was, because the commission's report underlined the profound implications of what had happened in August which, for many within Union's deeply traditional ranks, had not properly sunk in until then. Those who had scarcely come to terms with Union acceding to competitive leagues now faced new proposals for a radically different playing structure for the season. It was proposed that the Five Nations internationals should be moved to the end of the traditional season, in May, with the players involved having dual contracts with club and country; and arrangements for player transfers were also addressed.

If that was not enough for the traditionalists, the commission heard evidence from northern Rugby Union clubs, such as Wakefield, pressing for the lifting of restrictions on Rugby League players. They were to be allowed a free passage: "more, perhaps, than the commission's findings will receive" according to *The Times*.[233]

The commission's deliberations had been dogged by controversy long before the report was published, with England's 10 top Premiership clubs indicating their lack of confidence in it and stressing that their interests were being overlooked. Their nominee for the commission - a representative of Sale RUFC - had been rejected by Twickenham and there was anger also over an RFU executive decision to exclude them from European competition until the 1997-98 season because of suggested complications over television contracts. Alongside on-going rows over the control of top players' employment terms, the dispute over the operation of the commission added to media speculation that a permanent split between the top English clubs and Twickenham was imminent.

By early December 1995 the increasingly bitter battle within Union for television and advertising revenue had led to the top 10 clubs breaking away from the National (formerly the Senior) Clubs' Association in an effort to establish a stronger, independent negotiating position, particularly in respect of future television coverage of the European competition. The relationship between these clubs and the RFU became even more strained very early in 1996 after a special general meeting in Birmingham which appeared to put the brakes on moves towards a fully professional game in England. The meeting brought sharply into focus the fact that what was at stake was more than just access to funding. It was about Union's entire *raison d'être*.

Traditionalists and modernisers

Shortly after the meeting, *The Guardian* published two contrasting articles evidencing the battle for Union's soul. In the blue corner David Davies warned of the perils of going down a professional road that Union could not afford. Deriding Will Carling's insult, he happily ascribed to himself the status of one of the "old farts" who had rebelled at that meeting over what was happening to the game. "For we old farts recognise ourselves" he wrote, "...sometimes even when the other chap is not be-badged and be-blazered and dribbling down his chin." Summing up the essence of Union tradition he added: "We recognise ourselves because, maybe, in the dim and distant past, we played against each other, or because over the years, we have shared beers and bawdy songs: pies, pints and even punch-ups in the aftermath of defeat. We recognise each other because here we are, years on, still with the club that begat us, that gave us and gives us so much pleasure."[234]

In contrast, for Frank Keating, on behalf of the modernisers, it was "a final futile blazer flourish".[235] He suggested that these "buffers" had previously gathered regularly at Twickenham itself. "But that was before those new grandstands were filled by the hordes of corporate-hospitality City slickers in suits. If there were 800 in the hall on Sunday, at least 750 were in the regulation club blazer with faded twirly-wirly wire badge on the breast. This was their last collective round up and more than likely they knew it, too."[236]

From amongst the blazers at the Birmingham meeting there emerged a figure who was to become increasingly central to the heated debates over Union's control and direction in the aftermath of Paris. Cliff Brittle had defeated RFU nominee, John Jeavons-Fellows, for the post of chairman of the RFU executive by nearly 300 votes and was charged with overseeing the preparation of a five-year "business plan" for English Rugby Union. His election as a representative of the old guard was accompanied by widespread denunciation of the RFU Commission's report.

In challenging the motives of the leading clubs, Brittle was increasingly supported by Fran Cotton, the former England Union prop and chairman of the north's playing committee. At the RFU's second special general meeting, held in late March, Cotton spoke critically of the "posturing" of three or four clubs or "three or four individuals within those clubs".[237] He accused those concerned of disenfranchising their own members, being disunited and in most cases financially weak.

As the 1995-96 Union season drew to a close there were press suggestions that "the doomsday scenario of a breakaway by England's leading clubs remains"[238] after continued lack of progress in talks with the RFU over the key issues of player contracts, future television & sponsorship arrangements and competitive structures. Their formation of a separate body, the English Professional Rugby Union Clubs Ltd (EPRUC), which Twickenham was loath to recognise, cemented the growing divisions.[239]

The frustration of the top clubs became increasingly evident in April 1996 with what the media described as a "bitter propaganda war" between the clubs and the RFU. Mike Coley, the Gloucester club's chief executive, was quoted as suggesting that Brittle "couldn't take a decision to save his life" and "wants us to go back to the 18th century rather than forward to the 21st".[240]

The Observer's Mick Cleary questioned the common perception that the RFU was at war with the leading clubs. "They are not," he suggested. "They are at war with themselves." Brittle, he wrote, was being blamed by sources within the RFU for an intransigence that was in danger of splitting the game apart. "Rugby is nothing like as violent a sport as it once was. On the pitch that is. These days the blood is being spilt in the committee rooms."[241]

Rumours emerged to the effect that some elements within the RFU would be happy to see the conflict with the top clubs get considerably worse. Cleary outlined this conspiracy theory: "Then the clubs would break away and form a professional game leaving the old boys to get on in peace with their beloved amateur pastime."[242] *The Independent*'s Steve Bale claimed hard evidence to support this belief that there was a desire to see them go: "One member of that (RFU) executive has seriously suggested to me that there is a hidden agenda to oust the major clubs as a precisely similar exercise to that which entailed the departure of the northern clubs 101 years ago."[243]

Whether or not such an outcome had been in Brittle's mind, he was generally viewed as winning this initial battle with the leading clubs in the struggle for control of the English game. The issue, before the end of Union's 1995-96 season, of detailed plans for the first fully professional season's league and cup competitions along with a refusal to accede to the top clubs' pressure for a block on relegation from the First Division that year was perceived as him calling their bluff on breakaway threats. In a display of authoritative leadership the RFU had, according to David Hands in *The Times*: "asserted its right as a governing body to control the game in England".[244]

By that time Brittle clearly had some very real fears over the financial implications of professionalism and the possible consequences of having on board the increasing numbers of wealthy entrepreneurs taking sizeable stakes in various clubs. Shortly after what was reported to have been "an emotional confrontation"[245] between the Newcastle club's Sir John Hall and Brittle in early April 1996, the RFU executive chairman spoke of "welcoming some wealthy individuals into the game who are used to getting their own way and whose motivation and experience are not the same as our own."[246]

While Hall was arguably the biggest financial player among Union's new money men he was probably not the only one in Brittle's line of fire. Millionaire property developer Nigel Wray was reported to have put two and a half million pounds into Saracens, enabling them to recruit players of the calibre of Michael Lynagh, Philippe Sella, and later François Pienaar from South Africa.[247] Ashley Levett, a Monaco-based businessman, had sunk a similar figure into Richmond, the Japanese electronics giant

NEC had lent its name and funds to Harlequins and Gerry Sugrue, a computer magnate, was enabling Coventry to attract new players with lucrative deals.[248] Such investments, beyond just the confines of clubs in the top division, added to the very real fears of Union's traditionalists about the future direction of the game.

As the traumatic 1995-96 Union season drew to a close, efforts to hold the English game together led the RFU into a quite remarkable conflict with the other home Unions over arrangements for the television contract for the Five Nations Championship. England, through the RFU, argued for a bigger share of the new television contract, adopting a go-it-alone posture in an effort to achieve their aims.

The direct link to the dispute with its leading clubs was summed up by David Hands: "If the RFU can point to a substantial television deal (which would also help to repay the debt on the refurbished Twickenham) it would be a big incentive for clubs to remain under the Union's umbrella."[249]

By the end of April 1996 the press were claiming that Rugby Union was "in chaos"[250] with the top clubs at war with Brittle and the RFU, and England's future involvement in the Five Nations Championship increasingly in doubt. Eddie Butler highlighted the way the game's administrators were making what he termed a pig's ear out of a silk purse. "Amateurism," he wrote, "may have been corrupt, elitist and hypocritical, but damn it, it worked."[251]

But a month later, the top clubs appeared to have gained the upper hand in a temporary truce following day-long talks at London's Hilton Hotel on 24 May. The peace agreement gave them a major share of power in English and cross border competitions and, of even more importance, a role as signatories to future TV and sponsorship agreements concerning competitions in which they would be involved.

While Brittle spoke of there being "no winners and losers", *The Guardian*'s Robert Armstrong described it as "a significant policy defeat for Union traditionalists, who have attempted to prevent the clubs gaining greater control".[252] The deal clarified procedures for contracts between clubs and players, making provision for a release clause ensuring players were available for international matches. At that point, however, it was still far from certain exactly what international commitments English players would have because of the conflict over the RFU's position on television coverage.

Just over a fortnight after the Hilton Hotel meeting, the need to finance Union's new professional era in England plunged the game into a new crisis. On 10 June 1996 the RFU concluded a five-year £87.5 million television deal with BSkyB, separate from the other home Unions. Predictably the Scottish, Welsh and Irish Unions reacted angrily with suggestions that the deal would mean the end of the Five Nations' Championship. Of longer term significance was Cliff Brittle's outspoken criticism of the agreement and his claim that, as chairman of the RFU's executive, he had been kept completely in the dark on the matter.[253]

In a dispute that was to fester throughout Union's first professional season, he subsequently claimed to have been deliberately misled by Hallett over the BSkyB deal, prior to the RFU's 1996 AGM, held on 12 July. While there was considerable criticism of the deal at that meeting the fact that it remained unchanged led to the other Home Unions expelling England from the championship on the following day.

The sports writers had a field day in slamming the RFU's position in an affair which had brought Union's oldest international competition to its knees. Gerald Davies argued that despite Twickenham's line about each Union controlling their own destinies and claims of a major share of television audiences being English, they had "sounded disingenuous and blinkered: greedy even."[254] Colin Welland suggested that no one should be surprised over the RFU's position: "Anyone connected with Rugby League who suffered the arrogance of the English Union hierarchy over the years has wondered down those years how those other Unions willingly shared, apparently comfortably, their bed."[255] He singled out Davies's fellow countrymen for particular comment: "The Welsh RU, in particular, with their working-class base, should have recognised long ago that 'the Nigels', as they call them, while going through the motions of total acceptance of their rough and ready neighbours, always felt, deep down, that intrinsically, both on and off the field, the superiority was theirs."[256]

One hundred and one years after the great rugby split of 1895, the last bastion of sporting conservatism was approaching its first openly professional season. The four other Home Unions were at loggerheads with England over television payments. The RFU was in a tense stand off with the top clubs and itself was riven by internal wrangling between modernisers and old guard. The first anniversary of the historic Paris decision saw few celebrations in the Union game.

Rugby League at a traditional Union venue: London Broncos versus
Wakefield Trinity Wildcats at Harlequins' Stoop Memorial Ground in 1999
(Photo: Peter Lush)

London Broncos versus Leeds Rhinos at The Stoop in 1999.
The Twickenham Stadium dominates the skyline (Photo: Peter Lush)

12: Paris in the springtime

Union's final season of amateurism in England coincided with League's last winter competition before the advent of Super League in the spring of 1996. The Centenary season ran from August 1995 to January 1996 with a rather meaningless competition which was poorly supported by a somewhat bewildered Rugby League public.

In marked contrast, League's Halifax Centenary World Cup, played in Britain during the autumn of 1995, captured the public's imagination with excellent attendances for some highly competitive matches. For seasoned supporters like myself the public response to this series of matches was a breath of fresh air during an otherwise dismal period of great uncertainty. The international development of the game was shown by the attacking, flamboyant rugby played by Papua New Guinea, Tonga and Western Samoa. The tournament also had a huge impact in Wales, with the team reaching the semi-final after a memorable victory at Swansea over Western Samoa, and being chosen as BBC Television's Sports Team of the Year for Wales.

The spectator support for the Centenary World Cup was all the more remarkable because of the almost complete absence of any promotion, by the BBC in particular. The corporation surpassed even its own miserable standards of Rugby League coverage at that time by making virtually no prior mention of even the matches it had been scheduled to cover. Against this background I was incensed to hear a BBC *Breakfast News* interviewer, on the day before the England versus Australia final at Wembley, denigrating League's inability to fill the stadium for the first contest between the two sides at the start of the competition. There was, of course, no mention of the complete lack of any previous publicity. There was no mention of the fact that the BBC had found themselves rescheduling coverage to increase the number of televised matches because of the popularity of the contests or that the highlights packages were only shown in the north of England, much to the frustration of Rugby League fans elsewhere in Britain. And there was no reference to the subsequent apology for the corporation's failure to anticipate and reflect the obvious public interest in the Centenary World Cup.

The Parliamentary Rugby League Group had found it necessary to meet the BBC's then head of sport, Jonathan Martin, on more than one occasion to discuss our concerns over the way League was, in our view, consistently treated far less favourably by them than other sports. Martin's limited understanding of the game was particularly evident to the Group when he recalled the occasion he had worked with the outside broadcast crew covering a live Rugby League match from Headingley. He had been mystified to see Eddie Waring being booed and jeered by the crowd as he climbed up to the commentary gantry in the south stand. Martin had no conception of the fact that, despite his obvious love for League, Waring's popularity in the south was not reflected in the north where his comical approach to the coverage of a serious sport was deeply resented among grass-roots fans.

The support for the Wales team during the World Cup competition had provided clear evidence of the great potential for Rugby League in that country if a serious effort was made in terms of development. The Welsh had a squad of genuine international quality. Sadly, the Old Trafford semi-final marked the demise of that squad. However, League fans were heartened by the establishment of the South Wales club, playing in the Second Division in 1996, to prepare the way for a Super League side. This was the first professional club in Wales since 1985.

However, it was perhaps no surprise to anyone when, shortly after the end of the World Cup, the Welsh skipper, Jonathan Davies, switched back to Union, signing for Cardiff following a compensation deal worth around £90,000 to his former League club, Warrington. It was common knowledge that his wife Karen, who was seriously ill with cancer, wanted to return to live in South Wales and Davies left with the blessing of all in Rugby League who had been privileged to see his performances since he had "gone north" seven years earlier. He acknowledged numerous messages of sympathy from friends in Rugby League when Karen died some months later.

Davies's departure from Rugby League, and his subsequent welcome back to Wales with an intensity on a par with the Second Coming, marked the first of a series of Welsh players returning to their Union roots. Bearing in mind that professionalism was obviously well established in Welsh Rugby Union long before the IRB's decision of August 1995, the WRU had not thought it necessary to replicate Twickenham's one year moratorium to enable a period of adjustment to the new era.

Returning to Union

The immediate consequence was an interesting reversal of traditional roles, with Welsh Union clubs now enticing League players to switch codes and move south. During the lengthy campaign for a free gangway I had always accepted that would be likely to happen if Union went openly professional. But my concern as the process began was that I had not anticipated the extent to which Union apparently would be able to offer significant financial inducements so early in the new era.

Knowing the nature of the Union game in England, it came as no real surprise that their clubs could pick up such backers as Hall, Wray, Levett and Sugrue, but the news that "Welsh millionaires" were likely to assist with financing the return of other former Union stars who had "gone north" was unexpected.[257]

By the Christmas of 1995, besides Davies, St Helens's Jonathan Griffiths and Warrington's Kevin Ellis had returned to Welsh Rugby Union. John Devereux, David Young, Paul Moriarty, Rowland Phillips and Allan Bateman were, according to the press, all set to follow. Mike Nicholas, manager of Wales's national Rugby League side, put as brave a face as possible on these developments. "With respect, the players returning to Union are not in their prime; their careers are nearer the end than the beginning", he said.[258] Nicholas had been charged with both sustaining the Welsh national side, which faced four fixtures in the new year, and assembling the Welsh club side proposed for Super League within the next 18 months.

Nicholas faced difficulties not just in terms of a player shortage but also through continued hostility towards League from some within Welsh Union whose attitudes were unaffected by the International Board decision. Proposals for coexistence, with players turning out for League in summer and Union in winter, were opposed by the WRU, with its chairman Vernon Pugh insisting that players could only be contracted by one club at a time.[259] Nicholas was also hindered by BARLA blocking some northern amateur players from playing trial games for his fledgling South Wales club in the Second Division.

While Nicholas struggled gamely on with the national team in 1996 as well as developing the South Wales club in preparation for Super League, the RFL subsequently pulled the plug on proposals for a Super League side in Wales later that year by rejecting the South Wales club's application for membership of Super League, instead offering a place in the First Division, the one below Super League. This was despite the club having a financial backer in place and agreement to play at the Cardiff RUFC ground. The Welsh public are used to watching top class rugby and Nicholas and his colleagues believed that only Super League would have made the club viable. After the remarkable Welsh upsurge in the Centenary World Cup, Nicholas and the vision of a Welsh Super League side were perhaps the first League casualties of rugby's new "open" era.

While the first Welsh Super League side would fail to appear, the new Paris St Germain Rugby League team's first performance highlighted the arrival of Super League. It was a cool spring evening at the Charlety Stadium, Paris, for the team's launch on Friday 29 March 1996. The Paris side played Sheffield Eagles and won 30-24 in front of a crowd of 18,000 comprised largely of somewhat bemused Parisian spectators, watching Rugby League probably for the first time.

This was for me a night of mixed emotions. During the 12 months since the Murdoch deal had arrived I had shifted little from my original position of deep concern about the eventual consequences for Rugby League. But as a life-long fan of the game I knew I had to be present at the start of what was trumpeted as a bright new era. And I was delighted that the Parisian side, albeit including a significant number of Australians, not only offered a competitive performance but also recorded a victory in the face of media predictions that they would be Super League's weak link.

I had travelled through the channel tunnel in the company of pressmen who, according to Maurice Lindsay, "came for a funeral and had to write about a party".[260] Heading through France on the Eurostar towards the new vision of what, it was suggested, League could be like, I felt some emotion as well in reflecting on the past treatment of the game and its followers in that country. If League in Britain had faced a constant uphill battle for survival against a barrage of prejudice, malice and deceit since 1895, our experiences had been nothing compared to those facing Rugby League followers in France.

The familiar story of Union attempts to strangle League at birth was recorded by the *Paris Midi* as the game was launched in that city in 1934: "At last we were allowed this romantic and spectacular display, so much criticised by the orthodox players of Rugby Union," the paper reported. "The play, rapid and clean, without brutal shocks and confusion, completely conquered the Parisian public. Now we understand why so much hostile criticism has been launched from the Union authorities in England, who tried every possible means to prevent this match taking place in Paris."[261]

The period immediately prior to the Second World War had been one of real progress for French Rugby League but this advance had been checked by remarkable events in the later months of 1941, when the collaborationist Vichy government actually banned the playing of the sport and disbanded its structures, as outlined in Mike Rylance's excellent book *The Forbidden Game*. Years later an English writer asserted that by bombing the west stand at Twickenham in the 1930s British fascism would be destroyed for generations to come. And various sources have suggested that right-wing Rugby Union connections within the Vichy Government had seized the opportunity to block League's development, they hoped for years to come.[262]

The threat to Union's future in France posed by 12 professional and nearly 300 amateur League clubs was blocked by what has been described as "one of the most shameful events in the history of any sport". After the Vichy government's Prime Minister, Marshal Philippe Petain, signed a decree banning Rugby League on 19 December 1941, Axis forces destroyed the French Rugby League's headquarters in Paris and its records. The French Federation of Rugby XV, recognised by the Vichy government, took over League's playing resources.[263]

Such events, allied perhaps to a wider political view of the historical developments of the time, collectively constitute the soul of the game of Rugby League and its appeal to many traditional supporters, over and above the playing spectacle. I pondered that night over the way League had risen, literally, from the ashes of its burned down headquarters, and resurrected itself among the small towns and villages of south-west France. I wondered as well, as I sat high up in the Charlety Stadium, how the fireworks and glamour of the launch of Murdoch's Super League would be viewed by the surviving members of Rugby League's supporters in the wartime French Resistance.

Wigan and Bath

Comparisons of League with Union, noted in the *Paris Midi* so long ago, have been the bread and butter of sporting argument for generations. I will be among many who have spent a significant part of their lifetime engaged in such debates which generally conclude with the reinforcement of existing prejudices.

For such protagonists the moment of truth was on the horizon that spring as Wigan RLFC and Bath RUFC agreed to play two challenge matches, under League rules on Wednesday 8 May at Maine Road, Manchester, and Union rules at Twickenham on Saturday 25 May 1996.

The organisation of the two matches was primarily at the initiative of the two clubs concerned and the RFL in particular at first did not react with much enthusiasm, seeing the contests as a pretty unwelcome disruption to the early weeks of Super League. Nevertheless, by mid-April, the RFL had given its blessing to its controller of referees, Greg McCallum, and operations executive, Geoff Keith, meeting with the RFU's national referees development officer, Steve Griffith, and the disciplinary officer, Roy Manock, to discuss the refereeing arrangements for the historic double showdown.

The *Yorkshire Post*'s League correspondent, John Ledger, recorded that they had on their agenda issues such as wearing padding (not allowed in Union), shirt numbering, substitutions and disciplinary issues, "although whether Jeremy Guscott will be allowed to hold his mother's hand was not discussed at this early stage".[264] The England Union international had earlier reinforced his unpopularity among some League followers by indicating his unwillingness to turn out for Bath in the two challenge matches.

It was a couple of days after the first match had been played before I found out the result. Regrettably I had to miss this long awaited confrontation because of my involvement in a parliamentary delegation looking at global warming and environmental pollution to the north of Svalbard in the Arctic Circle. When our group returned to Oslo two days after the match, I asked the British Ambassador to Norway, at the end of a debriefing session, if he knew the result. He turned out to be a Union man professing ignorance of the fixture but his staff kindly supplied me with the previous day's *Daily Express* report of Wigan's 82-6 victory.

"Wigan prove they're in a different League,"[265] proclaimed the headline of the piece, describing the way Bath "were simply brushed away by a Wigan try blitz..." And, it suggested: "By the look of the commitment on the face of the Wigan captain, Shaun Edwards, each try was a blow for the bigotry and hypocrisy League has endured at the hands of Union for the last 100 years. The £3,000-a-man match fee was simply a side issue."[266] Indeed, many League followers felt that Wigan eased up, and could easily have scored 100 points. Sportingly, the one try that Bath did score was applauded by the League fans at the game. Later that day I travelled back to Britain in a plane full of London-based businessmen. I pinned the *Daily Express* report of the match to the top of the seat in front and chuckled all the way home.

After Wigan went on to win Union's Middlesex Sevens, subsequent press speculation was concerned with the likelihood of them also beating Bath in the 15-a-side return match. Their very obvious superiority in terms of physical fitness and basic handling skills led to League correspondents, in particular, peddling this line and even sowed the seeds of doubt among some in the Union camp. Such a scenario struck me as unlikely, but not impossible, because of the likelihood of Bath's dominance of possession through their control of line-outs and set scrums, rucks and mauls. The Wigan team, with Edwards absent through injury, included their 6feet 5inch New Zealand coach, Graeme West, in their side for line out purposes. Despite his somewhat advanced 42 years of age, he was playing club Rugby Union at the time.

The rugby historian would do well to listen to Ian Robertson's BBC radio commentary on that second match. From a condescending description of the litany of penalties awarded against Wigan for technical offences in the first half to near orgasmic relief at the end of Bath's 44-19 victory, in my opinion his performance that day will offer future generations remarkable oral evidence of the incredible depth of partisan feeling over rugby's great divide and how such sentiment among Union commentators was rarely constrained by the BBC's requirement for objectivity. 50,000 people were at Twickenham for the match and saw Wigan achieve a 19-19 draw in the second half, and have a marvellous try disallowed in the first half because of a marginal forward pass.

The outcome would have left the protagonists still arguing, but putting their case against a background of the almost embarrassing rapprochement from the top of both codes which followed the two matches. If Tony Hallett's conclusion that it would "be very difficult for the two codes not, ultimately, to merge",[267] raised blood pressures among his blazer brigade, Maurice Lindsay's reported suggestion of a merger within five years also would have done little to assist his rehabilitation within the League ranks, still seething over merger proposals and the imposition of Super League, although he later retreated from this position.

Beyond the traditional affiliates of both codes what lessons emerged from these unique matches? *The Scotman*'s Norman Mair, quoting Bath's Victor Obogu's admission that the latter contest was "the fastest, most tiring game I have ever played in," noted that the ball had been in play "for something like forty minutes, by comparison with maybe twenty to twenty-five in most of Bath's Courage first-division matches." He did not admit it but Union had been played League-style.[268]

Mair contrasted Lindsay's perspective on future developments with the parting comments of one northern reporter at Twickenham that day. In thanking the press-room tea ladies on his way out he "replaced the conventional 'see you next season' with a beautifully delivered, equally matter-of-fact 'see you in 100 years...'." Lindsay's five-year prediction might, he suggested, "be construed in some quarters as wishful thinking since it is partly conditioned by the money currently pouring into Union."[269]

The RFL's initial recalcitrance over the cross-code fixtures may indeed have been based on more than just concerns over fixture disruption. The Welsh developments had very clearly underlined the extent to which League was likely to lose several quality, if somewhat seasoned, players. Lindsay would have been more aware than most of the extent to which players' agents were looking at the impact of Union's changes in the context of their clients' future careers. He would have known that Union clubs, flush as Mair implied, with new money, were casting their eye over League talent. He was aware of the extent to which League's player contract system had pushed clubs into some impossible financial deals which could be unravelled by either allowing certain players a stint in Union during League's off season or completely transferring the contract to a Union club, perhaps even together with a transfer fee. He would have appreciated that these two matches, with other high profile shop windows such as the superb 1996 Challenge Cup Final and Wigan's victory in the Middlesex Sevens, had advertised the high quality of top League players to Union clubs with considerable purchasing power.

Wigan's financial situation at the time was clearly a major factor in their agreeing to release their former Welsh Union international, Scott Quinnell, to Richmond RUFC in May 1996. Their spectator support during the first Super League season had dropped alarmingly and, despite what the press called "unbelievable propaganda"[270] about increased attendances from the RFL, other clubs were clearly concerned that the new arrangements had yet to convince a sceptical public.

The Observer's assertion in early July 1996 that "Super League is a super flop"[271] had to be treated with caution in view of the paper's antipathy to Super League, but their writer Andy Wilson made some valid points about League stars being courted by wealthy Union clubs and the paralysis of the game in the southern hemisphere because of the ARL-Super League dispute. All League could offer in response to Union's wealth, influence and popularity, he argued, was a more entertaining and demanding game played at the right time of year for a handling code. "The game won't die," he wrote, "it's too strong in its pockets of northern England and the south of France and in two major states of Australia. But it's in a worse mess than ever."[272]

Union's potential impact upon Super League's prospects had, by August 1996, ended Maurice Lindsay's reported accord with Union. As Wigan's Va'aiga Tuigamala, Henry Paul, Jason Robinson and Gary Connolly were in the process of tying up short-term Union contracts, he was described as being "sick of reading about our best players moving to Union."[273] The Wigan-Bath games appeared to have opened the floodgates. "Now we must close them again," he said.[274]

With Wigan's Martin Offiah signing for Bedford RUFC and the London Broncos RLFC in a unique joint deal and Bradford's Robbie Paul also choosing to winter in the south playing Union, Lindsay's concerns contrasted very markedly with the consequent crowing of the Union ranks. Mick Cleary in *The Observer* suggested his game should welcome the League arrivals. "These are men used to exchanging bruises for a decent bank balance and will bring steel and edge to domestic competitions. Who knows," he suggested, "we might even see a few passes strung together in the Courage League as well."[275] He foresaw a more serious possibility which would also have troubled

Lindsay. Recognising that Super League contracts prevented them from playing Union much beyond January, he asked: "Who is to say that if, given a taste of international competition, the one real advantage Union has held over League, these players might not throw in their lot with Union full time?"[276] Beyond the pursuit of a basic sporting principle, I was also having doubts as to the possible long-term consequences of the success of the lengthy campaign for free movement between the codes.

Leeds in action in the August 2000 Middlesex Sevens. The club fielded a combined team from their Rugby League and Rugby Union squads, including Iestyn Harris, which attracted much media interest (Photo: Hugh McClean - SpedeGrafix 99)

Steve O'Neill (Crawley Jets) receives the Rugby League
Conference trophy from Harry Jepson in August 2000.
Rugby League Conference Chairman Lionel Hurst is in the background
(Photo: Peter Lush)

13: The Wars of the Rose

It's not just baffling to the outsider. To those of us who have followed closely the developments in Union and League since the remarkable events of 1995 what has happened in both games has been an astonishing cocktail of drama, tragedy and farce.

In Union the interminable battle between the RFU and the top English clubs has continued; the deep-rooted conflicts that have followed formal professionalisation have often been narrowed down by the media to the personalities of key individuals within the warring camps.

Some Union people felt a continuing deep resentment at the way the RFU was bounced into adherence to the August 1995 decision. With the financial realities of a professional sport becoming clear, Union's problems have centred on the crucial issue of who actually controls the game.

The *Yorkshire Post*'s Union correspondent, Neil Squires, suggested that anyone trying to understand what was happening should think of it as a conflict between the free market and communism. Alluding to the new club owners and investors on the one side and the RFU on the other, he suggested: "To the right are the aggressive advocates of the individual's rights to self-determination; to the left lie those who believe in centralised control."[277] It was essentially a clash of ideologies.

If it was the free market versus communism in Union, perhaps the analogy for League's problems was more the troubles of a newly privatised industry. Since the Murdoch takeover it had been one long story of controversial management and decisions alongside allegations of misuse of funding, personal extravagance and inflated expenses.

But those controversies, centring largely on the role of the man who delivered the Murdoch deal, Maurice Lindsay, were the tip of the iceberg beneath which were not dissimilar ideological battles over the ownership, control and direction of the game.

Like many others, I have felt very deeply the trauma of the unprecedented changes that have occurred since 1995. On its own, the advent of Super League, with its merger proposals and the move to a summer season, was enough to shake the game to its roots. But on top of this came the profound changes in Rugby Union and their largely unforeseen consequences for Rugby League.

Having contributed to the political pressure for change in Union, I make no bones about the fact that like most of those campaigning for the principle of free movement between the codes I had not anticipated the rapidity of that change when eventually it came. I also readily admit that I had not in any way fully thought through the extent to which Union's formal professionalism might impact upon Rugby League.

As I have made clear, I pondered upon the implications of the free movement campaign as Union's first full professional season saw a significant number of League's top players take the Union shilling on either short-term contracts or under longer-term arrangements. While there was no surprise in the return of former Union players, I had not expected those with no Union connections to move over, particularly the jewels in League's crown such as Gary Connolly, Jason Robinson and the Paul brothers, Henry and Robbie. I had also not expected Union clubs from the lower divisions, such as Wakefield, to be apparently able to compete financially with local Rugby League clubs in offering in some instances full-time contracts to lesser-known League players.

By November 1996, it was suggested that around 70 professional players had crossed from League to Union, with monetary reasons deemed the key factor. The new-found wealth of Union coincided with the close season between Super League I and II. Union clubs were desperately anxious to make an impact within their first professional season and, even on short-term contracts, established League players would not only add to their playing strength but also to spectator interest.[278]

While alarm bells were beginning to ring in some Rugby League circles, at the Wigan club, which had lost several key players to Union, the movements were apparently seen as the inevitable consequence of the contract system which would in turn impact upon that code as well. The Wigan spokesman, the former RFL's Public Relations Officer, Paul Harrison, said: "As usual, reports of Rugby League's demise are premature."[279] Nevertheless, when Super League's new World Club Championship was launched that same month there was press speculation that the competition would reduce the drift of players doubling up with Union.[280]

League's code-switchers, temporary and permanent, may have delivered a huge propaganda coup for Union's adherents but that sport's first official professional season was dominated in England in particular by the continuing battle for control of the game. While, at its start, the row over the Five Nations' Championship ended with the RFU making financial concessions to Wales, Scotland and Ireland, only three months into the new season English Rugby Union, according to *The Times*, was said to be "on the brink of open warfare".[281]

Conflict between the clubs

The uncanny coincidence of Union's formal professionalisation almost 100 years to the day after League's was to be followed by exactly the same kind of conflict between clubs and governing body that had lead to the great divide of 1895. At the heart of the conflict between the clubs and the RFU was the increasing realisation within Union that open professionalism cost a good deal of money. For some clubs the money was apparently there in quite substantial amounts but that fact added to the growing polarisation of different factions.

With access to the millions made from the Gateshead Metro Centre, Sir John Hall's Newcastle set a pace which many other top clubs and the Union game in general simply could not follow. The level of rewards offered in their recruitment of top Union players, including Rob Andrew, Tony Underwood, Doddie Weir and subsequently Wigan's Va'aiga Tuigamala, inflated the value of contracts commanded and raised serious questions about how clubs in the new Union set-up would finance the costs of a paid game. They were accused of doubling the going rate for players overnight.[282]

The earliest warnings over the direction in which Union clubs were going came from Wales. There had been similar arguments between the Welsh clubs and the WRU over control of the game; and access to money from TV deals and other figures produced at Cardiff RUFC's 1996 annual meeting underlined why. From a surplus the previous year of nearly £320,000 a loss of anything up to £500,000 was predicted for the first season of the professional game. According to a report in *The Times*, wage costs alone were put at £750,000.[283]

According to *The Guardian*, one senior figure in Welsh Union at club level was predicting in October 1996 that: "Without a significant financial injection, nine of the

12 first-division clubs would be asking their players by Christmas either to take a pay cut or rip up their contracts because they would have run out of money."[284]

If the English clubs had hoped to forge an alliance with their friends in other countries, the agreement reached by the WRU and Welsh clubs later that month was clearly a set-back. Coming on top of accords reached by the French and Irish with their respective governing bodies, and most of Scotland's leading players contracting with their union, the WRU deal made available to their clubs a minimum figure of between £6 million and £7 million for the 1997-98 season and, according to *The Times's* Union writer, David Hands, left the English clubs "in a vacuum of their own making".[285]

The October deal may have eased the Welsh situation but, by December 1996, Llanelli had announced that, in an effort to cut their wage bill by £200,000 and tackle their financial problems, eight players had to go. They were followed the following month by Swansea announcing that eight of their players had been given the choice of tearing up their contracts or moving on because of the club's financial difficulties. Their former international, Clive Rowlands, a past WRU president, argued for amateurs and professionals to play alongside each other in an effort to address the financial state of the game in his country. "Professionalism caught the game in Wales unawares," he said, presumably with tongue firmly in cheek.[286]

By the middle of the first official professional season, seven Welsh clubs were being bailed out to the tune of £750,000 by the WRU to prevent them falling into the hands of the receiver. They loaned the First Division clubs Llanelli and Swansea £200,000 each, Bridgend £170,000 and Newbridge and Treorchy £70,000 each, with the Second Division clubs Abertillery and Aberavon each receiving £25,000.

In the month following the Welsh clubs' deal, in the first of several reported resolutions to the on-going dispute in England, what a report in *The Guardian* dubbed "an uneasy truce"[287] emerged around EPRUC's agreement to a deal worth some £48 million to clubs over the next five years. They would be involved in negotiating TV deals jointly with the RFU and, in return, would support an updated divisional competition advocated by British Lions manager and former international, Fran Cotton.

The deal was criticised by several leading clubs with suggestions, according to *The Guardian*, that many others would only sign the agreement "because they are facing insolvency as a result of costly contracts with quality players they cannot afford".[288]

By early 1997, there was talk of vultures hovering over the newly professionalised game.[289] As well as facing the higher than expected costs of player contracts, the anticipated increases in spectator attendances had not in any way matched expectations or reflected the huge coverage Union was by then receiving in the media. But what was widely perceived as an impending financial crisis for the game only worsened Union's apparent conflicts. In Scotland, against a background of the SRU's sizeable overdraft, the three-tier structure of national, district and club rugby was increasingly the subject of vigorous debate. *Scotland on Sunday* reported in February 1997 that club attendances were down by 30-40 per cent[290] and the game was described as being in a state of civil war when, later that month, the former internationals, Gavin Hastings, Finlay Calder, David Sole and Jim Aitken, called a press conference to plead with the Scottish clubs to get rid of the controversial district tier.[291]

The disputes over the Scottish structure provided an interesting backdrop to the English debate around Cotton's idea of divisional competition and no doubt informed journalistic suggestions, quoted in *The Observer*, that: "those who still cling to the fallacy of divisional rugby should be shown forthwith to the nearest padded cell."[292]

Such comments were evidence of the strength of feeling around Cotton's emerging and increasingly controversial role within English Union conflicts. As the first professional season neared its end he was singled out for mention in press allegations of a whispering campaign against Tony Hallett, claiming the RFU secretary had mislead its membership over the TV contract with BSkyB and that elements in Union's hierarchy secretly sought to break up the Five Nations' Championship by forming an England-France alliance with leading southern hemisphere countries.[293]

As Lancashire's representative on the new RFU Council after its 1997 AGM, Cotton publicly criticised the decision to appoint Hallett as the RFU's first chief executive without outside competition. He also lambasted the game's approach to professionalism and said that Union had learned none of the lessons of Rugby League, despite taking on board significant numbers of new investors with successful business backgrounds. "Maybe these new Rugby Union men that have come in know more about business than we do, but all I can see at the moment is a large deficiency between what is being paid out and what is coming in,"[294] he said. The *Yorkshire Post* reported him saying: "Rugby League was there and available for us to see what they had done wrong and to look at some of the things they have done well but we don't seem to have learned an iota."[295]

Cotton attended the RFU's much trumpeted AGM at the London Hilton Hotel on Friday 11 July 1997, on the back of a highly successful British Lions tour to South Africa which had shown how much he personally had learned from Rugby League. His inclusion of several former League players in the side was to prove a key element in the British triumph.

The annual meeting was the subject of huge media interest, being billed as the long-awaited showdown between the warring factions of Union. "The War of the Rose," according to *The Times*.[296] Reams of newsprint profiled the protagonists and subsequently analysed the outcome, narrowing the conflict down to the contest for the chairmanship of the executive committee or management board, as it was to become, between the incumbent, Cliff Brittle, and his challenger, the executive committee member, Bob Rogers.

I read with some amusement the projection of Rogers as the candidate of the game's modernisers, having met him in the Commons four years earlier when, along with Dudley Wood, he was stoutly defending the last vestiges of the "amateurism" status quo. Now he was defending the progress made since the Paris declaration of August 1995 had ushered in professionalism and presenting himself as the unity candidate able to blend the interests of club and country within the game's new era.

He openly warned of the consequences of support for his opponent. "I fear that, if Cliff Brittle is re-elected, the existing problems and divisions will continue," he was reported as saying in *The Times*, "and the RFU image will continue to decline. The top clubs will become increasingly dissatisfied and will drift away from the RFU."[297]

But Brittle and his supporters were equally damning in their condemnation of what had happened to Union with Rogers's apparent compliance. "It has been a ripping yarn of clandestine meetings, treachery, deceit, duplicity, greed and power and it has split asunder a once respected and respectable governing body," wrote Chris Rea in the *Independent on Sunday*.[298] Club rugby, he suggested, was in financial chaos with the combined debts of the 24 leading clubs estimated at £15 million. "It is also estimated that next season's wage bills for a number of the biggest spending clubs will be approaching a staggering £3 million per club,"[299] he said. These were shortfalls which could not possibly be made up by sponsorship and television.

Presumably such concerns were shared by the majority of those who returned Brittle to his post by a majority of 599 to 357 and similarly supported a proposal that the position of chief executive held by Hallett on a trial basis until the end of October that year be advertised nationally. It was little surprise that less than a month later Hallett was gone.

If things were bad in that first professional season, they got a good deal worse during the subsequent 1997-98 season as the chickens came home to roost. By late September 1997, there were reports of investor unrest at Harlequins and serious difficulties in meeting wages in some Second Division clubs including Moseley, Coventry and Wakefield.[300] During October, Bristol announced a loss of nearly £500,000 and Bedford, with a wage bill of more than £1 million and gates of less than 3,000, shed eight contracted players in a bid to cut costs.

What the *Financial Times* deemed "desperate times"[301] for Rugby Union clubs had led, only two months into the new season, to no fewer than four club benefactors expressing publicly their concern over the way their expenditure was outstripping income. Bedford's Frank Warren was joined by Chris Wright at Wasps, Nigel Wray at Saracens and Ashley Levett at Richmond in warning of the seriousness of the game's position. Levett was quoted as giving "the starkest warning yet that he may withdraw his multi-million-pound backing because of 'mounting unsustainable losses'."[302]

As Cliff Brittle pointed to the All Blacks' sponsorship deal with Adidas, worth £28 million, as evidence of the importance of a successful international team in generating resources for the game as a whole, there were suggestions in the *Yorkshire Post* that some of these millionaire backers "were hinting at a breakaway in an attempt to recoup their investments". Wray said: "I don't want to pull out of the game but the finances are not adding up."[303] And, again in the *Yorkshire Post*, Warren was reported as saying: "The market level at which rugby players are being paid is more than anyone anticipated and we are disappointed that the crowds are not coming in."[304]

Dissatisfaction with the fixture and financial structure prompted a meeting involving at least five of the leading Union clubs in London on 20 October 1997 to consider the possibility of a breakaway tournament. Funding of around £20 million was reportedly available from Benfield, a company built up by the late Matthew Harding, formerly vice-chairman of Chelsea FC. A report in *The Times* suggested that the renewed threat of a breakaway "brings the sport full circle ... little appears to have changed from the uncertainty of a year ago."[305]

By late October, the scale of the financial problems which had beset Union clubs in the new professional era was becoming increasingly clear. According to the *Sunday Times*, Northampton, like Bristol, had lost £500,000 in that first season. Wasps recorded a £540,000 deficit, Harlequins £484,482, Leicester £276,000, and Bath and Bedford were also reported to be heavily in the red.[306] Peering over the fence from the Rugby League camp, Colin Welland suggested in *The Observer* that Union's much vaunted financial boom was not based on solid foundations, especially at club level.[307]

Brittle's response to the crisis came shortly before Christmas 1997, in a blueprint for the sport proposing professionalism's restriction to the English national side and the twenty-four Allied Dunbar Premiership clubs. His *Rugby Restructure 2000* document suggested that National League One and below would revert to amateurism, there would be an English amateur side, five semi-independent Unions and a revival of the county championship. Subject to RFU approval and consultation with member clubs, it was proposed that the changes should begin in 1999.

The general response from both traditionalists and modernisers was that Brittle was more than a little late with his barrow. For Chris Rea in the *Independent on Sunday*, what Brittle set out "was what had been blindingly obvious ever since Sir John Hall opened his cheque book and signposted the road to ruin."[308] But his vision was about two years overdue. "What the Brittle masterplan fails to recognise," reported the *Yorkshire Post*, "is that the genie of professionalism is already out of the bottle and galloping away down the street." If the previous amateur era was somewhat discredited, "the second coming will be even murkier."[309]

Brittle was ridiculed as well by Eddie Butler in *The Observer*, whose view was that amateurism was "as archaic as alchemy". It may have been cheap to run, he said, "but it was morally bankrupt, infested with a corruption that made Union the laughing-stock of the confessional. To miss amateurism is to long for scurvy or rickets."[310] I had to ponder on where Brittle had been before 1995 when I read his admission in the *Yorkshire Post* that, with his proposals, "amateurism will need to be clearly defined".[311]

1998 began with the announcement of an English club boycott of the next season's Heineken European Rugby Cup because of concerns over the apparent failure to accord sufficient prominence to the domestic League programme and with Brittle's masterplan under continued fire. Even traditionalist areas such as Yorkshire which had supported Brittle's re-election as chairman let it be known that they opposed the suggested return to "amateurism".[312]

The clubs were again at loggerheads with the RFU by late January as Fran Cotton, in his role as RFU vice-chair, unveiled plans to put some meat on the bones of Brittle's provincial union proposals. His *Vision for the Future* document suggested the establishment of four regional teams of Twickenham-contracted top players, in a revised form of the southern hemisphere Super-12s and based upon a franchise system for English club rugby.

He justified his model as offering a financially viable professional structure for England but its central principle of player contracts with the RFU met predictable club opposition. The English First Division Rugby group said in a statement reported in *The Guardian*: "It appears that the RFU want to strangle professional club rugby just as it breathes life into the game."[313] And, in echoes of steps taken in opposition to Super League in Britain, English First Division Rugby (EFDR) were also said, in *The Guardian*, to have reported the RFU to the Office of Fair Trading, querying their position as sole controllers of the English game.[314]

Cotton's plans to contract players to the RFU were firmed up the following month when it was revealed that Twickenham were targeting 16-year-olds to sign with them rather than the clubs. RFU contracts were also waiting for England players to sign when their club contracts expired. While the England squad met him on 23 February, except for representatives from Rosslyn Park, Reading and Newbury (all relatively minor clubs), the other clubs in the top three divisions were said to have boycotted the meeting because of their opposition.[315]

At the beginning of March, Northampton's owner, Keith Barwell, went on the record in the *Independent on Sunday* as describing Cotton's blueprint as "a cross between Karl Marx and Groucho Marx",[316] and announcing that his contracted players would not be available for England's proposed summer tour of southern hemisphere countries because of concerns about them being overplayed. His actions prompted the England coach, Clive Woodward, to omit the players concerned - Paul Grayson, Tim Rodber and Matt Dawson - from his squad for the remaining Five Nations' matches amid allegations that he had bullied players into choosing between club and country.[317] The 11 Premiership One clubs who had backed Barwell's stance were said in *The Guardian* to be "privately fuming"[318] when, in response to Woodward's actions, he climbed down ensuring the players would after all be available.

Later that same month, as the EFDR set out proposals to give their clubs greater access to TV and sponsorship rights and control over players and fixture arrangements, Cotton was rubbishing their proposed legal challenge over the powers of the RFU. The EFDR chairman, Donald Kerr, indicated that they had already begun an action, taking the RFU to the European Commission, on the basis that their plans constituted a restraint of trade and were against the Treaty of Rome.[319]

The power struggle continued during March with the clubs instructing their players to sign no new contracts with the RFU. The *Daily Mail* reported one First Division official as saying: "We are rapidly coming to crunch time. If the players are not prepared to support us, then the investors will say, 'Enough is enough', walk away and anything up to 500 rugby players will be out of work."[320]

Union's professional shambles and League's lawyers

As Brittle threatened to withhold some £6.6 million of funding from the clubs as a consequence of their refusal to take part in the European Cup, crunch time did indeed seem to have arrived by the end of March with Barwell proposing a breakaway from the RFU and describing its chairman as being like Boris Yeltsin, "sacking everybody who does not agree with him".[321] But less than a week later, Brittle himself was brushed aside by his own RFU council and cut out of further negotiations with the clubs over ending their dispute with the governing body.

That decision, along with a moratorium on the RFU discussing contracts with England players while negotiations were held, was too much for Cotton who resigned from their management board, and launched a bitter attack on the RFU president, Peter Brook. "What we are seeing here is the treachery of one or two people in the Rugby Union who have been trying to get at Cliff Brittle for two years because he had the temerity to stand against John Jeavons-Fellows in an election," he claimed in a report by the *Yorkshire Post*.[322]

It is worth noting, of course, that it was the very same Brook and Jeavons-Fellows who were party to the IRFU Board decision in August 1995, allegedly in direct contravention of the RFU instruction, to keep the game "non-vocational".

Of course Cotton had believed it could all have been very different if only the RFU had looked at Rugby League and learned from that code's mistakes. Chris Rea said in the *Independent on Sunday* in July 1997 of the shambles that was Union's professionalism, Rugby League "must be laughing its newly sponsored socks off".[323] It wasn't, because increasingly League was also splitting into various factions battling over the control and direction of their game.

As Union entered its traumatic 1996-97 season, Super League clubs formed their own limited company (Rugby League [Europe], later to become Super League [Europe]) and the First and Second Division clubs (those outside Super League), fearing further isolation and financial difficulty, hinted at a possible breakaway from the RFL.[324] The remarkable opportunities for expansion within South Wales shuddered to a halt when the South Wales club team was apparently unable to meet Super League's criteria for entry.

At that point, while Union's troubles had not significantly troubled the lawyers, League's entire international future rested on the outcome of the legal battle in Australia between Super League and the ARL. On 4 October 1996, the Australian Federal Appeal Court allowed Super League to operate freely in that country and whether one subscribed to the vision or not, the way was clear for the British game to move forward into the controversial new era. This was for Super League to run in Britain and Australia, and to stage a World Club Championship. It meant in Australia the game was split down the middle, with the ARL and Super League both staging senior club competitions, and the game being split internationally.

There was speculation over what would have happened to Rugby League if News Ltd's appeal had not been upheld. *The Guardian*'s Andy Wilson suggested that Murdoch would almost certainly have pulled out of Rugby League in Australia, concentrating on Rugby Union, a development that "would have left the game in the northern hemisphere staring into the abyss".[325]

Having been strongly opposed to the implications of Murdoch's effective take-over of Rugby League, I had at that stage very mixed feelings. The threat of breakaway by British First and Second Division clubs reflected their concern, after the initial Super League season, that the new elitist competition could do immense damage to the traditional roots of the game.

I shared those fears and remained firmly opposed to mergers of clubs such as Castleford, Featherstone Rovers and Wakefield Trinity, proposed on no firmer foundation than the inclusion of their communities in the same metropolitan district by a very dubious Conservative local government reorganisation way back in 1974. However, I did recognise by then that if the Super League funding had not come to the game when it did, Union's professionalism, with its multi-millionaire club sugar-daddies, would have almost totally cleared League of its finest players.

The League players who had guested with Union during the first Super League close season returned to prepare for the second season of Super League. Some players such as Tuigamala and Halifax's John Bentley, decided to remain in the other code for the time being, with Bentley emerging from the British Lions' 1997 South African tour with great distinction. Halifax claimed he was still contracted to them but, as a report in the *Rugby Leaguer* put it: "How on earth can they expect him to trot happily back to Thrum Hall [Halifax's ground prior to their 1998 move to The Shay] instead of going on an odyssey of fame, fortune and unbelievable glory with 'the other code'?"[326]

At the time, the national media's treatment of the likes of Bentley, Alan Tait and Scott Gibbs underlined the challenge League faced to hold on to other players who saw the chance of a national prominence denied to them by the establishment press's avoidance of Rugby League. But it was not long before the message got back to the League lads that the Union ticket didn't necessarily lead to a guaranteed pot of gold.

Gibbs's experiences in returning to his native Wales were noted by many in League. He had gone public on his boredom with the comparative lack of action in Union compared to League and there was concern that Swansea faced difficulties paying back the £120,000 loan from the WRU to land his signature.[327] The future of the former Wigan and Castleford player, Frano Botica, was also in doubt only months after he had joined Llanelli at the start of the first professional Union season because of the debts the club were facing during 1997.[328] Others were to be soon back in League after the Union financial bubble rapidly deflated.

As Hallett faced his critics during the summer of 1997, his Rugby League equivalent, Maurice Lindsay, was at the centre of controversy over suggestions that he was about to become the new chairman of the horse racing Tote. For reasons that were never made public the appointment went elsewhere but that episode and others led to growing demands for him to move on.

The role Lindsay had played in the Super League conflict with the ARL meant for some that his continuing presence in a key position would prevent any possibility of re-establishing working relationships within international Rugby League. In Australia the disastrous split was repaired after the 1997 season and the game was tenuously re-united by 1998. *League Express* suggested that: "the time may be coming when, for the good of the game, Lindsay should be thanked for his contribution and offered a pension and a thank-you dinner."[329] The Tote saga, the embarrassing defeats inflicted upon British clubs in the World Club Championship that summer and allegations that foreigners in the Paris St Germain squad had been playing illegally on tourist visas led to *The Observer*'s Andy Wilson also calling for "Mud Splattered Mo" to go.[330]

As Union's different groupings pulled their game this way and that, Lindsay's leadership was deemed responsible for not dissimilar conflicts in League. According to the *Yorkshire Post*'s John Ledger, a situation had been allowed to develop whereby the game had "more factions than a South American terrorist group with Rugby League Europe (RLE), the First and Second Division Clubs Association (FASDA), the RFL and BARLA and all the sub-groups contained within tearing it apart."[331]

In a move that even Union couldn't match, during August 1997, two anonymous businessmen professed themselves so concerned at what they termed the "gross mismanagement" of Rugby League that they paid £100 to register at Companies House and acquire for themselves the name Rugby Football League Ltd. Their view was that the present administration had brought the game into disrepute and were not deserving of the ownership of the Rugby Football League. "That name should represent quality, unity and tradition," they claimed.[332] Having made their point they subsequently offered to hand the title back to the game's ruling body.

The cudgels were taken up by the Rugby League historian, Robert Gate who, in an article in *League Express*, analysed Lindsay's near five-year record as chief executive. In addition to numerous criticisms already aired, he claimed that Lindsay's contacts with Rugby Union had been the equivalent of welcoming the Trojan horse. For long enough we were told that Union didn't represent a threat to League: "Mr Lindsay was seen in a television documentary consorting with Vernon Pugh, was heard to say we would face a combined game within five years, and sanctioned Wigan's games with Bath. Now," suggested Gate, "we gape at the TV contracts the rival code commands, complain bitterly at their superior media profile, actually lose players to Union ... and in Peter Deakin have begun to lose administrators who were thought of as Messiahs."[333] (Peter Deakin, a marketing director with both the Bradford Bulls and the RFL, subsequently returned to League as chief executive at Warrington Wolves, and then suddenly moved again to Union with Sale RUFC in August 2000).

On top of Andy Wilson's criticisms, there were tabloid allegations concerning Lindsay's expenses, the revelation of a forthcoming Charity Commission investigation into the possible misuse of funds within Rugby League and the growing perception amongst many League followers that Lindsay was first and foremost "Murdoch's Man". But of all the serious allegations that could be levelled at a Rugby League chief, in the eyes of traditional supporters, conniving with Union is by far the most damaging.

Lindsay responded by suggesting that his critics were presenting Union "with a supply of ammunition to bring us all down". He told *League Express*: "I want people to know that we face a great threat from Rugby Union. If we don't do something they will have our players, our grounds, and, most importantly, our fans."[334] But he strongly refuted the suggestion by Newcastle RUFC's Sir John Hall that: "The day Union went professional was the beginning of the end for Rugby League."[335]

Hall had spoken of looking forward to the day they took Wigan, St Helens and Leeds into Rugby Union. "It will be a long time coming," said Lindsay. "We will never go back to Rugby Union on bended knee. We will fight for our own code and we will get people in new areas interested," he told the *Rugby Leaguer*.[336]

The *Rugby Leaguer*'s then editor, Steve Brady, put a positive spin on Union's player raids by implying that their recruitment of top-line players on huge contracts was boosting League's finances as well as lifting the game's image. "The general public," he wrote, "will soon get around to the idea that League must be a fantastic game to be producing so many top players. And the inclusion of some of our best players in Union ranks won't make the game any less boring than it already is."[337]

His view was clearly not shared by Lindsay when, later in the year, England's Union coach, Clive Woodward, revealed that he might recruit from League to help his bid for the 1999 Rugby Union World Cup. Lindsay was reported in the *Rugby Leaguer* to have issued a stern warning to Union chiefs not to induce League stars to break their contracts.[338] This idea was raised again by Vernon Pugh in the *Observer Sports Magazine* in May 2000. He predicted that professional Rugby League would be subsumed by Rugby Union. The consequence of this would , he argued, be that "England will be world champions of rugby for the next 15 years because if they get the best players from league playing rugby union, there's such fantastic talent there."[339]

Whether Lindsay himself had also been subject to similar stern warnings relating to his stewardship of the game is unclear but following further calls for his resignation in the Rugby League press,[340] his departure was announced at a meeting of the RFL board by directors on 7 January 1998. But while he was allegedly "sacked" as chief executive of the RFL, taking what was termed in *Open Rugby* as "a pre-planned escape route",[341] he immediately re-emerged in the newly-created job of managing director of Super League Europe. As Dave Hadfield put it in *The Independent*: "With all the doors opening and closing, Brian Rix would have dismissed it as being too far fetched for farce."[342] But presumably News Limited had no objections to the arrangement.

Sadly for Lindsay, his earlier warnings to Union appeared to fall on deaf ears. Woodward's comments had been indicative of the way Union was by then looking to

League as one way out of the complex tangle with the clubs and its implications for the constitution of the national squad. The future of Wigan's Gary Connolly became embroiled in the whole affair as recruiting League players was seen as the possible solution to Union's impasse. As Union's feuding continued well into 1998, Chris Rea in the *Independent on Sunday* suggested that by signing Connolly and other top-name Rugby League players the RFU could, if need be, draw together a reasonably good national side in the short term, servicing franchised clubs in Cotton's regional structure. "It might sound the death knell for Rugby League but it would save the Union game from the utter madness that is now threatening its existence."[343]

At the Wigan club, as the 1998 Super League campaign began, there was anger at the way League was being drawn into Union's internal disputes. The club's chairman, Mike Nolan, claimed in the *Rugby Leaguer*: "The Rugby Football Union are just bluffing their own clubs in their battle for control and are attempting to use the Wigan club to do it."[344]

Both codes continued to face financial difficulties and other problems. In Rugby League, at the end of the 1997 season, the Paris side withdrew from Super League. After a fairly successful first season, the club had been plagued by administrative and structural problems, and had been based almost exclusively on Australian players who, it transpired, had not obtained the correct work permits to allow them to play in France. When this problem came to light, there was a possibility that they would not be allowed back into France from an away match in Britain. But they did overcome this problem and finished the season. The Oldham Bears, in one of League's traditional towns, also collapsed and withdrew from Super League, but a new club was started, and competed in the Northern Ford Premiership, which replaced the First and Second Divisions.

Two smaller clubs also departed the League scene at the end of the 1997 season. Prescot Panthers wound up after suddenly hitting financial problems connected with a loan from a brewery. Although one of the game's perpetual strugglers, they had a history under a variety of guises that dated back to the 1920s and had seemed to be on a more secure basis than for many years, when a sudden crisis forced them under. And the Carlisle Border Raiders, an expansion club from the post-Fulham period of the early 1980s, merged with Barrow, effectively taking the professional game away from another League outpost.

Gateshead Thunder

One positive point for the development of League was Gateshead Thunder's acceptance into Super League. Although it was disappointing that again no club had been established in South Wales, the game had put a great deal of work into the north-east for 10 years, including setting up an academy team at Gateshead and staging international matches at the Gateshead Stadium. Although the team was based almost exclusively on Australians, it had seemed to establish a base in the north-east and support appeared to be growing.

It was therefore particularly disappointing when after only one season Super League used more than £2million to implement two club mergers which undermined years of development work. Hull, one of the game's traditional giants, and based in a hot-bed of support for the game, were in financial trouble. David Lloyd had purchased both the

Hull Rugby League club and the Hull City football team, aiming to build a new stadium to stage both sports. For various reasons his plans had not worked out and the Hull club were now on the verge of collapse. It also transpired that the backers of the Gateshead club were running out of money, with the enormous set-up costs of a new team not covered by returns at the gate. So Super League's solution was to merge the two clubs, with Shane Richardson and Kath Hetherington effectively moving their Gateshead franchise to Hull, leaving the game's fans in the north east high and dry. However, at the time of writing a new Gateshead club, backed by a campaign of the club's fans, has been accepted into the Northern Ford Premiership, so all is not lost in the north-east.

There was a second merger involving a club from a non-traditional area. The Sheffield Eagles had joined the Rugby League in 1984, and had managed to establish themselves in Super League. Their marvellous Challenge Cup Final victory over Wigan in 1998 had inspired the game's supporters - a classic giant-killing at Wembley. But the Eagles had seemed to lose direction once Gary and Kath Hetherington, the club's founders had moved on. At the same time, the Huddersfield Giants, who had come into Super League when Paris pulled out, had also been struggling on and off the pitch. So a merger of the two clubs was agreed, although almost immediately Sheffield Eagles supporters and some players and club officials set up a new Eagles team and managed to join the Northern Ford Premiership. Player-coach Mark Aston, a central figure in the club since its early days, managed to recruit a team that held its own in the league, while the merged club initially played a couple of games at Sheffield United FC's Bramall Lane ground at the end of the season to keep a very nominal Super League presence in Sheffield.

In recent times, Bramley had become one of the game's struggling clubs, but one with a long and proud tradition. The sale of their ground had seen them playing at Headingley and, at times, having little separate identity from the Leeds Rhinos. Often Leeds players were loaned to Bramley for short periods when coming back from injury and it seemed the club was little more than a Leeds feeder team. Just before the 2000 season, the club's directors suddenly withdrew the club from the Northern Ford Premiership. A group of supporters set up a new Bramley Community Rugby League club, with membership based on co-operative principles. They applied to join the Northern Ford Premiership, but apparently their proposed ground, Farsley Celtic FC, was deemed not good enough, although it is not noticeably different from some other Northern Ford Premiership grounds. At the time of writing the future of Bramley remains to be decided.

For some Northern Ford Premiership clubs, the price of success has been disaster. The problems caused by a franchise system, and the lack of clarity over promotion and relegation caused major problems for Hunslet. They won a marvellous Northern Ford Premiership against Dewsbury in 1999, but were then rejected for Super League because the capacity of their South Leeds Stadium does not meet Super League's criteria. Subsequently most of their players left and crowds declined, as disillusion with the club's treatment set in. In 2000, Dewsbury have won the Northern Ford Premiership, again in a marvellous Grand Final against Leigh, but have withdrawn from trying to enter Super League because of the costs of competing at that level. I am aware of the financial problems some clubs have faced in trying to compete at the top level, and understand the need for Rugby League clubs to be financially sound, but by removing automatic promotion and relegation, Rugby League has removed the romantic possibility of a smaller club challenging the game's giants. In football, the Yorkshire clubs Barnsley and Bradford City have both recently competed in the top flight for the first time in many years, with Bradford's survival ironically dooming Wimbledon, the perennial small club survivor, to relegation. Rugby Union is in a very similar position, with promotion and relegation, all part of the romance and excitement of sport, no longer the automatic result of success and failure.

Rugby League's Summer Conference

During the long and bitter fight to end union discrimination against amateur League players, there have been many claims that these Union rules were at the heart of League's inability to expand. While the ban on playing League in the armed forces was a key factor in the code's limited international expansion, the Union ban on any involvement even with amateur Rugby League put the blocks on so many efforts to spread the game, as I have outlined earlier.

The Rugby League Conference, played in the summer, has provided cast iron proof of what could happen once these Union shackles were removed. Formally launched in 1998, it has expanded to include 24 clubs across the north, central and southern England competing for the Harry Jepson Trophy, won this year (2000) by the Crawley Jets from Sussex.

Although criticised in some quarters for sometimes relying on Union players competing in their off season, at the League's original launch in the House of Commons, its chairman, Lionel Hurst, described their participation in league as a kind of finishing school for fine tuning the skills of such players.

Along with his colleagues in the Summer Conference, Hurst – a veteran of the 1980s Freedom in Rugby Campaign – deserves great credit for demonstrating the extent of interest in Rugby League in non-traditional areas now participation in this sport is no longer the equivalent of "criminal" activity.

I genuinely believe that the establishment of the Summer Conference competition could well, in the longer term, prove to have been one of the most important developments in Rugby League's recent history. The successful sowing of the code's seed in previously infertile territory offers the best opportunity to solidly establish the sport – eventually perhaps at a professional level – way beyond its northern roots.

While professional League's move to summer was clearly a positive factor in the evolution of this new competition, its entry on the sporting scene shortly after the advent of Super League was in every other way coincidental. It was clearly the efforts of grass roots operators like Lionel Hurst and not the arrival of the Murdoch millions which were responsible initially, although Super League Europe do deserve credit for funding from this recent season the post of its full time administrator.

And it was the 2000 Summer Conference which revived memories of the old order. John Dudley, a Rotherham RUFC forward, who made a considerable impact with the town's Rugby League Conference team was allegedly banned from even attending their matches, let alone playing, under the threat of having his Union contract withdrawn. As Phil Caplan pointed out in *Total Rugby League*, this was particularly ironic as Rotherham RUFC have three former League players in their side.[345]

While the Rugby League Conference continued the spread of the amateur game, in the professional game, for the 2000 season the only club outside League's traditional areas was the London Broncos. After all the development work, the sport was back to where it was 20 years ago, when Fulham entered the League. Although Gateshead have been accepted into the Northern Ford Premiership for the 2001 season, the possibility of Super League clubs in South Wales, or Dublin, or Scotland or anywhere in Europe seems as remote as ever.

On the international level, League has continued to develop, and has started to overcome the international consequences of the Super League war. Although one or two of the sides for the 2000 World Cup, such as Lebanon, may have tenuous claims to a genuine base at home, the competition still offers a wider international base than the 1995 tournament. If the quality of the rugby is as good as 1995, it offers League an opportunity to promote itself to new audiences. Taking the tournament to Scotland, Ireland, Wales and France and some non-traditional venues such as Gloucester and Wrexham offers new supporters the chance to see World Cup matches live and hopefully appreciate the League code at its best. It is an imaginative approach that deserves to succeed.

The Union code has also had its problems. Faced with Richmond Council's refusal to allow them to develop the Athletic Ground, in 1998, the Richmond club moved 40 miles away to play at Reading Football Club's new Madejski Stadium. Their tenants, London Scottish, a club with a similar long history, moved down the road to share The Stoop Memorial Ground with Harlequins.

Neither arrangement worked well, although Richmond drew some reasonable crowds for Union club matches at Reading. So at the end of the 1998-99 season, London Irish effectively took over ("merged with") London Scottish and Richmond. This was after Bristol had bought a share in London Scottish to try to secure a premier league place by the back door. In fact, Bristol did manage to win promotion on the pitch. And as London Irish's Sunbury ground was inadequate for the crowds they were attracting, they moved in to share The Stoop with Harlequins.

So at a stroke, two senior clubs, Richmond and London Scottish, with years of tradition, were lost to senior Rugby Union - more casualties of the professional era. As Peter Stead and Huw Richards wrote in *More Heart and Soul*: "The reaction of the English Premiership clubs to the loss at top level of two identities with a combined history of 259 years was that this was excellent news as it facilitated their restructuring. The restructuring was, incidentally, a reversal of the ill-advised expansion the clubs insisted on only a season ago."[346] Both clubs reappeared, as amateurs, in the lower reaches of Unions' league structure in the 2000-2001 season

And ironically, London Irish are now moving to Richmond's former base, Reading, despite having attracted good crowds to The Stoop. Some Rugby Union followers believe that Harlequins were concerned about being overshadowed by their tenants, whose matches are often well supported. In the 1999-2000 season, Harlequins gates averaged 3,500, while London Irish, promoting their matches as "The Craic at the Stoop" were pulling in more than 6,000. How London Irish will now fare 40 miles from their traditional base remains to be seen.

Another problem facing Rugby Union has been a decline in the playing side of the game. One of Union's strengths, in my opinion, has always been that its senior clubs ran several open-age teams and junior sides. Interestingly, Harlequins now just concentrate on their 30 professional players, whereas, according to Stephen Jones: "in the early 1990s they ran five adult amateur sides as well as under-18 and under-16 teams". On the other hand, London Irish have six adult amateur teams and a thriving youth set-up. In a major feature in *The Sunday Times* in February 2000, Jones said that since 1996, there has been a drop of 25,000 in the number of players in Union, a decline of 12 per cent. Jones rejects the argument that professionalism is responsible for this decline, and highlights a number of other problems the game faces.[347]

In Wales, there was the remarkable spectacle of Cardiff and Swansea pulling out of the Welsh League in 1998-99 to play friendlies against English clubs, saying that this offered a higher standard of opposition. Although their matches did attract interest in the first part of the season, as pressures of league and cup matches told on the English sides, they often fielded weakened teams against their Welsh opponents in the second half of the season. They returned to a new Welsh-Scottish League competition in 1999-00 which included two Scottish district clubs, from Glasgow and Edinburgh.

In Wales in particular, as the millennium approached, there had been concern over the implications of the continuing vigorous debate about the structure of Rugby Union in England. In December 1999 English First Division Rugby (EFDR), representing the 12 leading English clubs, backed plans by Tom Walkinshaw, the millionaire owner of Gloucester RUFC, to form a British League. This proposed a cross border league competition featuring the English sides along with four from Wales and the two Scottish Super Districts.

Later the same month, as the Guardian claimed that "everyone bar Baldrick has weighed in with their own cunning plan of how to save Rugby Union",[348] a task group headed by Rob Andrew added its contribution. Its suggestion, subsequently backed by the RFU, of a twelve club English Premiership, to be held between September and January, was described as "a crushing blow" to the WRU's hopes for a cross border competition of the kind proposed by Walkinshaw.[349] The Premiership would be followed by the European Cup in February and March with the Six Nations moved back to April and May.

The relationship between the codes

And what about the relationship between the codes? Although there has not been any repeat of the Wigan and Bath cross-code matches, the relationship between the two codes has mellowed, although traditional League followers still have suspicions for the long term. The staging of the Challenge Cup Final at Murrayfield, unthinkable five years ago, combined with Super League "on the road" matches at Leicester and Newport have introduced League to new areas of Union followers. And for three seasons the London Broncos played at Harlequins, one of Union's more traditional clubs who spotted a new financial opportunity in the professional era.

And some players have continued to switch codes, including Paul Sampson signing for one season for Wakefield Trinity from Wasps, before returning to Rugby Union.

A more dangerous development for League is the drift of experienced coaches into Union. In *Endless Winter*, Stephen Jones attacks an article by Phil Larder which compared the involvement in matches of League's Shaun Edwards and Union's Rob Andrew, both international half-backs, as part of a comparison of the two codes. Jones says the article is "drivel".[350] Phil Larder was the RFL's national director of coaching and did much to develop coaching in Rugby League. If his views are so wide of the mark, why is he now working for the Rugby Union as a coach helping the England team develop their defence?

Another particularly interesting move from League to Union was Ellery Hanley's. One of the great League players of his generation, and arguably of all-time, he fell out with the St Helens directors early on in the 2000 season and left his coaching job at Knowsley Road. With no opportunities offered to him in League, he is now assisting with the coaching in Rugby Union at Bristol. Phil Larder had some background in Union before switching to League. Hanley had none. Similarly, Clive Griffiths, despite his record in League as a player and coach, has been working mainly in Union since 1997. While British coaches leave League for opportunities in Union, the Super League clubs almost exclusively employ Australasian coaches. This may bring success in the short-term, but League puts its future in danger if it continues this approach. And in September 2000, Joe Lydon left the RFL to join the RFU as manager of the England under-19 team. While the likes of Jones may not be happy, such moves are further proof of Union's desire to import yet more ideas, skills and techniques from League.

Writing on the 2000 Challenge Cup Final at Murrayfield, Eddie Butler, *The Observer's* Rugby Union columnist considered the position of both codes. In a considered article, he recognised the handling skills amongst Rugby League players, saying the game is "awash with such spinning, darting talent".[351] He said that Union had gradually changed its rules and style of play and "more and more resembles League".[352] He compared the two games, saying that "… union holds the geographical advantages of being a multinational sport; league holds the ace of being a bloody good game to watch". The whole tone of his article is that there is room for both codes and "they deserve to remain apart; but at the same time deserve to remain related."[353]

As League's 2000 season drew to a close and Union's winter season began, I was struck by the way the two codes still remained remarkably united in their continued uncertainty over the answers to key structural questions.

Shortly after Dewsbury Rams RLFC had been engaged in vigorous debate over their right as NFP Grand Final winners to promotion into Super League, which ultimately they decided not to pursue, the promotion/relegation question was also plunging Union into further conflict. Mid-August saw their First Division (i.e. the former Second Division) clubs taking steps to convene a special meeting of the RFU in an effort to reinstate the principle of automatic promotion to what would be the new Zurich Premiership. A few days earlier EFDR had voted unanimously to introduce a Rugby League style play-off system to decide the Zurich Premiership Championship.

By September, battles over the Andrew plan's two year moratorium on promotion and relegation were causing serious financial difficulties at several of the Zurich Premiership clubs. At the heart of the problem was the refusal of the RFU to pay the first three monthly payment of the £1.8million per club agreed within the plan until such time as the promotion/relegation issue was resolved. The First Division clubs, led by Cecil Duckworth, the owner of Worcester RUFC, were looking at the possibility of legal action to secure an automatic promotion place for the First Division winner, with a second place to be determined through a play off. Five years on from open professionalism, Union's internal feuding over its structures and direction continued.

14: One code mega-rugby?

Looking towards the future for both codes presents a truly formidable challenge because of the rapid pace of change that has seen the most remarkable developments in both League and Union during the last few years. Sporting history unfolds in both codes almost by the day, making accurate predictions about their future direction exceptionally risky. The past certainties of two deeply traditional games have gone out of the window, leaving anticipation of events over the period of even a few months a sheer impossibility.

While moves in the direction of a merged code have not occurred at the pace envisaged by some in the aftermath of the Wigan-Bath challenges of 1996, in my opinion a coming together of League and Union remains a possible outcome of Union's decision to go "open" in 1995.

Despite suggestions that Murdoch is happy to see year-round rugby - with League in summer and Union in winter - it is difficult to avoid the conclusion that commercial pressures will soon require regular contests between the top League and Union sides in both hemispheres on the basis of a common set of rules. Such a scenario will also be increasingly driven by the desires and ambitions of new generations of players at the top levels in both codes whose personal experience is not tarnished by the bitterness of the old divide.

But, despite the fact that Union would probably have to concede far more than League in the inevitable moves towards a hybrid code, I have very mixed feelings about such a prospect. On the one hand, I have to accept that the only way the oval ball will come anywhere near challenging the round ball in terms of seriously impacting upon our national sporting psyche is through one clearly understood set of rules. For those of the population who are rooted in the handling code, it would be so refreshing to turn on to a radio or TV sports bulletin that did not almost inevitably begin with the words "... and first, football".

But the other side of the coin is that the projection of a united rugby, in serious competition with Association Football, might require further unacceptable departures from the traditions of both codes. Top football has long ago moved from being simply a sport to a mega-bucks multi-national business, its clubs and players being less and less rooted in the local communities from which they originally sprang. Rugby, of both codes, has at top level moved rapidly along a similar route with those driving such moves assuming supporters will follow in greater numbers.

Manchester United offer perhaps the ultimate example of the transformation of a local sporting activity into, in my opinion, an impersonal and distant marketing operation not very different to that of the Spice Girls. I accept that I may be reflecting the view of the older supporter in raising a cautionary note over the possibility of such a culture enveloping top rugby clubs, but from a personal point of view I would prefer to live with my game being the last item on a sports bulletin (or, as usual in Rugby League's case, not mentioned at all) than lose the game altogether in the way that football has done in terms of its roots in local communities and its traditional supporters.

Both codes of rugby play a key role in the lives of the local communities in which they are based. Despite my past experiences with the Sandal Rugby Union club in my home area of Wakefield, I recognise and respect their contribution to the improvement of the quality of life in that part of the city through the opportunities they afford as a sporting and social outlet.

In Rugby League there are many examples of clubs providing a focal point for the pride and identity of local communities. There are few better examples than that of Featherstone Rovers, whose performances on the field offered the one beacon of hope to a proud mining community during the 1980s when the industry which had constituted the economic base of the area for generations was being systematically smashed to pieces by the Thatcher governments.

Just as that small town had fought to defend its pits, it can also take great pride for being in the front line of the battle against enforced club mergers ahead of Super League. More than anywhere else it articulated, through the strong West Riding accents of Ian Clayton and his fellow resistance fighters, just how important teams like Rovers are in such areas and what Rugby League is really all about.

Their appearance on the national news at the time may have embarrassed some of the suits grooming Rugby League for a different image, and may also have reinforced existing prejudices in the drawing-rooms of Surbiton, but it was a sincere and honest exposition of the game's relevance to many of its northern communities which its rulers ignore at their peril.

In restating, in the era of Super League, the importance of small-town clubs, I risk accusations of being rooted in the past and clinging to romantic notions of the great days of the 1950s and 1960s. I recognise that there is a need to address League's image and present it in a way that will sell it to a new market. I have no quarrel whatsoever with Sky TV's excellent presentation of League despite sharing the doubts of many in the game over Rupert Murdoch's longer term objectives.

My concern is that the whole concept of Super League profoundly misunderstands the nature of Rugby League in Britain. Having portrayed itself as: "the man's game for all the family", with League's community roots and the basic decency of the majority of the game's supporters, isn't the whole thrust of Super League one of moving the game away from just those qualities?

It is interesting that Castleford is now recognised as one of the successes of Super League, with the club having undergone a revitalisation over the past two years, despite clearly not fitting the Super League "Big City" model. Although renaming Wheldon Road as "The Jungle" to link with their new sponsors grates a bit, there is no denying the vibrant atmosphere there in the 2000 season. And their achievement in taking 5,000 supporters to their away match in London, with a vast fleet of coaches heading towards the capital, was remarkable. Halifax have also developed new links with their local community and the redevelopment of The Shay, when completed, will offer a comfortable home for them and Halifax Town FC, even if it does lack the historic tradition of Thrum Hall.

Pay-television

The logic of those concerned with the presentation of Rugby League as a product for future pay-television is understandable. Murdoch is on record as admitting his organisation's intention: "to use sports as a 'battering ram' and a lead offering in all our pay-television operations". His company need big-city contests in bright modern stadia. But with the turnstiles from Oldham RLFC's quaint former Watersheddings ground now on display in Twickenham's Rugby Union museum, do we have to accept the demolition of League's soul, as well as some of its admittedly ancient bricks and mortar, in the Super League transformation?

The big question is whether we really want the game of Rugby League to become part of the big-city mass sporting culture that constitutes football and if we really have any choice in the affair. Do we want to be just a marketing exercise that retains no community roots and identity and common values?

Rugby League is still a sport based predominantly in the working class and their communities. There is a key opportunity for the game to link with the Labour Government's commitment to ending social exclusion, and use the game to strengthen inner city communities. However, there is still a long way to go before the role that rugby league clubs can and often do play in such communities is fully recognised and properly rewarded in terms of Government funding and support.

An otherwise disappointing report from the Commons Culture, Media and Sport Committee late last year underlined the marked disparity in the lottery grants being received by the two codes of rugby with Union receiving nearly five times as much money as League.[354]

The Government's response to this particular concern defended the discrepancy on the grounds of there being more players involved in Rugby Union.[355] Such a defence is frankly more than a little naive. If there is a genuine desire to tackle social exclusion then more than a simple comparison of the numbers involved in the two codes is required. I would expect the Government to be looking at the nature of the communities in which individual clubs are operating, at the background of the players and supporters they recruit and taking steps to positively discriminate towards those clubs working in disadvantaged areas.

Although, in this context I am primarily concerned with the role of amateur Rugby League clubs, it is also important to underline the role of professional sides in such areas. I was particularly struck by points made in an article about the financial difficulties facing Featherstone Rovers RLFC, written recently by the *Yorkshire Post's* John Ledger. "It can be strongly argued" he suggested "that Rovers are equally if not more important to the town of Featherstone than, say, the Royal Opera House is to London, yet while the latter has received over £78million in support from the National Lottery, the rugby club has yet to receive one penny for its work in attracting young people to the sporting world."[356]

The Labour Government has, through recent legislation, attempted to address the tendency for Lottery funding to reward the more advantaged but there is still a great deal more to be done to support the important work being undertaken in many areas by both amateur and professional league clubs.

Some of the Super League clubs are now undertaking very effective community-based development work, especially in schools. Wakefield Trinity's Nigel Johnston had an impressive track record previously as Rugby League Development Officer working with youngsters in inner-city Dublin. I have been encouraged by his successful efforts to engage youngsters in constructive sporting activity in my own constituency and believe that the likes of Johnson ought to receive much more encouragement and backing from both central and local government for the work they are doing.

While League has made important strides in attracting women to both watch and play the game it is for me a matter of regret that a sport which has, throughout its history, prided itself on being genuinely inclusive has so far failed in many areas to actively involve our ethnic minority communities to any great degree in either of these capacities.

There are numerous examples in Rugby League's history of individual players from ethnic minorities coming to prominence long before their acceptance in other sports, especially Rugby Union. While, on a visit to Bradford not long ago, I was very interested to learn of a group of young Asian female school students playing touch and pass Rugby League, many professional Rugby League clubs - frequently themselves based in areas with sizeable populations of Asian origin - have made little real headway so far in engaging with such communities.

Bulls, Bears and other beasts

I would argue that reaching out to these groups of our local population is entirely consistent with Rugby League's traditions. My concern about the Super League concept is that it has deliberately set out to question some of the game's traditions and loosen some of the ties with traditional communities in the game's heartlands in an effort to break away from many aspects of a past of which we should be rather proud.

I fear that it has already taken us some way down the road towards the projection of a product that identifies less and less with the game of Rugby League and its traditions. The attachment of tacky Americanised animal labels to the names of great Rugby League clubs was part of a wider attempt to distinguish Super League as something "different" and to market the "new" product far beyond the immediate geographical area of the clubs concerned.

During the early days of Super League I persuaded my colleague, Gerry Sutcliffe, the MP who succeeded the late Bob Cryer in Bradford South, to table a motion in the Commons deploring the replacement of Bradford "Northern" with the new "Bulls" logo. It struck me that of all the great names in Rugby League Bradford's was the most historically significant, emanating as it did from the distinction of the club playing Northern Union, after 1895.

The Bulls have been by far and away the great success story of Super League with average attendances far higher than in pre Super League days. Under their chairman, Chris Caisley, they have successfully sold the Bulls concept to a new audience which has flocked to the Odsal bowl for the new summer rugby. Their marketing and presentation has won over a younger audience and the presence of a markedly increased number of women.

To those who favour the concept they offer a clear insight into what Super League could look like if other clubs had just a fraction of the marketing and promotional skills which they have shown. Their success has been watched as closely in Union as it has in League, with Peter Deakin, the Bulls former marketing director succumbing to an offer he could not refuse to move south to front commercial activities at Saracens RUFC under their multi-millionaire owner, Nigel Wray.

Under Peter Deakin's influence, Saracens managed to build a base in a new area for the club. The atmosphere at their matches was very familiar to visitors to Odsal in the Bradford Bulls era. Peter Deakin returned to League and achieved a great deal at Warrington, under the slogan "Our Town, Our Team", one that could be applied to most Rugby League clubs, before resigning to changes codes again, moving to Sale

RUFC. However, this last move was clearly linked to possible links and joint ownership in the future between Sale RUFC and Warrington. At the time of writing the future of both clubs is to be decided.

But did the abandonment of "Northern" signify more than just the advent of a new brand name and a sales gimmick offering a broader appeal beyond the immediate environs of Bradford? Has the symbolic departure from the club's unique roots in League a much deeper significance? It is interesting that in an interview in *Rugby League World*, Chris Caisley speculated about Bradford and Wigan starting Rugby Union teams, because if Leeds Tykes became a top Union side they would then have local opposition which League fans could watch in the winter.[357] Given that few League fans have been attracted to watch Union at Leeds, even when Wendell Sailor played a short guest spell with the Tykes, I think the idea of new Union sides in the north will not happen, certainly in the short term. An end of season Leeds Tykes match in May 2000 attracted a "crowd" of 200 people, an attendance usually exceeded by the Leeds Rhinos Rugby League A team. Unless Union moved to a franchise system and abandoned their present League structure, it is hard to see how these clubs could suddenly play at the top level.

I was not entirely surprised to be told personally by one leading Super League club official if his club's crowds dropped to a particular level, he would give serious consideration to the club joining Rugby Union if that represented a better business proposition, bringing in more spectators. While that club has achieved much in Rugby League, the complete absence of any apparent loyalty to his code is a sad fact of modern life in both League and Union and points the finger towards the distinct possibility of clubs crossing codes in the near future, or combining under merged rules.

I was struck by comments made shortly after Union's formal professionalisation by Leicester RUFC's honorary secretary, John Allen, when he resigned after 34 years involvement with the club as a player and administrator. He said: "By force of circumstance you are more likely in future to take on people who see rugby only as a business, without necessarily having an affinity for the game."[358] As *The Observer*'s Paul Wilson suggests: "League's destiny as well is in the hands of people who neither know nor care about its traditions."[359]

These new business men - without the baggage of Union's old fart blazer brigade or League's cloth cap, social-class perspective - are the ones who will drive both codes forward in the years to come and whose interests may well be served by drawing the best clubs from both games together. Deakin's position in switching between the codes, together with the above mentioned official's apparent willingness to jump codes, presents an interesting prospect although I strongly suspect a little market research among his club's supporters would indicate more than a little resistance to touch kicks and line outs.

There are other developments which have a bearing on the possibility of code-crossing. The involvement of the Yorkshire businessman, Paul Caddick, in the running of both Leeds RLFC and Leeds RUFC, who now share the famous Headingley ground, could be a significant factor in any moves toward a realignment. As a former Headingley RUFC player he has a strong affinity for Union and clear ambitions to project that code in Yorkshire on the national stage.

As well as Leeds sharing Headingley with a Union team, new stadium plans at St Helens and Warrington may involve sharing with Union teams. Some moves, such as the past discussions between my team Wakefield Trinity RLFC with Wakefield RUFC regarding the possible joint acquisition of a new ground, are essentially pragmatic, but may have a future relevance to any realignment.

Apart from the question of enforced mergers, there is serious dissent among many supporters about the consequent move of professional Rugby League to summer. Such a radical change had been mooted by some over a period of years, with the Leeds Rhinos and former Sheffield Eagles manager, Gary Hetherington, being at the forefront of those in favour. I found it ironic to hear him on the radio in the autumn of 1997 justifying the Leeds club's organisation of two out-of-season Christmas-new year derby friendlies on the basis that it was what the fans wanted.

Hetherington deserves great credit for much of what he has achieved in Rugby League but his admission of the importance of such traditional clashes in mid-winter and the fact that they have always attracted some of the biggest crowds of the season tends to considerably undermine the case for summer rugby.

Rugby League's professional arm switched to summer without any real effort whatsoever to consult those people who have sustained the game, year-in year-out, for generations. It switched as part of the Murdoch deal because BSkyB wanted year-round rugby on screen, and ran with the Australian season with the plan of a world-wide Super League play off.. The message to those who pay at the turnstiles was like it or lump it and initially there was considerable evidence from the attendance figures, in the lower division in particular, that significant numbers chose to do the latter. And having opted to be a summer sport it is little wonder that the casual observer was somewhat mystified when matches were still played at Christmas and the new year, the early Challenge Cup rounds in February, with the season completed by September and October, arguably the best rugby watching months of the year.

Perhaps the Bradford Bulls' marketing model will have an impact on other clubs and, along with the establishment of a more coherent season for Super League lasting into the autumn, prove summer rugby a success. Leeds Rhinos and Castleford have both experienced a growth in attendances, with Leeds playing on Friday nights. But I remain to be convinced and believe that new supporters must be drawn in, otherwise the spectator base will decline as traditional followers, who are unoccupied on Sunday afternoons in November, find themselves involved in myriad non-rugby alternatives during the summer months.

It is interesting that the Northern Ford Premiership will start its season at the beginning of December in 2000, and that its chairman, Bob McDermott, has predicted a complete return to a winter season within two to three years.

But League is not alone in facing fundamental divisions over the entire direction of the game. Rugby Union faces similar debates over "super league" concepts but is still wrestling with the hangover from the Reverend Frank Marshall's time, as to whether the game is "for exercise or exhibition". As Mick Cleary (then at *The Observer*) argued, not long after the IRB decision of August 1995, "Rugby Union has effectively been two games for half a dozen years at least."[360] There were the élite clubs, many of which as we now know were rewarding their "amateur" players rather well, and there were the rest. The latter have traditionally performed the perfectly honourable function of enabling an enjoyment of playing the game on the field and socialising off it.

Despite the sponsorship money pouring in from a variety of sources to fund both international and top club Rugby Union, there is some evidence in historically strong areas that the game is facing very serious difficulties in sustaining the lower levels of the game. The Yorkshire Rugby Union commissioned an investigation into the state of their game in the county following claims that an inability to raise sides has led to a spate of fixture cancellations at senior level.

It is in Unions such as Yorkshire that any attempt to develop a unified code of rugby would be vigorously fought by traditionalists who see such decline as a direct consequence of cavorting with the devil - professionalism. Things have already gone much too far from their point of view and the results are only too obvious.

Any attempt at drawing together one single game of rugby will inevitably at some point come up against the deep-rooted, social-class differences that have been at the heart of rugby's great divide since 1895. Despite some very important measures taken by the Labour government in terms of tackling poverty and unemployment, I see little evidence so far to suggest we are likely to witness the British class-system being brought to its knees. And a united set of rugby rules will not alter the fact that League clubs - especially amateur ones - generally inhabit the poorer communities and Union clubs, in England at least, the leafier suburbs.

Class loyalties

In the short term it will also come up against the fact that the strongest adherents of both codes will not easily forgive the enemy for sins perceived to have been committed during the 100-year war. Such attitudes are, understandably, particularly apparent in the League camp. They could be seen, for example, in the vigorous debate which has taken place among supporters about the venue for Challenge Cup Finals while Wembley stadium is being modernised. In terms of the required spectator capacity, Twickenham meets League's requirements but many traditional League followers will not be seen dead there. For traditional followers of both codes, the staging of England's opening match against Australia in the 2000 Rugby League World Cup, and the 2001 Challenge Cup Final being played there is an event for rugby football as momentous as the collapse of the Berlin Wall was for eastern Europe. Having said that, the 2000 Challenge Cup Final at Murrayfield, the home of Scottish Rugby Union was acknowledged as a great success, being supported by fans from the traditional Rugby League areas and many others who had a Union background. And Wales will play a World Cup game at the Millennium Stadium in Cardiff, the home of Welsh Rugby Union, only 11 years since the Union authorities stopped Jonathan Davies being interviewed on the pitch before a Union international because he had switched to Rugby League.

The traditional League attitude towards Union could be seen, as well, in the welcome given to Nigel Starmer-Smith, the BBC's Rugby Union commentator, by a Wigan Rugby League club steward at Central Park when he went to watch Orrell RUFC play in a short-lived experiment to stage major home matches there. According to Rugby Union journalist Ian Malin, he was told to "fuck off".[361] And the experiment failed - Wigan's Rugby League followers had no interest in Orrell, and some Orrell supporters could not bring themselves to set foot in Central Park. Basic class loyalties are sometimes expressed in a less than articulate form but such anger is aimed at all those individuals in Rugby Union down the years who did everything humanly possible to kill off the game of Rugby League, and that will not be quickly forgotten.

The flood of sponsorship money and big business now supporting professional Rugby Union has reinforced such "them and us" attitudes, underlining the belief that social stratification continues to underpin rugby's great divide. From a League viewpoint this has come as no surprise because what Dudley Wood termed Union's "freemasonry" has always guaranteed strong links with corporate support.

But while the consequences of such connections could have been anticipated, many League followers have been genuinely surprised by the way such connections have ensured that Union's media profile, especially in the national press, has hugely increased since the game went "open".

It is particularly interesting to note how the comparative coverage of League and Union does not in any way reflect respective attendances at actual matches. As the fifth Super League season concluded and Union's 2000-01 season started, Ray French put things into perspective: "Rugby League put its rival code firmly in place over the weekend when just six Super League matches proved the equal of all twelve of the elite Rugby Union clubs in England, Scotland and Wales." He outlined that 49,936 fans watched the six Super League matches, with 27,142 watching the six Zurich Premiership Union matches and "a pathetic" 21,000 went to the six Wales/Scotland league Union games.[362]

The average attendances for the top clubs in the two codes are as follows:[363]

Rugby League	1999 season	Rugby Union	1999-2000 season
Leeds	13,703	Leicester	12,691
Bradford	13,398	Northampton	7,282
Wigan	9,446	Saracens	7,250
St Helens	8,460	Bath	6,973
Castleford	6,877	Gloucester	6,820
Warrington	5,110	Bristol	4,958
Salford	4,505	Wasps	4,917
Halifax	4,483	London Irish	4,372
Hull	4,346	Harlequins	4,314
Wakefield	4,235	Newcastle	3,367
Gateshead	3,895	Sale	2,763
Sheffield	3,590	Bedford	2,718
Huddersfield	3,727		
London	2,935		

For French and others who observe both codes it remains a mystery why huge news coverage is given to a game which at top club level frequently draws less spectators than Rugby League. It is easy to conclude that the discrepancy is a straightforward consequence of Union being more widespread nationally but, returning to the social-class divide, perhaps the real issue is not how many watch the respective codes, but **who** is watching. The former England Union international, Stuart Barnes, has argued that the popularity of Union is a "vastly overrated thing", suggesting it is not the audience's size that is important but its nature. In *The Times*, he noted: "Rugby Union is watched by ABC1 males aged twenty to thirty. Advertisers love 'em; or at least they love their disposable income."[364]

Despite League's efforts to broaden its support-bases in terms of social class and the remarkable progress made, for example, in the development of the game in the armed forces, colleges and universities, the public and private schools stick with Union with the consequences Barnes describes. Breaking into the sporting agenda of such schools requires parental support for Rugby League which is unlikely when today's parents at such establishments are often themselves the ABC1 Union products he identifies.

Those who enthusiastically predict the demise of Rugby League, like the Scottish Rugby Union's Jim Telfer, point to the consequent stark fact that: "The focus for business people is on Rugby Union."[365] Of course, very largely it is, because those running the business community are the very same ABC1 males that Barnes identifies and this fact is confirmed by the wealth of sponsorship deals pouring money into Union in recent years.

In looking to the future, any objective analysis of the positions of the two codes is likely to conclude that in nearly all the key elements off the pitch Union clearly has the upper hand. In the crucial area of media coverage it wins hands down, creating, as Stuart Barnes concedes, a largely false picture but one which is of enormous importance in influencing corporate sponsorship and television time.

But there is one area where Union does not have the edge which is arguably the most important of all, particularly in the context of possible future pressures towards the establishment of a merged game. On the field of play League offers the spectator a much greater opportunity to witness the handling skills which represent the icing on the cake of both games. The ball is in play more, there is more action and it is easier for the new watcher to understand. As the future of both codes is now largely in the hands of TV broadcasters, its advantages in terms of entertainment could prove crucial.

League's separate existence from the late 1890s necessitated a continuing review of the rules to attract the spectators who paid the players' wages and the modern game constitutes the end product of a series of revisions distancing it considerably from Union. To League's opponents, like Telfer, the result is insufficiently complex. "Rugby League is such a simple game; any simpleton can watch it and it can be very boring," he was reported as saying in the *Guardian*.[366] But others in the Union camp believe that their game is in desperate need of similar simplification if it is to become spectator friendly. The *Independent on Sunday*'s Chris Rea has argued that Union's arcane laws "are too much even for the players and arbiters to comprehend let alone the casual bystander."[367] Such a situation didn't really matter when the game was just a players' pastime but the introduction of professionalism requires a duty to entertain.

At a very senior level in the Union game however there have been dire warnings about the direction of the game on the field. "We are coming perilously close to following the same road as Rugby League", warned Vernon Pugh, chairman of the IRB, recently. In almost Telferesque terms, he added, "The uniqueness of Rugby Union must be preserved and we must ensure that Rugby [Union] remains a physically challenging and intelligent game."[368]

It will give Pugh no comfort to learn that I would be the first to concede that by bringing in a range of changes in recent years - several, such as restrictions on direct kicking into touch, taken directly from League - the Union game has improved considerably from a spectator's viewpoint. The Super-12s competition, televised from Australia, has convinced many Rugby League enthusiasts that, played adventurously, Union can entertain in ways the old Five Nations Championship and British club rugby have never done. The 1997 All Blacks showed during their matches in Britain that quick ball turnover in the ruck can ensure a greater continuity of play than has ever seemed possible in British Rugby Union. The 1999 Rugby World Cup semi-final between France and New Zealand also showed that attacking Rugby Union could produce a very exciting game.

The increased dependency of Union on TV contracts will inevitably bring pressure here to improve the spectacle, as Gerald Davies has suggested in an interview in *The Times*: "What, the television executive may ask, is the point of kicking the ball so often into touch when what our audience wants is for the ball to be in and not out of play."[369]

While all these Union writers recognise the need to make their game less complex that code faces a real dilemma in taking such steps because of the very existence of Rugby League. A common analysis of Union's ills on the field pinpoints the issue of too many players and frequently identifies the two wing forwards as the most dispensable positions. As well as creating more space, the loss of these positions would have the added attraction of reducing the number of occasions that open play arising from a set scrum is ended with the half-backs of the attacking side still in possession. But for many in their game, reducing teams to 13 players would be just too much to swallow after also following League in so many other areas, including professionalism. Increasing the pitch's dimensions has even been suggested as a possible alternative![370]

The future of the line-out has been similarly questioned and concerns underpin debate about the methods of restarting play after a player is caught in possession because, at the moment, penalties often seem the end result. Jonathan Davies identified rucks as the main problem in Union, "killing the game stone dead as a spectacle".[371]

While Union's options for change are limited by the way the other code has evolved, without in any way arguing for a fusion of the rules, I would accept that there are areas where League could improve and perhaps even learn lessons from Union. One does not have to subscribe to the Jim Telfer school of thought to recognise that on occasions League can be too repetitive and one-dimensional.

League's tactics

The play-the-ball rule does introduce an element of stop-start although few top sides ever stand still when the game is restarting this way, whether they are on attack or in defence. The six-tackle rule transformed the game for the better when it was introduced but tactical alternatives to a handover on the last tackle can sometimes give the game a predictable air, being often restricted to an 'up-and-under' or kick for touch, although a confident team will run the ball if in an attacking position and "keep it alive". The introduction of the 40/20 rule has given an incentive for accurate touch-line kicking in League. It is interesting that Eddie Butler, writing on the 2000 Challenge Cup Final, wrote: "And how long will it be before union starts to copy the tactic of the kick from hand close to the line which produced so many tries at Murrayfield."[372]

One factor in the introduction of the handover was spectator frustration at the scrummaging used previously to restart play if the ball was not kicked on the last tackle. Rather than reinforce clear scrummaging rules, the RFL encouraged referees to turn a blind eye to scrum-halves feeding their own team's feet in an effort to ensure that the game was restarted with a minimum amount of fuss. The end result is entirely predictable, emerging from scrums that offer no contest but afford the forwards a welcome and, with the speed of the modern game, very necessary breather. It also frees the backs from the forwards for one play.

To retain the edge in spectator appeal, League would be wise to take a leaf out of Union's continued fostering of scrummaging skills. The proper application of the rules to ensure correct binding and straight feeding - if necessary by the referee - would restore contested scrums and an element of unpredictability at the conclusion of a set of six tackles. If a defending side faced the prospect of losing a scrum well inside its own half it would ensure that it made much greater efforts to prevent a ball finding touch. It would also sharpen up the attacking side's kicking skills if they knew that their opponents were likely to do all they could to avoid a subsequent scrum.

The prospect of the attacking side regaining possession from a scrum following a kick would ensure that Rugby League as a whole revived the scrummaging skills that have been gradually lost over the past 20 years. And a welcome side-effect of the re-invention of specialist front-rowers would perhaps be some slowing down of what seems on occasions a rather helter-skelter modern game.

I have been encouraged by League's return to giving the restart after a score to the non-scoring side and also by a gradual increase in the number of these restarts actually being contested by both teams. I have fond memories of contested restarts being an important feature of Rugby League during my early days as a spectator and player, with both sides having the opportunity to gain possession. A high ball from the centre spot just past the defending side's 10-yard line guaranteed a fascinating clash between opposing forces. This tactic has started to be used again by some teams.

Union has retained such restarts but League had generally lost them as part of its de-skilling of specialist forwards. To encourage a revival of this element of the old game, a possible new requirement to kick the ball into the area between the 10 and 20 metre line would encourage the team kicking off to try to gain possession with the consequent unpredictability which League is lacking at the present time.

The fact that I advocate a return to such contested phases of play and the rediscovery of specialist forwards is in part a reflection of my belief that modern League suffers as a result of the game being far less overtly physical than it was even 20 years ago. The introduction of the limited-tackle rule contributed to the demise of many of the heavyweights whose forte was intimidation and confrontation and I have no qualms with a development that considerably speeded up the game and enhanced ball-handling skills. While the cleaning up of Rugby League at both an amateur and professional level is obviously to be welcomed, I do regret the way the game has lost some of its bite in the process. It is in the nature of collision sports for there to be occasional explosions and I am not alone in mourning the fact that their gradual passing is perhaps some comment on the make-up of the modern game.

The spectators who cheered on the victorious Great Britain Rugby League side at Old Trafford in the second 1997 British Gas Test against Australia were not just recognising a greater effort than they had seen a week earlier at Wembley. They were responding to a team rising to its coach's call for a physical confrontation within the rules. They were applauding a return to what Test matches are all about: torrid forward confrontations alongside fast, open play - in short, real old-fashioned blood-and-guts Rugby League!

It is my privilege to see marvellous sporting exhibitions at Rugby League matches most weeks. I regularly admire the increasingly high standard of amateur Rugby

League and the obvious lessening of the gap between the amateurs and lower-division professional clubs. While that gap has narrowed, the one between the Northern Ford Premiership and the Super League has grown quite markedly, reflecting the remarkable advance in the skill levels and fitness of full-time Rugby League players at the game's top clubs.

Such qualities earn the admiration of the vast majority of fair-minded adherents of Union and it is a great tribute to League that many top Union clubs are increasingly playing to League rules in training as a means of sharpening up their handling and defensive skills.

League's innovations go to Union

An interview with Chris Caisley in *Rugby League World* highlighted some of the tactical innovations that Union has borrowed from League in recent years. He noted the following: "Attacking formations based on League patterns, with the first receiver standing flatter and more stationary; the modification of the penalty law so that the side who are awarded a kick to touch also get the line out throw [and usually possession]; promoting values such as physical confrontation, continuity of play and 'big hits'; in the southern hemisphere, the selective application of the ruck and maul laws to devalue the contest for possession, thus allotting teams a certain amount of possession; devaluing the contest for possession at scrums and line outs to ensure the ball is shared out and Union's leading coaches now preach tactical values such as ball control and field position - an approach directly taken from League." [373]

He also highlighted 10 other innovations in how the game is run that Union has adopted directly from Rugby League, including professionalism, world cup tournaments, league structures, video referees, defensive systems, tactical substitutions, the sin-bin, protective equipment, conditioning training and allowing minor injuries to be treated on the pitch while play continues.

The League game clearly, therefore remains in the driving seat on the field but, regardless of whether a merged code is an early, distant or non-existent prospect, to stay in pole position it must continue the process of review and reform which has ensured its evolution towards the spectacle of today and marked it out from Union. If it continues to build upon the general excellence of the modern game, the well-established pattern of Union eventually conforming to League's arrangements both on and off the field as shown above will continue, with any merged rules being predominantly based upon Rugby League.

15: And was Jerusalem builded here...

So who won rugby's class war?

In terms of dominating the nation's sporting agenda the answer is neither Union nor League because football was the key beneficiary of rugby's great divide. During the 100-year conflict it came through the middle to establish in Britain and elsewhere in the world a sporting predominance which appears unassailable in the foreseeable future.

Narrowed down to the two codes, the simple answer to the question is that it is far too soon to know. Both codes remain in a state of almost permanent revolution with an eventual outcome some considerable distance away and far from certain. And I suspect that establishing the ultimate answer to the question will be as subjective an exercise as all the countless other debates about the comparative merits of the two codes throughout their existence. Despite the changes in both codes, at the time of writing they are still two separate sports, putting different demands on the athletes who play them at the top level and providing enjoyment for those who play in the amateur ranks.

In short, establishing the victor is dependent entirely upon the criteria on which the judgment is based and also perhaps where the judge is coming from. However, when there is a conflict over issues, the side that is defeated is the one that concedes the issues. And almost entirely, both on and off the pitch, that has been Rugby Union.

Where I am coming from in terms of this debate will be fairly clear. For me, Rugby League has always been more than just a game. Growing up where I did it was, and to some extent still is, a manifestation of the collective pride of the communities from which it emerged. Geoffrey Moorhouse summed it up for me in his literary celebration of the game, *At the George*: "League has my allegiance... because it is an expression of who I am and where I come from, the history of my people and our ancestral lands. It is of the culture from which I spring...".[374]

In suggesting ethics, morality and basic sporting decency as a fairly reasonable criteria for coming to an evaluation, I would take it even further, because the more I have given thought to the historic relationship between Union and League the more I have been sustained in my pride at being born on what some would term the wrong side of rugby's blanket. Such an assessment leaves pre-Murdoch League as the only possible winner.

Rugby Union's sporting apartheid was a unique product of the British class system, an indefensible elitism sustained for a century by anachronistic rules underpinning a perceived superiority. What was a by-product of the social stratification of late Victorian Britain was fostered by educational and occupational elitism, snobbery, vindictiveness and even hatred.

For those of us coming into contact with elements of the culture which encouraged such attitudes there was no surprise when, in the face of an almost world-wide sporting boycott of apartheid South Africa, Rugby Union (as well as cricket, it has to be said) gave that racist regime particular support. There was no surprise when Union's top amateur players in Britain took substantial payments in breach of the game's rules to help "the white man's game" in that country celebrate its centenary. And there was no surprise when Vernon Pugh's report into their actions was quietly buried by Union's authorities, in quite remarkable contrast to their diligence in pursuit of those with even the vaguest connection to Rugby League.

League took the honourable route in 1895 and its demise has been predicted by the sporting establishment ever since. I have played, watched, loved and lived the game for more than 40 years and I have been told it was dying throughout that time. But when a game's entire history has been peppered with the most vicious attacks from that establishment - throughout broadcasting networks, the southern-based national press, educational institutions, the armed forces and even Nazi collaborators - and it still survives, there is perhaps something quite unique in its soul.

League's future lies in defending that soul, in remaining true to those communities which have sustained it and to those ethics that have underpinned its inclusiveness and essential decency throughout most of its history. It lies in balancing the perfectly proper desire for vigorous marketing and expansion with positive attempts to take the joy of sporting activity to the disadvantaged in those less fashionable areas and communities that some of the game's big thinkers would have us leave behind in the search for more middle class appeal.

It lies in valuing, celebrating and keeping faith with a very honourable past in determining the direction it will take in the future.

Chronology

1871	Foundation of the English Rugby Football Union
Dec 1877	Introduction of Yorkshire Challenge Cup "although no medals were to be presented to players because it was felt that this smacked too much of professionalism".[1]
1878	The Wakefield Trinity three-quarter, Harry Hayley, believed to be the first player without a public school background to be selected for the Yorkshire County side. [2]
1879	Press reports claim that, against the rules, a Yorkshire club had a paid player. Possibly the first ever professional rugby player was said to be Wakefield Trinity's C.E. Bartram. [3]
1892	The formation of leagues in both Yorkshire and Lancashire, despite the RFU's opposition
20/12/1893	The northern clubs' proposal that players be allowed to receive 'broken time' payments for loss of earnings is rejected by the RFU.
29/8/1895	22 clubs from Yorkshire, Lancashire and Cheshire break away from the RFU, forming the Northern Rugby Football Union (NU) and allowing the practice of 'broken time' payments
1898	NU allow professionalism within strictly regulated working clauses.
1905	Unrestricted professionalism allowed by NU.
1922	The Northern Union changes its title to the Northern Rugby Football League.
19/12/1941	Collaborationist Vichy Government in France ban playing of Rugby League. Axis forces destroy French Rugby League's headquarters in Paris and its records. French Federation of Rugby XV, (RU) recognised by Vichy Government, take over League's playing resources.
23/1/1943	After the RFU temporarily lift the restrictions on League players playing Union, Northern Command Rugby League defeat Northern Command Rugby Union 18-11 at Headingley, playing under Rugby Union laws.
24/4/1944	Rugby League Combined Services defeat Rugby Union Combined Services 15 -10 at Odsal in a game played under Rugby Union laws.
4/3/1973	British Amateur Rugby League Association (BARLA) formed to separately administer the amateur game.
1981	RFU propose acceptance of amateur League players into Union, provided they have "ceased to be involved" in League.
1983	IRB allow full time students to play either code of rugby, provided it is part of the named sporting activity within their college or university.
March 1985	Freedom in Rugby campaign launched to take on Rugby Union over its attitudes to both amateur and professional Rugby League.
Sept 1985	Introduction of League tables and commercial sponsorship in Rugby Union.
27/11/1985	Welsh Union player, Steve Ford, banned from the sport after playing three trial matches with Leeds RLFC for which he had received expenses.
11/12/1985	Parliamentary Early Day Motion tabled by Roger Stott M.P., condemning the RFU block on a free gangway between the codes and calling for an end to Sports Council grants to Union while there is continued discrimination against League players.
24/2/86	Roger Stott M.P. draws attention to Rugby Union's failure to meet Sports Council criteria for the receipt of capital grants as a result of their exclusion of Rugby League players.
April 1986	IRB relaxes rigid restrictions on earnings from books, radio and TV appearances by those involved in Union.
1/5/1987	RFU announces it is to propose that players should be free to play amateur Rugby League while still members of Rugby Union clubs.
10/2/1988	Formation of Parliamentary All-Party Rugby League Group signals the start of a series of parliamentary initiatives aimed at ending Union's discrimination against League.
1991	Australian RFU press for changes to IRB regulations on reinstatement of Rugby League players after legal advice received that, as they stood, the regulations were unenforceable.
1993	Wasps Rugby Union fullback, Steve Pilgrim, banned from Union for 12 months after a trial with Leeds RLFC for which he had not been paid. The issue is drawn to parliamentary attention through an Early Day Motion.

---

[1] Tony Collins, Rugby's Great Split, p.22
[2] Ibid. p.29
[3] Ibid. p.49

1/4/1993	Senior RFU officials meet All-Party Parliamentary Rugby League Group in Commons
28/4/1993	Debate on proposed amendment to National Lottery Bill, aimed at blocking funding to Rugby Union while discrimination against League continues.
1993-1994	Stuart Evans, the former Welsh Rugby Union and St Helens RLFC prop, examines a proposed "restraint of trade" legal action against the WRU and the IRB for their refusal to reinstate him in Rugby Union. He believes that the widespread payments being made in Rugby Union can be exposed through court action.
June 1993	After representations from All-Party Parliamentary Rugby League Group and parliamentary questions, Inland Revenue investigate financial arrangements at several Union clubs.
15/4/1994	Just before the dispute comes to the supreme court, the New South Wales RU agree to reinstate former Eastern Suburbs League player and Union international, Brett Papworth.
1994	Inland Revenue officials advise officers of the All-Party Parliamentary Rugby League Group that their investigation of Rugby Union had shown that at top level the game was "at least as professional as Rugby League."
27/4/1994	Ministry of Defence announce lifting of ban on playing of Rugby League in armed forces after vigorous parliamentary campaign.
21/6 1994	Sports (Discrimination) Bill - an attempt to make it illegal for one sport to discriminate against another, introduced by David Hinchliffe M.P. in the House of Commons.
1/7/1994	Sports (Discrimination) Bill gains unopposed second reading in Commons.
13/7/1994	Sports (Discrimination) Bill completes Commons committee stage.
August 1994	Magazine interview by Scott Gibbs, the St Helen's RLFC and former Welsh Rugby Union international, gives detailed information about payments within Union.
October 1994	Scottish RU international, Gavin Hastings, alleges widespread breaches of "amateurism".
21/10/1994	Sports(Discrimination) Bill's progress in Parliament is blocked at report stage.
Late 1994	Parliamentary EDM contrasts comments of Bath and England Union player, Mike Catt, about his earnings from Union in South Africa with the banning by the RFU of the Cambridge University RU player, Adrian Spencer, for having played Rugby League as an amateur with London Crusaders.
January 1995	Press reports of meeting being arranged between Vernon Pugh, the WRU Chair and IRB member and Maurice Lindsay, Chief Executive of RFL. Pugh confirms speculation that a key reason for seeking meeting is concern over implications of Sports (Discrimination) Bill.
2/3/1995	National Heritage Select Committee Inquiry into relations between Rugby Union and Rugby League begins.
14/3/1995	IRB announce that former Rugby League professionals will be allowed back in Rugby Union after a three year stand-down period.
21/3/1995	Press reports that IRB amateurism working party had found breaches of amateurism "rife".
8/4/1995	Rugby Football League agrees Super League deal with News Corporation with proposed club mergers and move to a summer game in 1996.
19/4/1995	National Heritage Committee report on relations between Rugby Union and Rugby League finds " the attitude of Rugby Union to Rugby League both discriminatory and indefensible" and proposes a block on public funding to Rugby Union until the sport amends its rules.
19/4/1995	Revised Sports (Discrimination) Bill introduced by David Hinchliffe M.P. in the Commons and the Earl of Swinton in the Lords. Bill completed its stages in the Lords, later blocked in the Commons.
26/4 1995	Parliamentary debate on Super League.
27/8 1995	IRB announce Rugby Union's acceptance of professionalism.
29/8/1995	Rugby League celebrates its centenary.
1/11/1995	London Broncos versus St Helens at The Stoop - first professional Rugby League match on a ground owned by a Rugby Union club.
March 1996	Start of Super League
May 1996	Wigan RLFC win Union's Middlesex 7s, Bath RUFC & Wigan RLFC cross-code matches
August 1996	Start of first full professional Rugby Union season
May 1998	Rugby League Conference starts
29/4/2000	Rugby League Challenge Cup Final at Murrayfield
28/10/2000	Rugby League World Cup England versus Australia played at Twickenham - the first time professional Rugby League has been played there.

A brief guide to parliamentary terminology

How a bill goes through the House of Commons, before it goes to the House of Lords:
(A bill can also be introduced in the House of Lords, where it follows a similar procedure before going to the House of Commons.)

First Reading: Starting point for a Bill, with MP or Minister responsible being called by the Speaker to formally give notice of the Bill's title and the intention to introduce it on a future day.

Second Reading: The first opportunity for a debate and vote on a Bill. Sometimes uncontroversial measures can receive a Second Reading without either a debate or a vote.

Committee Stage: When a Bill passes its Second Reading it is next considered by a Committee which is responsible for the detailed examination of its content clause by clause.

Report Stage: After a Bill has completed its Committee Stage, where it may have been amended, it comes back to the Commons Chamber where there is a further opportunity for changes to be made. All M.P.s have the opportunity to contribute by speaking to amendments at Report Stage.

Third Reading: The final stage for a Commons Bill before it goes to the Lords. There may be a debate and vote on the final amended form of the Bill.

Types of Bills:

Government Bills: Proposed new laws, initiated by the Government, often implementing political commitments set out during a general election.

Private Members Bills: Proposed new laws initiated by MPs who are not Government Ministers, addressing a specific issue with which they may be particularly concerned.

Ballot Bills: Private Members Bills arising from a draw that takes place shortly after the start of each parliamentary session, whereby the winners are given time on Friday mornings to present their bills.

Ten Minute Rule Bill: Procedure whereby an MP can speak for up to ten minutes in prime parliamentary time and argue for their Bill to make further progress. These slots used to be obtained by a typically obscure procedure that at one time entailed MPs spending the night queuing in an upstairs room to be the first to present their parliamentary measure to the Clerk responsible. Now they are allocated through the whips of each party.

Parliamentary procedures and committees:

Pairs: M.P.s from opposing parties who may arrange to miss certain votes so that the required absence of one (e.g. for a speaking or campaigning commitment) is neutralised by an arrangement for the opponent also to be absent.

Whips: The terms is said to owe its origins to the "whippers in" looking after the hounds at fox hunts. In the parliamentary sense, the Whips have a similar function in dealing with the discipline and attendance of each party's MPs but they also are responsible for arranging much of the order and content of parliamentary business.

Standing Committees: The group of M.P.s appointed in numbers proportionate to party representation in the Commons to undertake the Committee Stage of a Bill.

Select Committees: Permanent committees of MPs similarly appointed to undertake the detailed scrutiny of policy areas covered by each Government department.

Early Day Motion: An expression of opinion on an issue, set out in writing on the Order Paper by an individual MP or group of MPs which attracts the signatures of others, evidencing the extent of support. Originally the procedure was a mechanism for pressing for parliamentary time to debate the issue concerned on an early day.

Appendix 1:

Debates in Parliament on Rugby League

The National Lottery Debate

28 April 1993

Clause 24

CONTROL OF DISTRIBUTING BODIES BY THE SECRETARY OF STATE

<u>Amendment made:</u> No. 42 in page 10, leave out lines 26-32 and insert -

(1) A body shall comply with any directions given to it by the Secretary of State as to the matters to be taken into account in determining the persons to whom, the purposes for which and the conditions subject to which the body distributes any money under section 23(1).
[Mr Key.]

Mr Hinchliffe: I beg to move amendment No. 1, in page 10, line 32, at end insert

except that in exercising their functions under section 21(2) above, the sports councils shall in no circumstances distribute money to any organisation which practices discrimination as between players in amateur and professional sport.

I appreciate that it is late and that hon. Members have had a long and hard day. However, the issue with which the amendment deals are serious, and some of us have been waiting a long time for a proper debate on them. People have been waiting since 1895. The amendment is an all-party attempt to address discrimination in sport. Were it to relate to women or people from ethnic minorities, such discrimination would be illegal.

Mr Maxton: That is not correct, because private clubs and sporting organisations can and do discriminate against women in many ways, and are not breaking the law in doing so.

Mr Hinchliffe: I did not expect an intervention before I had put the arguments in support of the amendment. It addresses specifically what is deemed amateurism within the regulations of the Rugby Football Union and concerns the relationship between that and Rugby League players, not just professionals but amateurs. The vast majority of Rugby League is played by amateurs, not professionals. The professional game is a small part of Rugby League and it annoys many of us interested in the game to hear it described as a professional code.

Some hon. Members will recall a recent early-day motion, 1342, on some of the issues with which the amendment deals - in particularly, the case of Steve Pilgrim, a Rugby Union player who until recently played for Wasps in London. He also played as an England B team Rugby Union international. He had the audacity to go for an unpaid amateur trial with Leeds Rugby League football club. As a consequence, he was automatically banned by the Rugby Football Union from playing Rugby Union football for two years.

The interesting point is that, if Mr Pilgrim had gone to the Headingley Rugby League ground in Leeds, but appeared on the other side of the main stand, on the Yorkshire cricket ground, for a professional trial for Yorkshire cricket, he would not have been banned. Had he gone to Elland professional trial for Yorkshire cricket, he would not have been banned. Had he gone to Elland road, and been paid for playing for Leeds United, he would not have been banned. Had he been playing professional tennis, professional golf or even American football, he would not have been banned. Unfortunately, he played the game of Rugby League.

He has not received a penny for playing Rugby League, although he has had trials since then with the Halifax Rugby League club. Neither club has signed him on, and he is now between the devil and the deep blue sea - not signed on by Rugby League but banned from his previous sport. In the view of many decent, thinking people in sport as a whole, including many in the sport of Rugby Union, that is unacceptable in this day and age.

I mentioned 1895 because that was the year when what was then the northern Rugby Union split away from the rest on the issue of broken time payments. They are related to the fact that in the industrial north, and elsewhere, working-class people could not afford to miss time from work to play Rugby Union; therefore, young men were paid to cover the money that they could not earn in their normal course of employment because they were playing rugby. The ultimate result was the development of Rugby League football.

Unfortunately, since 1895, some in the 15-a-side code have attempted, right up to the present day, to kill off the game of Rugby League - both the amateur and the professional games. Many who have been involved in both rugby codes feel that that is unacceptable in this day and age. It is some measure of Rugby League's strength and popularity that, despite all those attacks over nearly a century, the game continues to thrive and prosper, at both the amateur and professional levels. I shall be pleased to attend the nation's main sporting event on Saturday, to watch Widnes win the Rugby League cup, along with the 75,000 other people who will pack Wembley to witness a great sporting occasion.

It is some measure of rugby's league greatness that, despite the obvious prejudice of the establishment, the media, the education system and the armed forces against the 13-a-side code, the professional sport of Rugby League is second only to association football as the most popular spectator team sport in Britain. It would be encouraging if media coverage of Rugby League reflected the fact that it draws crowds second only to those attracted to soccer. In terms of spectators, it is more popular than Rugby Union and cricket. The House has not considered the fact that Rugby League is such a popular sport.

Amendment No. 1 attempts to address the discrimination against those who play Rugby League football as amateurs or professional that is still evident nearly 100 years after Rugby League's break with Rugby Union.

Some years ago, when I played both League and Union, I participated in a game of Rugby Union at a club in Otley, which is an area that the hon. Member for Keighley (Mr Waller) knows well. When I entered the club house, I noticed a painting of the team that had won the Yorkshire rugby cup two years before the 1895 breakaway. A number of the faces had been blanked out. They were players who had, after 1895, moved from northern rugby to play in the new northern union. They have never been forgiven. I want to see the day come, before too long, when the faces of those players are painted back into that picture, and an end to the nonsense of the past 100 years.

I speak with some passion because I, as an amateur League players, was banned from playing Rugby Union. Many of my friends and peers in Wakefield of a similar age still retain the letters that they received from local Rugby Union clubs saying that they were no longer welcome because, after the age of 18, they had played Rugby League. We were considered sporting lepers. I will never forget that experience for as long as I live. Sadly, that attitude still prevails. Tonight, we hope to do something about making a long-overdue change to that period of history.

I pay tribute to those of my hon. Friends who, some years ago, achieved - at least in theory - a free gangway between the code of amateur Rugby League and Rugby Union. I say 'in theory' because I could give example after example to show that, often, that free gangway does not exist in practice. I shall cite just one that came to attention as joint secretary, with the hon. Member for Keighley, of the Parliamentary Rugby League group.

In Reading, an attempt was made to form the Unity Rugby club, to play both Rugby League and Rugby Union under the same banner. That is entirely reasonable. Plenty of clubs play cricket and Rugby, or soccer and Rugby. Why not Rugby League and Rugby Union? Why should they not use the same facilities, pitches and equipment? It would be sensible. However, permission could not be obtained from Twickenham, simply because, they were told, they were playing Rugby League. Had it been cricket, soccer, or any other sport, there would have been no problem. There were many examples of the Rugby Union establishment leaning on the game of Rugby League.

My hon. Friend the Member for Warrington, North (Mr Hoyle) has had to leave the Chamber, but before he did so he drew my attention to correspondence that he had received about a Rugby League tournament that is held at Swansea Uplands [Rugby Union] ground in Wales. Amateurs from both codes are involved in games there each year. Rugby union players received letters threatening them with action if they took part in an amateur tournament, where the trophy was presented by Jonathan Davies, who, it just so happens, has left the Rugby Union code and gone north.

There have been many examples of what can only be described as blatant discrimination in the armed forces against people who want to play the game of Rugby League football. We met Lord Merlyn-Rees, a former Defence Minister, who headed the delegation. The prejudice with which we were confronted at that meeting had to be seen to be believed. We were told that the armed forces could not afford to fund the game of Rugby League. We made the point that the same balls, jerseys, shorts, boots, socks and other items that rugby players wear are used in both codes, but we were told that, because of insufficient resources, Rugby Union, not Rugby League, was played i the armed forces. It is high time that we did something about that prejudice.

Mr Hargreaves: Many of my hon. Friends probably share the hon. Gentleman's concern, and what he has said is enlightening. Those of us who served on the Committee probably missed out by not having this matter drawn to our attention earlier in the debate. However, at this stage of the proceedings on the Bill, is this the right place to raise such an important issue concerning Rugby? Ought it not to be the subject of a debate?

Mr Hinchliffe: I should be only too happy to initiate such a debate. The reason for the amendment is that many of us feel that although the Rugby Union game receives substantial public funding, particularly from the Sports Aid Foundation, the Sports Council and the education system, it practises blatant discrimination against Rugby League players. That is why we feel that the Bill is an appropriate mechanism to get Rugby Union to take account of the strength of feeling in the nation about the way that it treats Rugby League players.

The rules relating to amateurs appear to apply only to people who are concerned with Rugby League, not to Rugby Union, although those people are, to all intents and purposes, professionals. We know for a fact that Rugby Union players are paid and that they receive rewards often far in excess of what is payable in the Rugby League game. In France - which is a party to the International Rugby Board's rules on amateurs, which forbid professionalism in rugby - entire Rugby League teams have transferred to playing Rugby Union because they can get more money from playing Rugby Union. In New Zealand and Australia, payments are commonplace. Can anyone tell me that David Campese is an amateur? Does he go to Italy every winter to play for nothing? Of course he is a professional, and rightly so. He is an excellent rugby player, so why should he not be rewarded for his skills and for the fact that he, like many others, entertains vast numbers of people?

Payments are also commonplace in South Africa. Recently, my own team, Wakefield Trinity, was in the process of signing a Springbok Rugby Union players called Albertus Einslin. He pulled back from signing the deal because he had been offered £200 a match and a job playing "amateur" Rugby Union in South Africa. It is absolute nonsense to suggest that Rugby Union is an amateur code. Many of us are annoyed that the South African Rugby Union has attempted to stamp on the development of Rugby League in the black townships on the basis that its amateur code there will lead to professionalism although, as everyone knows, the South African Rugby Union is semi-professional, if not wholly professional.

In this country, the Pugh report considered the British Rugby Union players who went on the so-called centenary tour of South Africa against the advice of the various home unions. The Pugh report, which has been suppressed, suggested that those players received about £30,000 each. Let us remember that that was an 'amateur' game.

Week In Week Out, a BBC Wales programme, recorded a player - I seem to remember that he was an international player - saying that, to his knowledge, payments were made in Wales in the dressing room, in front of a Welsh Rugby Union official, an official from the Union that banned Jonathan Davies from commenting for the BBC at Cardiff Arms Park because he had gone north to play for Widnes Rugby League club. That is the union that continues to ban Stuart Evans from returning to playing Rugby Union in the valleys because he flirted with St Helens' Rugby League club but unfortunately did not have a very successful career in the 13-a-side code.

We have in the House an hon. Member, who is not here tonight, whose main distinction in life was not arriving here some years ago but playing in my team, Wakefield Trinity. He told me one night that he had received far more money playing Rugby Union than playing for teams such as Wakefield Trinity.

The parliamentary Rugby League group, which comprises about 70 members from this place and another place, has become rather impatient about this matter. We contacted the International Rugby Board to ask it to explain what its rules on amateurism meant in this day and age. Last Wednesday, we met Mr Dudley Wood, the secretary of the Rugby Football Union, and Mr Bob Rogers, the chair of the English Rugby Football Union amateurism committee. On behalf of the parliamentary group, I must say that we were most grateful that they were prepared to meet us. They had a fairly hot reception.

The two gentlemen said that the problems which they conceded were occurring in certain unions - not the English union - were due to interpretation of amateurism, not the principle. They insisted that, although there were problems in Wales, France and here, there and everywhere, in England everything in the garden was fine. They said that there was no evidence of any payments to players in the English Rugby Football Union.

The most memorable part of our meeting was a comment from the right hon. Member for Westmoreland and Lonsdale (Mr Jopling), who told us of his experience of standing as the Conservative candidate in Wakefield against my predecessor's predecessor in the 1959 general election. Because of contacts with the local Conservative party - at that stage, the chair of Wakefield Trinity was a prominent member of the Conservative party - the right hon. Gentleman was allowed to kick off the Wakefield Trinity versus Hunslet league match.

I was present, and there was a crowd of about 15,000. The local Conservative parliamentary candidate was allowed to kick off, which would be a huge boost to anyone campaigning in an election in that area. The right hon. Gentleman kicked off, the incident was reported in the press, and he found that he had professionalised himself and was banned from playing Rugby Union. The right hon. Member for Westmoreland and Lonsdale - he is not an Opposition Member; no hard lefty he, but a former Minister and Government Chief Whip - is still banned by the Rugby Union. Thirty years of anger came out in the right hon. Gentleman last Wednesday in Committee Room 14 - and right so. That nonsense is still with us. and we are sad that such attitudes prevail.

There have been one or two developments since last Wednesday's meeting; things have moved quite rapidly. First - I believe that it happened the day after we met the two gentlemen - in Edinburgh the International Rugby Board came to the decision that Rugby League professionals who have never played union would be allowed to play Rugby Union within two years of making their desire to switch codes known, but union players who have turned to league are still banned from returning to union. That reads like a Monty Python script.

The news was picked up in *The Independent* yesterday, when Alan Watkins wrote about what nonsense it was: "Religious conversion is much in the air these days, with several Anglicans going over to the Church of Rome. If we regard Rugby League players as Anglicans, and Union players as

Catholics, it will be as if Anglicans can become Catholics and Catholics Anglicans. But Catholics who become Anglicans will not be allowed to revert to their original faith. As Winston Churchill once said of his own early shifts of political loyalty between the Conservative and Liberal parties: anyone can rat once, but it takes a man of character to rat twice."

Alan Watkins makes the important point that the lack of equality between the codes means that 'While Jonathan Davies', who, of course, will play for Widnes at Wembley on Saturday, cannot return to Llanelli, or Martin Offiah to Rosslyn Park, there is nothing to prevent Ellery Hanley, say, from signing on for the Harlequins as Peter Winterbottom's successor, playing a couple of seasons at the Stoop, and then returning to Leeds or some other Northern club to see out the autumn of his days.

What absolute nonsense - yet that is the present position.

Another development following the denials of Messrs Wood and Rogers in Committee Room 14 last Wednesday is reported in *The Times* this morning. The main article on the sports page is headed: "RFU find breaches of amateurism rife'"

That means breaches of amateurism in the same English Rugby Football Union that we were told last Wednesday was totally amateur. We were told that amateurism was its members sacrosanct principle, and the most important thing in their game. Yet according to the article in *The Times*, a report circulating in English Rugby Football Union clubs has forced the RFU to confront a situation it denied existed to any serious extent. It reveals numerous illustrations of disregard for the amateur principles which officials at Twickenham insisted had more to do with imagination than reality.

A working party set up by the RFU to investigate growing allegations of financial benefits for amateur players has found the claims to be substantially true. Its report ... says many examples of such payments have been received.

Is that not interesting? Yet at a meeting attended by many hon. Members who are in the Chamber now we were given clear assurances that everything in the garden was lovely in the English Rugby Football Union.

To put it mildly, there appears to be some inconsistency between the official position and reality. The official position is clearly in conflict with what we know and what the union, too, knows is happening. The worry is that the rules of amateurism as administered by the RFU apply only to those who have contact with the game of Rugby League. It seems that anything is allowed to go on in Rugby Union.

I emphasise again the fact that many of us have no objection to Rugby Union players receiving payments. We have no with to prevent funding from going to Rugby Union clubs. I have two - Sandal and Wakefield - in my constituency. I played discreetly for both teams many years ago as a Rugby League players. I have friends who are involved in both clubs. They are two excellent Rugby Union clubs which are a credit to the game of rugby as a whole. I have no wish to see them deprived of funds that may accrue from the national lottery. However, the amendment would affect them only if the attitudes to Rugby League continued. Through the amendment, we are saying, 'For goodness sake, address the issues about which all of use here are concerned and back off. Let us have some common sense after 100 years.'

I am grateful to the House for tolerating a fairly lengthy contribution at this late hour. It is an important matter. The London-based media largely disregard Rugby League. Many of us in the north are used to that. We can manage without them. From the point of view of the media, it is sad that they do not see the great sporting spectacle - some say the greatest sporting spectacle and I concur with that view - of Rugby League football. What is more worrying is that the media fail to cover the civil liberties questions raised by the issues I have described. They do not cover the way in which players are refused their basic civil rights by those who run Rugby Union.

I pay tribute to the Rugby League press for the way in which it has pushed the matter. I pay tribute to the *Rugby Leaguer* newspaper, to *Open Rugby* magazine, which has had a continuing campaign for freedom in rugby, and to the *League Express* newspaper for its campaign on the issue.

I shall read from the editorial in this week's *League Express* because its comments put more succinctly than I can the feelings that many people have about the matter. The editorial says: "If the Union actions did not impinge on League, they could go to hell in their own hand-cart, at their own pace, without any comment from us, but the Union's hypocrisy, dishonesty and blackmail - to give it an honest name - prevent many people would like to try our game from doing so. The message goes out to schoolboys and adults alike, that playing Rugby League can seriously damage your health and career prospects." As we have endlessly pointed out, professional soccer players, golfers or cricketers, don't need special dispensations from Twickenham to play union. And league players, union players or players of any damn sport at all, should not need permission from Dudley Wood and his cohorts to take some exercise on a football field. They have no moral, legal or any other right to pronounce on the sport of Rugby League, or prevent free men and women playing whatever sport they like. No amount of window-dressing ... will alter the fact that their game is continuing to use unjust and illegal discrimination against a sport they perceive as a competitor to their own.

There is great anger on the issue. I hope that the Government will grasp the nettle and end this nonsense once and for all.

Mr Gary Waller: I strongly support and warmly commend the words of the hon. Member for Wakefield (Mr Hinchliffe). Some people - this point was made by my hon. Friend the Member for Birmingham, Hall Green (Mr Hargreaves) - may consider that the issue does not relate easily to the Bill. As the hon. Member for Wakefield explained, the Rugby Union is in receipt of substantial public funds through the Sports Council, so public policy issues arise which the Government cannot thrust to one side.

As an adherent of both Rugby League and Rugby Union, like many other hon. Members, I do not seek to adjudicate between the qualities of the two codes. I congratulate Ilkley Rugby Union football club in my constituency on its achievement in gaining promotion this season. I also pay a warm public tribute to Keighley Rugby League club, which had a magnificent season, winning the third division of the league and, equally importantly, attracting massive gates in the process. In the town and in the club there is enthusiasm to go on to greater things. Wigan and St Helens should watch out.

It is regrettable that the policy of disallowing a free gangway maintained by the International Rugby Board, which, despite its title, has no responsibility at all for the league game, should still mar the reputation of rugby after so many years. The Rugby Football Union claims that it wants to protect its amateur status. That makes no sense whatever because everyone with eyes to see and ears to hear knows that, in the top echelons, amateurism is an absolute sham. Many international Rugby Union players quite clearly have the benefit of a car and other benefits - including, perhaps a job - simply because of who they are and because they are exceptionally good at the game they play.

As the hon. Member for Wakefield said, it cannot be right that a senior player like Steve Pilgrim should be banned from playing Rugby Union, possibly for life - certainly for a year from the time when he applies for reinstatement - just because he had a trial with a professional league club. That is a case about which Sir Peter Yarranton, chairman of the Sports Council and a past RFU president, has expressed concern.

The hon. Member for Wakefield referred to the fact that my right hon. Friend the Member for Westmoreland and Lonsdale (Mr Jopling) was banned from playing Rugby Union many years ago because, as a parliamentary candidate, he was invited to kick off a Rugby League match. I am sure that goes a long way towards explaining why my right hon. Friend has such strong feelings about the issue.

Some forms of the discrimination practised by the administrators of Rugby Union may eventually be tested in the courts, where a finding that they are illegal may bring the whole house of cards crashing down. That may apply in relation to differential treatment of former union players who have played Rugby League. The payment of money and inducements to move from one union club to another, revealed in the newly circulated RFU report, to which the hon. Member for Wakefield also referred, also casts doubt on the possibility that the present situation can be maintained indefinitely. Not for nothing did an article in today's issue of *The Times* refer to a "malaise among administrators". One day soon, the little boy who pointed out the king was not wearing any clothes will prove impossible to shut up.

Tennis, cricket and athletics eventually came to terms with professionalism and in no way was the amateur sport harmed - quite the reverse. In due course, Rugby Union will have to do the same. In the meantime, however, the Government should take a leading role in making it clear that discrimination - even if well-intentioned but misguided - is not acceptable in any sport.

Mr John Maxton: As an ex-Rugby Union player, I find little with which to disagree in the remarks of my hon. Friend the Member for Wakefield (Mr Hinchliffe). Unlike him, however, I am not happy about the way in which Rugby Union is moving towards becoming a professional sport. As its rules - or, rather, its laws - stand at present, it is far too dangerous a game to be played for large sums of money. Unlike Rugby League, Rugby Union has not adapted its rules to ensure that people are not in a position to injure other players and, if people were playing for large sums, it could be an extremely dangerous game. People could be seriously injured; there might even be deaths. I deplore that state of affairs. I repeat, however, that I find little with which to disagree in the tenor of my hon. Friend's remarks. If I have an objection, it is to the wording of the amendment. The hon. Member for Keighley (Mr Waller said that athletics has sorted out the problems of professionalism. That is not true. The so-called professional Powderhall sprints are held in Scotland every new year. The prize money is about £150 to £200. But someone who wins that race and accepts the £200 is barred for life from taking part in amateur athletics.

If the hon. Member for Falmouth and Camborne (Mr Coe) had run in any of those races, he would have been banned from taking part in any other race, yet we all know that, as a result of his prowess as a miler and a half-miler, he made enormous sums of money out of athletics. Not all sports have done away with that kind of discrimination, and athletics is one of them. As it is worded, the amendment would hit athletics as well as Rugby Union. That may be right.

The discrimination to which I have referred is not the only discrimination that occurs in sport. A very well-known gold club in my constituency is celebrating its centenary this year. It applied to Glasgow district council to ask whether it would hold a civic reception to celebrate its centenary. quite rightly and very honourably the district council said that it was not prepared to give a civic reception to the Pollok golf club because the club would not allow women to become members.

That gold club actively discriminates, openly and blatantly, against women. However, it also discriminates much more subtly, without any openness, against Jews. There is racial discrimination in individual golf clubs and also in other sports. The House and the sports council will have to address that problem.

Bowls is another very popular sport in my constituency. However, in many bowling clubs, a woman can become a member only if she is the wife of a male member. She cannot join as a woman in her own right. there are other discriminations of which I hope my hon. Friend the Member for Wakefield is aware and they, too, should be addressed.

I fully support what my hon. Friend the Member for Wakefield said. However, I am concerned that the amendment would cover a much wider range of sports than simply Rugby Union and Rugby League. I hope that Rugby Union will finally come to its senses and find a better way of dealing with players who play the two codes.

Mr McCartney: As chair of the All-Party Rugby League group, I support the amendment. I formed the group in February 1988. I had never played Rugby League, although I had played in many positions in Rugby Union. As I grew older and slower, the positions seemed to change with regularity.

We formed the group to promote Rugby League in an amateur and professional way, to try to build bridges between Rugby Union and Rugby League and to use our activities in the House to develop links between the codes in the hope that they would assist to break down the prejudices that have existed for 98 years and continue to exist.

It took five years - until last Wednesday evening - for the English Rugby Football Union to agree to the first meeting. That meeting came about because of the publicity generated in the House over the discrimination against Steven Pilgrim. He has not been banned for one or two years. As Dudley Wood pointed out the meeting that I chaired last week in Committee Room 14, Steven Pilgrim has been banned for life from playing Rugby Union.

That ban does not just apply to playing: it applies also to coaching - whether of young children or adults. Steven Pilgrim's ability and right to play the game he loves has been taken from him by a group of elderly and out-of-touch gentlemen.

We did not simply call the meeting because of Steven Pilgrim. As a parliamentary group, we had amassed a growing dossier of evidence of the discrimination at an amateur level with respect to the attitudes towards playing Rugby League. I am pleased that the Minister has been able to listen to this debate, because the Government, in relation to Ministers at the Ministry of Defence, have a case to answer. I do not make the point in a partisan way because Ministers at the MOD under the last Labour government had the same case to answer.

Current Ministry of Defence policy is to try to ensure a complete blackout in the playing of amateur Rugby League in the forces. The Ministry does that in two ways. First, Rugby League is not allowed assistance from MOD sporting funds for development or insurance purposes, or to cover expenses in connection with playing the game. Secondly, when any attempt is made to organise Rugby League - whether it is in the RAF, the Army or the Navy - senior officers take a number of steps to ensure either that the games do not take place, or that they can be quickly stamped out through the issuing of orders at specific stations.

The Ministry of Defence has been provided with the evidence on numerous occasions. We met the Minister of State and came to what we believed was an agreement on the development of the sport and its right to be treated in the same way as Rugby Union. Last week, in a meeting in Committee Room 14, we asked the Rugby Football Union to join us in agreeing a common approach to the right of armed forces personnel to play Rugby League. Mr Wood refused to participate and indicated clearly that the union, along with its colleagues in the MOD, would continue to oppose the introduction of the playing of Rugby League in the armed forces.

Last year, the Government gave the Royal Navy alone some £35,000 in development funds for the full-time employment of Rugby Union coaches in the MOD. Resources has also been provided for the RAF and the Army. We are not opposed to that; we are saying that people who join the armed forces should be allowed to engage in the sport of their choice and should be given the time and opportunity to do so rather than being discriminated against.

We are concerned not only about the discrimination, but about the web of the deceit involved in sham amateurism. At the meeting, Mr Wood and his colleague Bob Rogers were questioned in detail about the role of their organisation in relation to payments, or substitute payments, for playing Rugby Union. Mr Wood made it absolutely clear that there was no evidence whatever of any payments, direct or indirect, for Rugby Union played in England under the direction of the Rugby Football Union.

We now know that that was a direct untruth. Not only did Mr Wood mislead Committee members; when questioned, he deliberate did not inform us that Mr Rogers - who was also present - had chaired the investigation into the payments made to Rugby Union players. At the time when he told us that there was no proof whatever, the report was already on his desk awaiting his consideration. That report - commissioned by Mr Wood and prepared by Mr Rogers - is dealt with in great detail in *The Times* today.

Mr Deputy Speaker: Order. I am listening attentively to the hon. Gentleman; he has not once mentioned the national lottery, to which the amendment is supposed to relate. I do not think that it is in order to deal in depth the pros and cons of evidence given to a parliamentary Committee. The hon. Member for Wakefield (Mr Hinchliffe), who moved the amendment, related his speech firmly to the lottery; even that was stretching it, but I was prepared to be lenient in his case. I do not think that a repetition is necessary.

Mr McCartney: I made it clear at the outset, Mr Deputy Speaker, that I was speaking in support of amendment No. 1. The wording is quite clear -

Mr Deputy Speaker: Order. The wording of the amendment is, indeed, quite clear. The hon. Gentleman began by saying that he was speaking to it; that was the last we have heard of it so far.

Mr McCartney: I am not challenging your ruling, Mr Deputy Speaker, but I feel that, in saying that this was an anti-discrimination amendment, I made it clear that I was trying to explain the reasons why an all-party group tabled the amendment and to give evidence. There is no point in tabling an amendment without being prepared to give detailed reasons for doing so. Some Conservative Members may, for whatever reason, find it uncomfortable to hear the evidence. But the evidence must be heard in support of the amendment.

The evidence that I have is not a repeat of that put forward by my hon. Friend the Member for Wakefield (Mr Hinchliffe) or the hon. Member for Keighley (Mr Waller). It is the evidence of the Rugby Football Union. The evidence should be placed on the record in the debate because the RFU was given an opportunity by an all-party group in the House to put its views on the matter. In the confines of the House, it made it clear and set out in crystal clear terms that there was no evidence of sham amateurism. It said that there was no need, therefore, for an amendment such as amendment No. 1. It is for that reason that I wish to quote the evidence in the report that Mr Wood has received, produced by his colleague Mr Rogers, whom we interviewed on 21 April.

The evidence is contained in an article today in *The Times*, which is not known as a newspaper that supports the game of Rugby League. The report was entitled 'Inducements to move, incentives to stay and other illegal payments'. It produced a 'brief but not exhaustive' list of the evidence that it uncovered The newspaper article said that payments to amateur players in England had arisen through the following: "excessive expenses, cars, ... fictitious employment, cash-playing bonuses, clothing, fictitious expenses, housing-mortgage support, writing rugby articles, appearance money, overseas trips, luxury items, free or subsidised accommodation, car passenger expenses, fictitious appearances, sponsorship holidays, and family support."

If that list does not suggest a professional sport, I do not know what is. The list shows hypocrisy. I know of few Rugby League players even at the highest level of the game who are provided with such inducements to play their sport.

It is also interesting to note that when members of the Committee raise the issue with the Chancellor of the Exchequer he said that he could not investigate it or put it to the Inland Revenue because Rugby Union was an amateur sport and, therefore, payments did not exist. Perhaps the report of the debate should be passed on to the Treasury so that it can investigate what is known to go on but is not reported for tax purposes by the Rugby Football Union.

On bank holiday Monday, at Wigan's Central Park, a race will take place between Martin Offiah, a former Rugby Union player and now a Great Britain international winger who plays for Wigan and hopefully will be man of the match at Wembley on Saturday, Andrew Harriman, the man of the tournament at the seven-a-side world championships at Murrayfield two or three weeks ago, and Rory Underwood, the current English international wing forward.

They will race to find out who is the fastest rugby player in Britain. Under the rules described by Mr Wood, the players will not be playing rugby and, therefore, will not be banned. They will be in a Rugby League ground running against a Rugby League player, but because they will not be playing Rugby League, it will be OK. They will turn a blind eye to it. Yet Mr Steve Pilgrim, who played a trial match as an amateur on a Rugby League ground has been banned for life from playing the sport in which he wishes to participate. It is a human rights issue and one which for far too long has been swept under the carpet in the House.

Through the Bill we want to put on notice the Rugby Football Union, the Welsh Rugby Union, the Irish Rugby Football Union and the Scottish Rugby Union that unless they end discrimination no resources will be used from either the lottery or public funds to benefit those who, through discrimination, prevent others from playing the game of their choice.

Mr Davidson: I wish to speak briefly to this amendment. [Hon. Members: 'Hear, hear!'] I thank hon. Members for their enthusiastic response.

I do not represent a constituency in which Rugby League is played, but I was brought up in an area in which many Rugby Union players went on to play Rugby League. It always struck me as extremely unfair that those layers, when they reached the end of their league playing days, were not allowed to return to Rugby Union to put something back in the game as coaches or in any other capacity.

It is absurd to talk about the national lottery as a means of raising money for sport, when a certain sport refuses to allow former players to put something back, voluntarily, into their sport. Such behaviour should be subject to public policy. We should also question whether public money should be given to organisations that discriminate so blatantly against one group of citizens simply because they chose to play one sport rather than another.

I know that the Bill gives Ministers a number of reserve powers. They should tell us their intentions regarding those powers. My hon. Friend the Member for Glasgow, Cathcart (Mr Maxton) has expressed his reservations about some sports clubs that discriminate on the grounds of race and other hon. Members have alleged that clubs discriminate on the grounds of sex. That matter, too, should be a matter of public policy. The Minister should make it clear that he wishes to have a level playing field so that all can benefit from the public moneys distributed through the lottery.

Hon. Members have done the country a service by bringing certain issues about Rugby League into the open. I hope that the Minister will give a clear statement to the effect that discrimination will not be tolerated. I hope that we can look forward to swift action and pressure being exerted on the English Rugby Union in particular, as well as on the other Rugby Unions and other sports that practise similar discrimination.

Mr Pendry: I commend what my hon. Friends have done and I am pleased that, after some battle, their amendment was eventually selected for debate.

The late hour may be inconvenient to some, but that is tough. My hon. Friends have raised an important issue and it falls within the context of the Bill, because the Sports Council should not be allowed to distribute lottery money to a body that actively discriminates. The Minister for Sport cannot stand aside after hearing about that discrimination. He should agree with his hon. Friend the Member for Birmingham, Hall Green (Mr Hargreaves), who thought that a full debate on the issue should be held in Government time. The Minister should institute that debate.

The Minister is the custodian of sport and he should call for an inquiry into the matter. The House is indebted to my hon. Friend the Member for Wakefield (Mr Hinchliffe and my other hon. Friends for raising the issue. I hope that the Minister's response will be constructive, and I am as anxious as my hon. Friends to hear what he has to say.

Mr Key: It will come as no surprise to hon. Members to learn that I see myself as the custodian of the Bill. I shall be unable to recommend to the House that the amendment should be accepted for reasons I shall cite. I am grateful to the hon. Member for Wakefield (Mr Hinchliffe), however, for drawing attention to such an extremely important issue.

We discussed the matter briefly in Committee, and I am aware of its importance to our clubs and those beyond our shores. My hon. Friend the Member for Keighley (Mr Waller) and the hon. Members for Glasgow, Cathcart (Mr Maxton), for Makerfield (Mr McCartney) and for Glasgow, Govan (Mr Davidson) have also contributed to a debate in prime Government time - some might find that hard to believe, given the lateness of the hour - during the important Report stage of an extremely important Bill. The issue has been put firmly on the agenda, and I recognise its importance. I undertake to the hon. Member for Wakefield that I shall see whether I can do anything appropriate about it, although it would not be appropriate to accept the amendment.

I believe that this is best left to the determination of the distributing bodies subject, as regards this amendment, to directions laid down in the Bill by my right hon. and learned Friend the Secretary of State. It would be quite inappropriate to make it an inflexible exclusion on the face of the Bill.

The policy pursued by a governing body in respect of excluding participation by professional players in its competitions is a matter for it to determine and not a matter on which the Government should seek to dictate through access to lottery funds. Applications for lottery funds should surely be judged on their individual merits.

The sports councils are well aware of the policies of the governing bodies of sport in the United Kingdom. To rule out whole classes of body in statute on the ground that some hon. Members were unhappy with one of the policies of the governing body, whatever the merits either way, would prevent an individual club from ever being able to apply for lottery funds for worthwhile projects and projects which would extend the general sport provision in their communities, for example, for children at local schools. Surely these potential beneficiaries should not be punished because of their local rugby institution which belongs to the Union and not to the League.

The Government want to keep the arm's-length principle intact. It is tempting to be drawn into exploring suggestions that I can intervene in the governing bodies of sport to make them change their rules and laws, but I do not find that attractive. It is against the spirit of successive Governments of a political colours over many years. What matters is that there is a proper public debate of the issue, and the governing bodies of the sport perhaps need to have their heads knocked together.

Mr Hinchliffe: I thank the Minister for his response, and I thank my colleagues, particularly my hon. Friend the Member for Glasgow, Cathcart (Mr Maxton), for their contributions. I did not expect the defence to come from this side of the Chamber and was interested to find that it did. Nevertheless, I understand the points that he made, although I disagree with him. I also thank my hon. Friend the Member for Glasgow, Govan (Mr Davidson) for raising the matter in Committee. We take the points that he has made about the situation, especially in Scotland.

I appreciate the Minister's response. I believe that he has taken close note of the comments made by those who have spoken tonight and that, privately, he shares many of the misgivings of hon. Members about the present situation.

I made it quite clear when I moved amendment No. 1 that there was no desire whatever to block funding to the Rugby Football Union, but the discrimination that has gone on now for nearly 100 years is unacceptable. I make it clear that there are hon. Members on both sides who are not prepared to tolerate this practice any longer.

I will in a moment beg leave to withdraw the amendment, having secured this important debate, but I make it clear that this matter may well be raised in another place by those who feel equally strongly about it. There are also moves in the European Parliament, where there is a well organised and successful Rugby League group, to raise it at a European level. But I fear that what will happen to bring this matter to a head will be action taken by particular players through the course, and that will be to me a matter of great regret. I hope that we can reach a common-sense resolution of the issue after this conflict of nearly 100 years.

Having made these points, and having expressed my gratitude to those who have stayed to take part in the debate, I beg to ask leave to withdraw the amendment.

Amendment, by leave, withdrawn.

Debate on the future of Rugby League
26 April 1995 (A selection of speeches)

Mr. Deputy Speaker (Mr. Geoffrey Lofthouse): The next debate is on the future of Rugby League. Before I call the hon. Member for Wakefield (Mr. Hinchliffe), I remind hon. Members that court proceedings are to take place on Friday which concern the subject matter of the debate to some extent. I trust that hon. Members who wish to speak will be careful not to trespass on the specific matters of the court hearing and, in particular, on whether Keighley should or should not be a member of any proposed Super League, but will concentrate on the general issues. This is a short debate and I hope that I shall not have to remind hon. Members of the sub judice rule. At present, nine hon. Members have indicated that they wish to speak in this hour and a half debate. The Chair will be more than pleased if they are all successful.

Mr. David Hinchliffe: I express my appreciation for the fact that this morning we have the opportunity for a brief debate on some serious developments in the game of Rugby League football, specifically professional Rugby League football. There are two separate organisations; the amateur game, run by the British Amateur Rugby League Association-- BARLA--is largely unaffected by the issues that we are talking about this morning.
I declare at the outset an interest in this debate. As is declared in the Register of Members' Interests, I have 500 shares in Wakefield Trinity Rugby League Football Club. I am not sure what they are worth at present.

The issues are simple and straightforward. Why should a battle between two Australian media magnates result in my constituents losing something very important which we have had for 122 years--Wakefield Trinity Rugby League Football Club? Why should a power struggle on the other side of the world mean that I should lose the team that I have supported through thick and thin since I was a small child?

It is very appropriate that you, Mr. Deputy Speaker, are in the Chair this morning. You have risen from humble origins in my part of the world to be a highly respected Member of the House. You have achieved a great deal politically but, most importantly to the people who matter, you once played for Featherstone Rovers. I have here your autobiography, *A Very Miner MP*. The front shows a Castleford miner and a Featherstone miner together. There is a gap; perhaps a Wakefield Trinity miner should be included.

I refer to the book because it is clear from it that you, Mr. Deputy Speaker, more than anyone understand the community in which Rugby League is played. You more than anyone understand how the events of the past two and a half weeks have shaken some of us to our roots because your roots, like mine, have been intertwined with Rugby League football from the word go.

On Sunday, I attended what may well be the last match that my team, Wakefield Trinity, will ever play. Grown men wept. That grief has turned to anger at the way in which those ruling the game of Rugby League in this country--Mr. Lindsay, the chief executive, Mr. Walker, the chairman, the club chairmen and others--seem to have allowed us to be used.

As you well know, Mr. Deputy Speaker, the root of the problem is that Rugby League has become a pawn in a power struggle between Kerry Packer and Rupert Murdoch over first, television coverage of Rugby League in Australia and secondly, the expansion of satellite television. When Packer won the right to show Australian Rugby League on his Channel 9 station, Murdoch's News Corporation retaliated by planning a super league in direct opposition. Murdoch bought up many of Australia's and New Zealand's top Rugby League players. When that strategy failed, he turned to Europe and to Rugby League in this country.

After the £77 million deal between the Rugby Football League in Britain and Murdoch a couple of weeks ago, Packer's representatives came to Britain trying to lure our best players away. The prospect of Murdoch's money being stuffed into players' pockets to outbid Packer is clear; that is the reality of Rugby League's present situation. Martin Offiah may become much richer than he is already, but the game of Rugby League will be poorer as a direct result.

What could be achieved if the money being offered to some of the players was used instead to develop the game? As my hon. Friend the Member for Makerfield (Mr. McCartney) said to me this morning, it could be used for balls, shirts, boots and the other equipment that the kids in the community who want to play the game need. I hope that the likes of Ellery Hanley, who come from a social background that is pretty deprived, do not forget where they come from and what the money that they may receive could do for kids who have origins like theirs.

The implications are clear for many of us who are deeply concerned with the game of Rugby League. Mergers have been agreed by club chairs of certain teams which will combine to enter, supposedly, the Super League. I am aware that we cannot refer to certain issues on this point, but I shall refer to one or two matters that are especially relevant to the Wakefield area. There have been proposals for the destruction of long-established teams. There are practical questions of particular concern, such as the implication for jobs in an area that does not have many jobs.

There are more than 2,000 professional Rugby League players in this country whose family incomes are substantially dependent on what they can earn in the game of Rugby League. Many of them will no longer have a job as a direct result of the changes. People such as the coaching staff, the groundsmen and the people who, at my local club of Wakefield Trinity, work behind the bar have asked me what will happen to them if the club folds.

It is proposed that Wakefield Trinity, Featherstone Rovers and Castleford should merge and be called Calder. I am ashamed to say that Trinity's shareholders voted 2:1 in favour of a merger; I argued against the proposal. Perhaps the fact that the club had lost 86-0 to Castleford two days before had an impact on their judgment that day. It is interesting to note that when the local paper, the *Wakefield Express* , conducted a telephone poll, the result was 9:1 against any merger and to keep Wakefield Trinity as a separate entity.

Mr. Kevin McNamara: I come from origins as humble as yours, Mr. Deputy Speaker, so I have only two £1 shares in Hull Kingston Rovers compared with the 500 shares that my hon. Friend the Member for Wakefield (Mr. Hinchliffe) has in Wakefield Trinity. When the question of the merger of the three clubs arose, was there any suggestion of a pecking order--of one club being more dominant than the others--or did the Rugby League urge the clubs to go in with equal status and to merge their interests equally?

Mr. Hinchliffe: I cannot answer that question in detail. I have no information that any pecking order was ever suggested. My hon. Friend understands the passions in Hull which has a great history of Rugby League, with Hull Kingston Rovers and the Boulevard. I suspect that he has shared in the debates, the arguments and the anger, as we have in Wakefield.

As you know, Mr. Deputy Speaker, a book has already been published, emerging from Wakefield, about the anger and the grief of people who are affected by the proposed mergers. The book talks of "the merger from hell" because that is the view of people in my area about the proposals. I congratulate the Yorkshire Arts Circus on its book, *Merging on the Ridiculous* and on its work to get across to people outside our area and in the game at high level just how passionately local people feel about what is going on and about the way in which they have been treated.

Mr. Spencer Batiste: As the hon. Gentleman has rightly said, the whole problem has arisen because of the battle between two Australian media magnates, Rupert Murdoch and Kerry Packer, over their interests in Australia. Does he agree that the right way to deal with the problem here is by a reference to the Monopolies and Mergers Commission?

Mr. Hinchliffe: The hon. Gentleman may be aware that my right hon. Friend the Member for Copeland (Dr. Cunningham) has already written to the Office of Fair Trading about the matter. Perhaps the Minister may reflect on that when he responds to the debate.

May I for a moment crave your indulgence, Mr. Deputy Speaker, and quote from the book that I mentioned a few moments ago to show the House the strength of feeling in my area about this matter, especially about the way in which people have been treated over proposed mergers? One anonymous supporter sets out passionate feelings about such treatment. The book quotes him: "A couple of dozen suits making a decision on behalf of God knows how many followers of the game is a disgrace. It's a bit like coming home one day and finding that your walls have been knocked through, and from now on you and your neighbour are all sharing one house. What do you say? `Thanks very much. Another time, perhaps you'd like to ask me first.'" That sums up the feelings of so many.

If I may briefly stray into Featherstone, if my hon. Friend the Member for Hemsworth (Mr. Enright) will allow me, I would like to quote a comment about Calder: "What is Calder to the people of Featherstone, but a river somewhere to the side of Normanton, as remote as the Ganges or the Volga... Why not call it Thatcher? She did more for the region than anyone else and you could really get some buzz on the opposition terraces when our team came out."

The central point of that comment is that 20,000 mining-related jobs have gone since 1979 in the Wakefield area; the area of Wakefield Trinity, Featherstone Rovers and Castleford. People have lost their identity, their self-respect, their standard of living and their way of life. For many, the one thing left which gives them pride is the local Rugby League team. The same philosophy of greed is about to take away that as well.

People in my area are fighting back. For the first time in history, in the pubs of Wakefield last night, people drank a toast to the people of Featherstone, because your members, Mr. Deputy Speaker, in Featherstone, voted by a large margin against the merger. I pay tribute to my many friends and colleagues in Featherstone for the way in which they have campaigned--rightly-- against what has been handed down to them on a plate without any kind of consultation.

Mr. Kevin Hughes: I am grateful to my hon. Friend for giving way while he is on the subject of mergers, relating to what is happening around Yorkshire in particular and describing the anger in the communities. He knows that in my community of Doncaster, it has been suggested that the Dons should merge with the Sheffield Eagles. The same anger prevails among the Dons' supporters about that proposed merger and 3,000 of them have signed a petition against it. A meeting in Doncaster last week with Gary Hetherington from Sheffield Eagles was attended by 400 supporters and only 16 voted in favour. The feeling is the same up and down Yorkshire on this issue. Local communities feel that they are about to lose their local rugby clubs and they will not have that. They will not sit down and take that and they are fighting against it.

Mr. Deputy Speaker: Order. I appreciate that the hon. Member wants to make a point, but interventions are supposed to be brief and not mini-speeches.

Mr. Hinchliffe: I pay tribute to my hon. Friend for working hard to try to sustain Doncaster. I know that behind the scenes he has done an immense amount and he is as aggrieved as I am at the way in which the affair has developed. I think that Gary Hetherington is genuinely doing what he believes to be in the interests of Rugby League in south Yorkshire, although I disagree with his strategy. I shall move on to some of the wider implications of the recent deal and developments of which the House should be aware. First, I find it particularly galling, having worked hard along with many hon. Friends, given that Rugby Union has for more than 99 years disgracefully discriminated against Rugby League, to find out, on the very day that I reintroduced the Sports (Discrimination) Bill, that my sport of Rugby League will in future, through the Murdoch deal, be discriminating against people who are not involved with Murdoch. It is not on for people to say that the future Great Britain Rugby League team will be exclusive to

161

Murdoch. I give a commitment here and now--the Minister is aware of the issues and that my Bill will, I hope get its Second Reading on Friday--that if the Bill goes into Committee, I shall certainly try to amend it to ensure that such discrimination is made illegal. Frankly, we cannot be hypocritical and say that union is wrong in doing what it is doing yet do the same in our own game.

Dr. Norman A. Godman : May I point out to my hon. Friend that many Australian Rugby League fans have very deep reservations about these developments? A few days ago I spoke to two such fans on the telephone and they expressed their concern. Incidentally, before they migrated from Scotland they were Glasgow Celtic supporters so perhaps, now that they are in Australia, they have come to their senses.

Mr. Hinchliffe: Time spent in the south of England has taught me that Rugby League is indeed a civilising influence and I concur with my hon. Friend's comments. Let us consider--this issue is being discussed in Australia--the wider implications, for example, for news management because of the way in which Mr. Murdoch has moved into Rugby League. Indeed, he is moving into other areas too. [Hon. Members:-- "What about Channel 5?"] Indeed, as my hon. Friends say, I was interested to note that Mr. Michael Grade, the chief executive of Channel 4, only yesterday demanded parliamentary action to check Murdoch's tentacles. Frankly, it is not his tentacles that we are after in my part of the world. I spoke last week to a Rugby League correspondent whom I have known and respected for a long time. He told me-- and I believed him--that certain writers and broadcasters are no longer free to report the facts about the super league. I shall be interested to see tomorrow's reporting of this debate by certain television stations and newspapers.

There is another side to the coin which is worth flagging up. It is fairly common knowledge to a number of hon. Members that at least one non-Murdoch tabloid is planning a highly personal attack on a key figure in British Rugby League. I shall say no more about that. I am sad to say that in Rugby League we are involved in a dirty business. I pay a sincere tribute to my hon. Friend the Member for Makerfield for the way in which he has from the word go set out a principled position on behalf of the parliamentary Rugby League group. My hon. Friend's line of opposition to the deal because of its wider implications was endorsed at a meeting of about 40 members-- including hon. Members of another place--of the group last week. My hon. Friend, in particular, has pinpointed a number of implications.

My hon. Friend and I had a three-hour meeting on Monday with the chief executive and the chairman of the rugby football league, Mr. Maurice Lindsay and Mr. Rodney Walker. If my hon. Friend catches your eye, Mr. Deputy Speaker, he will no doubt talk about that meeting and cite some detail of the comments that we made and, indeed, their responses. In response to my belief that they were widely seen to have sold the game's soul, they said that they had had no alternative. Their response was about the current financial difficulties facing the game.

I concede that such difficulties have to be addressed at club and board level. There are difficulties arising from the contracting system, which of course came from Australia in the first place, and difficulties with the safety at sports grounds legislation. Soccer's problems have cost Rugby League clubs such as mine £13 million since that legislation was introduced. With respect to the Minister's noble efforts, we are still waiting for some real help on that front and no doubt he will comment on that later.

Mr. Gerry Sutcliffe : Many local authorities have supported the development of Rugby League clubs' grounds because of the esteem in which those clubs are held in the communities. Local authorities are hard pressed and they have spent money that they do not have.

Mr. Hinchliffe: My hon. Friend is right. I pay tribute to Wakefield district council for the effort that it has made to support the three Rugby League clubs. Wakefield Trinity is certainly criticising the council at present, but I said at the shareholders' meeting last week that there is a lot to thank the local authority for in terms of the support that it has given to Rugby League and Wakefield Trinity in the past. I hope that the Minister will also mention the impact of the national lottery, which has wiped out the fund-raising efforts at local club level for teams such as Wakefield Trinity. We have lost thousands of pounds as a direct result of the lottery, and the compensation that is supposed to arise from the lottery funds has not yet filtered down to the game of Rugby League.

Following our discussions with Mr. Lindsay and Mr. Walker many questions remain unanswered, and I hope that we shall have further meetings with them and with the Minister. The central question that fans, supporters and people throughout the game ask me is how on earth a deal of such magnitude could be concluded without consultation with the various interested parties that surely have a role to play in the game. The players, in particular, are affected, as is the amateur game and as are a range of other organisations concerned with development.

The parliamentary group has worked hard in this place to press the interests of the game of Rugby League, but we have been treated with contempt. For nearly a fortnight, no attempt was made to advise us about what was happening. The most important development in the game for 100 years was taking place, yet there was no fax, no telephone call, no letter. I feel rather aggrieved by the way in which we have been treated, and it is worth putting that on the record. Much more important are the members of clubs, the people who pay for their season tickets and go through the turnstiles. Those are the people who fund the game where it matters-- through the gates of the Rugby League clubs. They feel that they have been treated with complete and utter contempt by the game's rulers, and in many areas they are angry.

I want to give my hon. Friends and Conservative Members the opportunity to make contributions, so I shall finish soon. But before I do I shall raise one or two specific questions that the Minister may be prepared to reflect on and perhaps to answer. My first question is: can the Government sit back and allow British sport to be taken apart in the power struggle that we are witnessing within the game of Rugby League?

I know that the Minister's background is in Rugby Union, although I think that he has realised that there is a better form of rugby now that he has been to one or two Rugby League matches. I am sure that he has worked it out for himself, but I must emphasise the fact that what is happening to Rugby League now will be like a vicarage tea party compared with what will happen to Rugby Union. I do not think that many people involved with Rugby Union who know what is happening to Rugby League are laughing about it. Despite the historic rivalries, when those people watch what is happening now they know that Rugby Union will be next. It will be hit in a big way and the game will be fundamentally changed.

What steps will the Minister and the Government take to defend British sport, and to alleviate the additional burdens imposed by the sports grounds legislation and by the national lottery, so that clubs such as Wakefield Trinity will be able to go it alone without Murdoch money and without the bribery that is bandied about to make people forget about their principles and forget about the history and heritage of the game of Rugby League?

Mr. Barry Sheerman : Is that not the crunch? Many of us share my hon. Friend's reservations about the way in which the deal was done, about Murdoch and about the lack of consultation, but there is one thing that we all know. I represent Huddersfield, where the modern game began 100 years ago, and I know it. We have to grasp the reality that we desperately need money and more spectators, and that we probably need a super league of some kind.

Mr. Hinchliffe: We need money, but do we need to prostitute ourselves on the street? That is a simple question that many of us feel deeply about. Rugby league is a game of principle, which I have supported all my life, but there are certain questions to be asked about the way that we have left some of those principles behind this time. I hope that the Minister will support the calls for an independent inquiry into the way in which the affair has been conducted. I know that the Select Committee on National Heritage has already been approached by its own members to consider the matter, and many hon. Members here today would support that request. To be fair to the Minister, he knows about the game of Rugby League and its qualities. It is primarily a local game, rooted in local communities and based on family relationships. We do not have problems at Rugby League matches, and we do not really need police, whether the crowd is 77,000 or 500, because people are well behaved and have decent values. One of the strengths of Rugby League is that the game itself oozes the values of decency and friendliness, and I believe that those qualities are well worth defending.

Mr. Roger Stott: My hon. Friend will be aware that my local club, Wigan, will play at Wembley on Saturday.

Mr. Hinchliffe: Just by way of a change.

Mr. Stott: It is like playing at home. At last year's fixture Wigan were playing Leeds, the same club that they will play on Saturday. There were about 70,000 people at Wembley Stadium last year for that cup final, and there was not one arrest.

Mr. Hinchliffe: My hon. Friend makes my point for me. there was a capacity crowd, yet I saw a police report on the match that questioned the need to police that Wembley event in future. For the record, even if Wakefield Trinity never appear at Wembley again, on the two occasions when we played Wigan we beat them.

This is an emotional issue for me - I make no bones about it. My team, Wakefield Trinity, began in 1873, based around the YMCA at Trinity church. It had its roots in Christianity, and I shall finish by quoting what one of that team's lifelong supporters, Elaine Storkey, said about the Super League two weeks ago on Radio 4's *Thought for the day*:
"It concerns the central values of our culture. When everything can be turned into a commodity for financial gain, it seems that nothing other than money has any ultimate meaning. Jesus asked 'What good will it be for someone to gain the whole world but to lose his soul?'. It warns us that something of soul could be lost in the north if the pleasure of local contests between neighbours is exchanged for global commercialisation. The cost may be the very meaning of the game, for even Rugby League can lose its heart before the tyranny of Mammon".

Mr. Gary Waller (Keighley): I am mindful of your reference to the sub judice rule, Mr. Deputy Speaker, so I shall choose my words with care. Recent days have seen much conflict and many expressions of anguish; indeed, there have been explosions of anger, and those are entirely understandable. The Rugby Football League has brought all that about by acting with unseemly speed and above all by failing to allow spectators to have their say, as they undoubtedly should.

Decisions have been rushed in a way unworthy of an organisation that celebrates its centenary this year. It took 100 years to create the Rugby League in its present form, and surely it must be disloyal to those who have supported the sport week in and week out, year in and year out, to decide on revolutionary changes in a matter of hours.

Bearing in mind the origins of Rugby League, and its creation in 1895 because of discrimination practised against Rugby League players in the north of England, I, like the hon. Member for Wakefield (Mr. Hinchliffe), find it a matter for deep regret--indeed, I find it tragic-- that the Rugby Football League has allowed itself to be drawn into a structure in which discrimination will be endemic. I object especially to the element of the deal with Mr. Rupert Murdoch whereby a Great Britain team will not play international matches against an Australian team containing players not contracted to the Murdoch organisation. Some of us have fought against such discrimination, and will continue to do so.

Last year, the Rugby Football League published a far-seeing document entitled *The Way Forward*, proposing better facilities and ways in which clubs should develop and promote themselves to a wider audience. We all support those objectives.

I want to say a little about my club. I shall not talk specifically about the composition of the super league, or give the reasons why my club should be part of it. As urged to by the Rugby Football League, the club has adopted a community-based approach. It has promoted in the ground every day what it calls the Cougars classroom, delivering the national curriculum to pupils. It has attracted families. It has admitted youngsters free of charge. It has initiated a scheme in which schools and pupils are encouraged to follow the pursuit of excellence. In two successive years, it has taken 1,000 schoolchildren in 20 or more coaches to Wembley to see an international match.

Now we see some of the results. Some 40 per cent. of spectators at home matches are women. Juvenile crime is said to have decreased in the town as a result of initiatives taken by the club. At Rochdale last Sunday, where the Cougars won 104-4 against Highfield, it was not just the achievements on the field that impressed. The stewards were amazed at the lack of problems among the huge crowd and the absence of litter after the game.

That community-based approach, matched by the creation of a superb team, has led to a dramatic increase in attendances from an average of 445 in 1986-87 to an average of 4,119 in the present season. Indeed, attendance has quadrupled in the past four years. A top coach, Phil Larder, and top players such as Daryl Powell, have been willing to come to a second division club to share in the excitement of reaching for the top. Obviously, however the league is organised, they expect to operate and play in the top flight.

In general terms, the exclusion of top-class teams which are doing now what some clubs still aspire to, epitomises what is wrong with the proposals. It is surely ridiculous to include teams which in some cases do not even exist yet or are incapable at present of playing top-class rugby, merely because they happen to be in the north-east, London, Humberside, Wales or, indeed, France. It is not surprising that the majority of the mergers which Maurice Lindsay has advocated for a long time are already breaking down. How does he expect people who have followed historic clubs such as Castleford, Featherstone and Wakefield Trinity all their lives to give their loyalty to something called Calder? The hon. Member for Wakefield spoke feelingly on the matter. I know how he feels and how so many clubs and supporters feel.

Mrs. Alice Mahon : It is interesting that, when the people who have supported the game all their lives were asked their opinion in a poll in the *Halifax Evening Courier*, in just an hour or two more than 3,000 voted against a merger with Bradford Northern and just 300 voted for a merger. So when they were given the opportunity to say whether they wanted to stay in Halifax, they chose to do so overwhelmingly.

Mr. Waller: I acknowledge what the hon. Lady says. Unfortunately, what she says is so accurate. Sadly, the chairmen of some clubs such as Bradford Northern and Halifax are among those who have been carried away by the hype that they have heard. Justifying the stance that he took in favour of the proposals, Chris Caisley, the chairman of Bradford Northern, wrote: "now and again, there is a need to step out of Cougarland, put your feet on the ground, and get into the real world." That was from the chairman of one of the clubs that have beaten a path to Cougars' door to find out just what Cougarmania is all about so that they can impart a little of it to their own promotion.

Mr. Sutcliffe: Does the hon. Gentleman agree that it is Mr. Caisley who ought to be in the real world and recognise that in 1985 there would not have been a Bradford Northern without local supporters and the local authority, just as there would not have been a Keighley Cougars without local supporters and the local authority? That is the real world. It is a bottom-up, not a top-down, process.

Mr. Waller: The hon. Gentleman is so right. He might be interested to know that Mr. Caisley, writing presumably about Members of this House who belong to the all-party Rugby League group, many of whom are in the Chamber today, wrote:"Don't be fooled by these wolves in sheep's clothing; they will disappear from the scene as quickly as they arrived. If they carry any real interest in Rugby League they would be better employed minding their own business and looking after the genuine interests of their electorate."

Well, I think I know my electorate reasonably well. My guess is that, in a contest between Chris Caisley and me or any of a dozen hon. Members who are here today, I or they would win hands down. I think that Mr. Caisley owes an apology to the supporters of the Cougars and an acknowledgement that the all-party group has been around for a good few years and its members are in touch with the views of Rugby League supporters from many clubs.

There are many educationists who seem to devise plans for schools which would work splendidly without any pupils. There are health professionals who reckon that the health service would be wonderful if there were not any patients. There are also some Rugby League administrators who have great theories about the organisation of the game, but attach scant importance to the need to keep the fans it has right now.

Rugby league is about emotion. It is about appreciation of skill. Above all, it is about people. After all, it is the people's game. So let us have some rethinking. Let the Rugby League start listening and open up the super league to fresh applications. Rugby league can still be the greatest game.

Mr. Ian McCartney (Makerfield): I am speaking as chair of the parliamentary group, in a debate which I hoped would never happen. I hoped that today we would be debating the National Heritage Select Committee report which concluded that, after 100 years, the Rugby Football League had been treated disgracefully by organised sports such as Rugby Union on the issue of sham amateurism.

Unfortunately, that will not be the case because, days before that report was published, a secret deal was done between a small group of administrators who control the rugby football league and the Murdoch organisation. The deal that was struck was clearly and simply to undermine, damage and destroy the Australian Rugby League--an affiliated international organisation legally standing on its own with a constitution and a right to manage the affairs of Rugby League in Australia--and to pick up the pieces and control Rugby League on a world-wide basis as a franchised outlet of the Murdoch organisation. As a supporter of Wigan Rugby League Club, I could take a cynical approach and see the matter in the short term. A small but significant number of clubs which are already successful will gain access to huge sums of money in a short five-year period. I could say to hell with the rest of Rugby League. However, if we are real supporters of Rugby League committed to the ethos of community and the honesty of the game, we have a responsibility to ensure that, in promoting itself, the game cherishes the reasons why Rugby League is anti-racist, why it does not have a criminal element and why it is a community sport.

It is an outrage that the Taylor report has bankrupted the game of Rugby League. As a result of horrific incidents that took place in soccer, there was a need to change the law in Britain to make sporting stadiums safer. We all supported that. The report also covered Rugby League, but no resources were given to bring its clubs up to the standards set out in that report. In the intervening years, football has received £130 million. Who says that crime does not pay? Until a few weeks ago, Rugby League had been given a paltry £2 million. Yet the accumulated debt of the sport as a whole is less than the cost of implementing the report. That left Rugby League unable to resist the way in which the Murdoch organisation moved in.

In this debate I shall not criticise Maurice Lindsay or Rodney Walker. Maurice Lindsay is a good friend of mine whom I have known throughout my public life in the north-west. I have been traumatised by what this matter has done to our friendship. My trust in the views of him and other people on the future of Rugby League was wiped out in three days because of Murdoch's ability to move in and place a gun at their heads. The gun was simply that if they did not sign up the sport exclusively to him, once he had destroyed Australian Rugby League and the international boards, he would be back for the UK game, would pick it up for nothing and would bankrupt it.

Players are to be cherry-picked and millions of pounds will flow out of the game in the coming weeks, both here and in Australia. A small group of players will become instant millionaires while the sport at the grass roots will wither away, clubs will be left to go bankrupt and communities will see their teams and players made redundant. How can Martin Offiah honestly hold up his hand and say that he did a deal because he wanted to play for his country? The money secured in that contract alone would be sufficient to plough into an investment programme for the clubs left in the first division.

If we are serious about a super league, why will the first division be starved of capital resources, sponsorship and income, as well as the right, even if teams are successful, to apply to join the super league? A head cannot survive if the body is destroyed.

If, in Great Britain today, the Football Association announced that Terry Venables's' English international team could not play a country unless that country had secured a deal giving Murdoch exclusive rights to that international programme, there would be international and national outrage. But this deal means that Great Britain cannot play rugby internationally unless the game is with a team that has a contract exclusive to Murdoch. What would be the reaction if David Platt, the England captain, could not play for England ever again because the club that he played for did not have an exclusive deal with Mr. Murdoch? That is precisely the position for Great Britain players. Phil Clarke from Wigan is a top international athlete, not just in the international Rugby League. Last year, he signed a contract, of his own volition, to play Rugby League in Australia. In the past two days, he has discovered that his club has not signed up to the Murdoch deal in Australia. So the best loose forward in the world today will be banned forthwith from playing for his country unless he breaks his contract and turns his back on a legally binding document. How could such an arrangement be allowed to happen? It means that the sport has been purchased lock, stock and barrel. For the first time in Britain's history, a media magnate has bought not just a sporting event but a sport and, with that purchase, he will manipulate that sport on an international stage for the long-term aspirations of his company at the expense of the short and longer-term aims of Rugby League, both here and internationally.

There are serious implications for the United Kingdom outside Rugby League. The House must consider whether it is right that Mr. Murdoch or any other media mogul can decide the shape, size and rights of any sport. Is it right that a media mogul from outside the UK can control virtually every major sporting event in the United Kingdom? Is it right that a media mogul can contract individual players and sports and, with those contractual arrangements, operate a virtual monopoly--a restraint of trade on individuals--which prevents access to that sport for any other sponsor or media agency without his prior approval?

If hon. Members want to surrender British and European sport to Mr. Murdoch, they should say so. He should not be allowed to use Rugby League as a Trojan horse to undermine all those public issues.

Ms Kate Hoey: Does my hon. Friend share my concern that someone--it is difficult not to mention names and personalities--who is involved with this deal, namely Mr. Walker, is the chairman of the Sports Council? Does he feel that people are confident in how sport in this country will be handled when the same person so quickly sells out a major sport?

Mr. McCartney: My hon. Friend makes an important point. Rodney Walker is a man of integrity but the deal seriously compromises the whole of rugby football league and the ability of its administrators to be regarded as independent in their role in other non-governmental agencies. The Minister must be clear about the future for Rugby League outside the super league. Rugby league outside the super league is massive, and not just on the M62 corridor. With more than 50,000 players and thousands of teams, Rugby League is played from Scotland to every constituent part of the United Kingdom. What happens to clubs that currently receive support from non-governmental agencies? They must not be treated as a franchise of Mr. Murdoch's and excluded from investment from other sporting bodies. Rodney Walker and others should consider whether, before making their hasty decisions, they should have thought the issues through more thoroughly.

If we are honest about the future of the game, we must also be honest about the fact that Rugby League is virtually a bankrupt game. It is short of capital investment resources, and it is sometimes short of vision. But cherry picking and an international battle for a few players will cause millions of pounds to seep out of the game into the bank accounts of a few players, their agents and the lawyers who represent them, and the game will not be able to survive in the long run. The most damning indictment of the whole issue is how Rugby League has lost control of events and the international rugby board has been smashed. The game can no longer be played unless Murdoch says that it can. Each day, the meter ticks on and the only people who ultimately will gain are the agents, a handful of players and a lot of solicitors.

The Rugby League family must come together quickly. Some sanity must prevail in Australia and here to end immediately the cherry picking, bans and prescriptions. Unless that happens immediately, none of the £70 million will be left to invest. It will have gone for ever.

Dr. Norman A. Godman: Some hon. Members may wonder why I, as a Scottish Member of Parliament, wish to speak in the debate. However, I played Rugby League as a boy--I was too slow to be a wing three-quarter and not big enough to be a forward--and I number among my family friends the late Mick Scott, Johnnie Whitely, Harry Markham, Tommy Harris, and many others whom you would recognise immediately, Mr. Deputy Speaker.

My father was a bit of a bigoted supporter. He always went to the Boulevard and he refused to enter Craven Park, even when Hull played there. As someone who played the game as a boy and who follows it still, I am deeply concerned about the recent developments. I plead with the Minister to set up an independent inquiry to examine the whole murky affair, particularly the role played by Mr. Rodney Walker.

I visited Australia over Christmas, and my wife and I stayed in Manly, which has a very famous Rugby League team--as you well know, Mr. Deputy Speaker. I spoke to many Rugby League supporters who are concerned about the way in which the game is shaping up in both Australia and England--it is still very much a Welsh and an English game. Nevertheless, they were concerned about what was happening in Britain and Australia. They told me to beware of Mr. Murdoch and not to trust him an inch.

I make a plea to the Minister to set up an inquiry and to play the game with Rugby League, as, God knows, its players and supporters deserve it. If the Minister does not set up such an inquiry, the Select Committee should take on board forthwith this deeply disturbing affair.

The Minister is highly regarded in Rugby League circles and has my genuine recognition for that, which makes it all the more surprising that he should have remained silent about the matter during the past two weeks. I do not know whether he has been muzzled by the Secretary of State, but that will become clear when he replies to the debate. I hope, therefore, that he will not take lightly my points in respect of the history of the deal and the degree to which it is divisive and discriminatory and jeopardises the future well-being of the game. We should remember why the deal was put on the table in the first place.

It did not result from Mr. Murdoch's altruistic desire to help a sport in undoubted difficulty. Instead, it arose from a battle taking place thousands of miles away in Australia, where Murdoch's interests created the breakaway Star League as a way of poaching the coverage enjoyed by great numbers of Australians, but shown on the networks of Murdoch's long-standing rival, Kerry Packer. That has already been said, but now it is on the record and it is as well that everyone knows it.

We have seen that battle before. I am sure that hon. Members will remember Kerry Packer's television coverage which caused the first manifestations of pyjama cricket in the late 1970s. If the battle is allowed to rage on unchecked, we shall end up in circumstances similar to those in the United States, where commercialism is rampant.

I remind the House that Murdoch paid almost $400 million nearly a year ago for the rights to screen the National Football League in America on his subscription Fox TV channel, ending 34 years of universal coverage. Murdoch is in the right position to build up a monopoly with Rugby League as a pawn in his game. He has access to vast funds by cross-subsidising his sports broadcasting with other areas of media activities. We can rest assured that once he has built up that monopoly, he will use it to generate sufficient profits to finance a bid for world domination in another sphere of his activities, which could mean sports fans paying through the nose. In the deal before us today, although it changes from hour to hour, Rupert Murdoch's News International will effectively become Rugby League's governing body. He will decide who plays where and when, taking to the extreme the developments within the Premier League in football, when matches are moved to suit BSkyB.

The deal is the precedent that could set us on a slippery slope as it involves much more than television rights negotiated through the sport's own governing body. Restriction and discrimination run through the deal like words through a stick of rock.

The players are likely to be contracted to play only against other players also contracted to News International. Individual players are being asked to pledge their contractual allegiance to a single broadcaster as if they were actors in yet another Australian soap opera. It seems that that restriction is to be extended even to national teams, such as those for the forthcoming test series.

On the basis of that deal alone, we now face a clear progression to the day when a broadcaster buys the rights to athletes, for example--the hon. Member for Falmouth and Camborne (Mr. Coe), an eminent athlete, is in his place--and can then say, "You can run the 100 m for Britain at the next international meet only if you sign for me." The governing bodies themselves will be reduced to near puppets, implementing the broadcaster's every whim.

Viewers will be discriminated against in an obvious fashion. If they cannot afford a dish or a subscription, they will not be able to watch the sport. It is that simple. What message does the Minister have for pensioners, among millions of others, who will be denied yet another sporting opportunity?

What about those who have enjoyed the BBC's coverage of the Silk Cut Challenge cup since 1964? The BBC's contract comes up for renewal next year. Although the event may remain, what will happen to its coverage? I have heard some favourable comments, but I should like some cast-iron guarantees from the Minister.

The Department of National Heritage made its position clear in response to the National Heritage Select Committee's report on sports sponsorship and television coverage, when it reasserted its faith in the market and the general public were as far from the top of its list of priorities. The Department stands condemned by its inaction. Fans from families who have supported the same club for generations will suffer from the spectre of those clubs being consumed in some cases and left by the wayside in others just to fit Mr. Murdoch's five-year master plan. If he decides to move on at the end of those five years, what will happen to clubs that have been forced to abandon their core support?

My hon. Friend the Member for Wakefield expressed his profound concern about the proposed merger of three clubs to form Calder--a merger already rejected by one of the clubs involved, accepted by another and now rejected by a ballot at Featherstone Rovers--a ballot, a club and a history about which you, Mr. Deputy Speaker, also care passionately, and only the traditions associated with the Chair prevent that passion from surfacing during the debate.

The deal's rejection by Featherstone Rovers serves only to highlight the lack of consultation and the hurried nature of the deal. Secret negotiations in smoke-filled rooms are no way to treat a game with such loyal and committed popular support.

The Minister would do well to remember that the anger of the Rugby League fans that was reflected in some of the comments we have heard today is very real and justified. Rugby league clubs provide a focus for many communities often not provided by other means. Professional and amateur clubs alike offer opportunities for young boys and girls to learn all that the sport has to offer.

That is all at stake. Whole communities have been shattered. Although that may be of no concern to some hon. Members who feel that there is no such thing as a society, who could doubt the sincerity, passion and heartfelt commitment of the communities where Rugby League is as much a way of life as a sport?

There can be no doubt that all those who have spoken in the debate have the best interests of the game and their constituents at heart. I recognise that before the deal the game was in a poor state financially and that has been accepted by many hon. Members. Clubs are in no position to try to hold on to their best players when there is a bidding war for Australian clubs, and the Government are by no means blameless in that state of affairs.

The House will no doubt recall that interventions were made by a number of hon. Members when we debated football ground safety in 1989 and 1990. It was pointed out that Lord Justice Taylor's report into the Hillsborough stadium disaster had exonerated the Rugby League supporters who moved freely without trouble around the terraces, coming largely from the same socio-economic group. It was a shame that the Government felt unable to draw the same conclusion before imposing the burden of safety improvements without financial assistance. Consequently, Rugby League clubs spent £30 million on ground improvements but received only £1 million from the Foundation for Sport and the Arts. Meanwhile, football was aided by more than £132 million from the Football Trust. The unacceptable financial burden on Rugby League left many clubs on the brink of bankruptcy--although I recognise again the Minister's contribution to redressing the balance, albeit belatedly, by persuading the Treasury to forgo some revenue from the pools and expanding the remit of the Football Trust to Rugby League.

When the Minister replies, perhaps he will say whether he was aware of the Murdoch negotiations with Rugby League at the time of his or the Treasury's decision and give his views on the possibility of public funds being used to cross-subsidise that bid.

We heard today of huge sums of money being offered to individual players. What is the Minister doing to ensure that smaller clubs prosper, community schemes are maintained and the game flourishes in schools? What consideration has the Minister given to fulfilling those needs? He will know from last week's business questions--at column 340 of Hansard for 20 April--that my hon. Friend the Member for Dewsbury (Mrs. Taylor) received from the Leader of the House a commitment that the Minister would reply to that point in this debate.

Does the Minister believe that the predicted widespread player redundancies will help to improve the game? Sport has the potential for being a great leveller, breaking down barriers and bringing communities together. That should be the aim of the Minister. In the past, Rugby League has been an example of how much good sport can achieve, yet it is threatened by commercial discrimination and the restrictions of Murdoch's proposals and Packer's counter-proposals. My right hon. Friend the Member for Copeland (Dr. Cunningham) asked the Secretary of State for Trade and Industry to refer the matter to the Monopolies and Mergers Commission. I hope that the Minister will back that call, which has been made also by Conservative Members, including the hon. Member for Elmet (Mr. Batiste).

Only yesterday, none other than Martin Offiah said of his signing to Murdoch that he wanted to play for Great Britain--which is something that he could not do outside the super league. If that is not a trade restriction, I do not know what is. If the MMC's terms of reference do not fit that particular case, the Government should alter its terms.

I urge the Minister to use his good offices even at this late stage to bring about a better deal for this great game.

The Parliamentary Under-Secretary of State for National Heritage (Mr. Iain Sproat): In this extremely important debate, the passions deeply felt were well controlled. I am sorry that we do not have time today to consider the matter in the detail and depth that it deserves. However, this is just the beginning of the debate and discussions that we intend--and I will return to that point later.

I thank the hon. Member for Wakefield (Mr. Hinchliffe) for initiating the debate and for something that he said on 28 April 1993, when I was sitting on one of the Back Benches, wondering how there could be a promised debate about rugby when the House was considering the Report stage of the National Lottery etc. Bill. The hon. Member for Wakefield made a powerful speech about what he saw as powerful discrimination by Rugby Union against Rugby League. As a keen Rugby Union supporter, I was hearing for the first time the other side of the story. When, to my amazement, I became Minister responsible for sport shortly afterwards, I asked the hon. Gentleman to come to the Department for National Heritage to help sort out some of the difficulties that he had mentioned. I say that so that the House will know some of my bona fides.

At that meeting, the hon. Members for Wakefield and for Makerfield (Mr. McCartney) and my hon. Friend the Member for Keighley (Mr. Waller) made three points above all. They were, "We want Rugby Union and Rugby League to talk, which they have not done since 1895. We want to get Rugby League into the armed forces, where it is currently kept out. We want something done about the ludicrous situation whereby the hooliganism and other problems in association football results in it getting help with problems of safety, whereas Rugby League, which causes no problems, is paying the price." The hon. Member for Wigan (Mr. Stott) mentioned that not one person out of a 70,000 crowd was charged even for swinging an odd punch after drinking at a Wembley cup final or international.

As a consequence of that first meeting, there was a meeting between Mr. Pugh and Mr. Rowlands, representing Rugby Union, and Mr. Walker and Mr. Lindsay representing Rugby League. I do not say that it symbolised a great deal, but it was a start. Rugby league is now played in the armed forces, although perhaps not at the level that everybody would like, and the Foundation for Sport and the Arts has a sum of £8 million, some of which will be available to Rugby League to sort out ground safety problems. We have made progress.

I thank the hon. Member for Stalybridge and Hyde (Mr. Pendry) for his kind words. When I arranged for the FSA to make £8 million available to games other than soccer, I did not know what Mr. Murdoch was up to.

Even in a one and a half hour debate, it is important that the House has a chance to air its views and to let loose the passion that is felt--even though it is clear that we will not reach any conclusions today. However, the world outside can see the passion that has been aroused. One hon. Member said that he went to Belle Vue and had seen grown men weep at what was happening to Wakefield Trinity. Those deep emotions must be expressed and the House is the best place for that. Serious principles are involved. The hon. Member for Makerfield referred to Phil Clarke, one of the finest loose forwards in the world, who, unless he breaks his contract, may find himself unable to play for his own country. One could mention many players and clubs, but that example encapsulates the problem.

As to restrictive practices and the Monopolies and Mergers Commission, letters have been written to the Director General of Fair Trading and to my right hon. Friend the President of the Board of Trade. I am not allowed to say that the implications of what is proposed for the super league are being looked at because lawyers say that if one is looking at something, one is implying that there is a conclusion. In any event, normal people would say that those letters are being looked at without prejudice, and no doubt we will shortly hear the sage advice of the director general and of my right hon. Friend. The hon. Member for Wakefield said that what is happening in Rugby League may turn out to be a vicarage tea party by comparison with what may happen to Rugby Union. With the world cup in South Africa in May and June, I am sure that Rugby Union will be the next target on which Mr. Murdoch and Mr. Packer will set their sights.

The hon. Gentleman and many others talked about an independent inquiry. As Minister responsible for sport I have a restricted locus in the matter. The Select Committee has already said that it may return to the subject. I suggest that it should do so. I will reply to the previous Select Committee report in the middle of June, if I can knock it out in time. It might be helpful if the Select Committee turned its mind to this other matter.

If I understood him correctly, the hon. Member for Huddersfield (Mr. Sheerman) said that he thought there was a role for a super league. I pay tribute to the integrity of Mr. Rodney Walker and Mr. Morris Lindsay, who believe that, with half a dozen clubs or more having gone into receivership in the past few years, and with the total debt of the 32 club amounting to about £10 million, and with few clubs turning a profit this year, something must be done. We have heard today that Rugby League needs an overhaul; it needs an injection of cash. It is not for me to tell Rugby League what to do, but so much is fairly clear. We have to balance the financial problems of the game against the emotions, the community links, the culture of the game and the oozing of values to which reference has been made--decency, for one. All these are important.

I suggest that the Select Committee turn its mind to this subject again and conduct a forensic inquiry--that can be done quickly. Secondly, the hon. Member for Wakefield may like to bring a delegation to discuss the matter further with me.

Debate on the Future of Rugby League 3 Nov 1999

Mr. David Hinchliffe: Let me begin by expressing my gratitude for the opportunity to initiate the debate, and my appreciation to colleagues who have remained in the Chamber until this late hour owing to their concerns about certain issues relating to Rugby League. I know that many of them--my hon. Friends the Members for Leeds, Central (Mr. Benn), for Leeds, North-West (Mr. Best) and for Halton (Mr. Twigg)--hope to make brief contributions later.

Let me begin by declaring certain relevant interests. I hold 500 shares in Wakefield Trinity Rugby League football club; I also chair the league's professional players consultative committee, which negotiates between the professional clubs and the players' union. The post is not remunerated, and pays no expenses. I am secretary of the all-party Rugby League group, which has about 80 members from the House and another place.

I welcome the Minister to her new post. She has my personal good wishes for the work that she will do. I know that she has a great passion for sport of all types. She has been a member of the all-party Rugby League group and, in 1995, participated in the previous debate on the subject, so she is aware of the background to many of the issues about which we are concerned. I believe that this is her debut on the Front Bench in her new position. She could not make it on a more important issue, as I am sure she appreciates.

The title of the debate implies some doubt and questions about Rugby League's future. I want to express a personal view. The sport, in both an amateur and professional sense, has a positive future. I will express no doubts about its future. I have concerns merely over the implications of Rugby League's administrative structure, particularly the controversies over the merger of certain professional clubs.

In stressing the positives, I recall that, in 1995, when the announcement was made in Paris that Rugby Union had gone openly professional, Ian Robertson, the BBC's "rugby"--that is, union--correspondent, implied that it signalled the end of Rugby League--that it had no future.

Several years on, we see the contrasting fortunes of professional Rugby Union and professional Rugby League. Those of us in Rugby League believe that the league game has proved its supremacy and will continue to do so over the years.

Certainly, attendances at professional Rugby League matches are far higher than at equivalent professional Rugby Union matches. Therefore, we can stress many positives. This season, attendances at several league matches topped 20,000.

Mr. Colin Burgon: Will my hon. Friend take the opportunity, even though he comes from Wakefield, to commend Castleford Tigers, a small-town club with average attendances of 6,000-plus? Does he agree that the club's community-based approach shows the way forward for Rugby League? In his much-valued opinion, what can the game learn from "classy Cas"?

Mr. Hinchliffe: Although they have had a successful season, Castleford were beaten by Wakefield Trinity, but I pay tribute to Castleford's work. I stress my hon. Friend's point: Rugby League is essentially a community sport. Clubs such as Castleford are rooted in the local community and have been successful as a consequence of their connections with that community. In the context of mergers, links with the local community are crucial, as my hon. Friend has said.

Let me make one or two other positive points on the future of Rugby League. The amateur game has spread throughout the country since the barriers in relation to union were lifted. The summer conference league, which has existed for the past two years, has spread like wildfire across central and southern England. Clubs are queuing up to join the league. Players who have played only union have not had the opportunity to taste the great game of Rugby League. That expansion throughout the country is encouraging.

The game is expanding in the armed forces. It was banned in the forces until 1994; a campaign in this place lifted that ban. The armed forces Rugby League is growing.

On the issue of bans, I draw hon. Members' attention to early-day motion 972, which is in my name and deals with the position in France during the second world war, when Rugby League was banned in disgraceful circumstances. The sport operates against a background of some vindictive treatment, especially from Rugby Union in recent times.

The game is expanding in colleges and universities. I stress that there is far more female involvement in Rugby League. When I go to matches as a spectator, certainly Super League matches, I reckon that, on average, about 50 per cent. of spectators at many of the clubs are female. Now, vast numbers of women are playing Rugby League, enjoying a great game that I have enjoyed over many years. Rugby league's future looks very positive.

I should like to deal in this debate primarily with current proposals, some of which have been formally agreed, on the merger of some professional Super League clubs. My hon. Friends and I are here today primarily to voice the concerns of Rugby League fans in the communities that we represent about the proposals.

One element in the controversy over the club mergers is the difficult financial position of some of the clubs. Player costs were certainly inflated by the initial professionalisation of union, in 1995. Although it is easy to criticise those who are involved in pushing for the merger of clubs, I appreciate that many business people and individuals with a commitment to the game have spent great sums keeping clubs afloat.

Additionally, Super League clubs have been receiving less from Sky Television. Consequently, Super League clubs have developed an agenda to reduce their number, from 14 to 12. As a further consequence, this year, £1.25 million was made available to clubs that were prepared to merge. The key issue--I hope that the Minister will address it today--in the proposed mergers is the way in which, in the past few years, three separate administrative arms have developed in professional Rugby League. The first is Rugby Football League, which is the game's constitutional governing body, comprising all the professional Rugby League clubs. The second is Super League Europe, which was introduced after the 1995 introduction of Super League. Originally, Super League Europe was simply a marketing arm of Super League, but now has its own headquarters, chairman and chief executive. The third is the Association of Northern Ford Premiership Clubs, effectively comprising the old first division. The problem with the current proposals have been caused by the division of responsibilities between those three bodies.

Currently, there is a proposal to merge the Huddersfield Giants and the Sheffield Eagles. I should say that I have a constituency interest in the Huddersfield Giants because my constituency includes two Kirklees wards containing significant numbers of Giants supporters. The Giants are based, of course, in the town where the game was founded, in 1895. It is one of the greatest teams in the history of Rugby League.

The Sheffield team was established only 15 years ago, in virgin territory. However, it has done excellent development work and--less than two years ago, in 1998--won the challenge cup.

We also have proposals to merge the Hull and Gateshead teams. Hull has another of the greatest teams in Rugby League. Its recent demise seems to coincide with the involvement of the tennis player David Lloyd--who has recently bought shares in the Gateshead side, thereby driving forward the merger between the two clubs. Last season, Gateshead was admitted to Super League as a new franchise. Another piece of the jigsaw that will concern my hon. Friends who have attended this debate is that, next season, a new Sheffield club may be admitted to the Premiership. Mark Aston--the former Sheffield Eagles player--is proposing admission of the team, entailing the possibility of a team dropping down to the Premiership and competing there. However, that will depend on the agreement of the Premiership clubs, which have an organisation and constitution separate from those of Super League.

Another factor is the position of the Hunslet Hawks--my hon. Friend the Member for Leeds, Central (Mr. Benn) may want to mention that team--which won the Northern Ford Premiership. The team is not quite sure whether it will be in Super League or in the Northern Ford

Premiership. Ultimately, however, its position will depend on whether Hull drops out of Super League.

The situation is complex. Thousands of Rugby League fans are baffled and angry about what is happening to their much-loved local sides. I want to stress the connection between Rugby League teams and the local community, because it is essentially a community game. More than any sport that I know, Rugby League is rooted in local communities and is part and parcel of them, particularly in the north of England.

Many professional players do not know whether they have a job for next season. Some clubs have reneged on their contract because the club has been contracted to disappear. They do not know whether they have a living. I am concerned about their circumstances. The situation does not reflect well on the game. I want to conclude in time to give some of my hon. Friends a chance to have a brief say in the debate. The heart of the problem with the current mergers is the administrative split between the key elements of the sport. It is crucial that professional Rugby League should get back to one coherent whole under its constitutional body, the Rugby Football League. The Government have a role to play in assisting the process and I look forward to the support of my hon. Friend the Minister in bringing that about.

Appendix 2:

The National Heritage Select Committee 1995 Report: Inquiry into the relationship between Rugby Union and Rugby League

Memorandum submitted by the All-Party Parliamentary Rugby League Group, written by David Hinchliffe M.P.

I have been asked to make a submission to your Committee on behalf of the All Party Parliamentary Rugby League Group for use in your Inquiry into the relationship between Rugby Union and Rugby League. My Group very much welcomes the establishment of this short Inquiry and would wish to set out our views on the key areas for consideration by your Members.

In short, I would summarise these as

(a) The denial by the governing bodies of the Rugby Union of basic rights and freedoms to exercise individual choice in terms of lawful sporting activities.

(b) The selective interpretation of the International Rugby Football Board's "amateurism" regulations to outlaw involvement with the sport of Rugby League rather than professionalism within Rugby Union.

(c) The wholly incorrect assertion by the various governing bodies of the Rugby Union that theirs is a strictly amateur sport despite extensive evidence to the contrary from various sources including the Inland Revenue.

The All Party Parliamentary Rugby League Group was established in February 1988 to promote the interests of the sport of Rugby League within Parliament and we now have around 80 M.P.s and Peers in membership. We meet on a monthly basis while Parliament is sitting.

Our Minutes indicate that perhaps the most central concern of the Group since its formation has been the consequences for Rugby League of difficulties in the relationship with Rugby Union. *Specifically, these have related to the Rugby Union's regulations on ..Amateurism" which we believe are interpreted not to prevent the growth of professionalism but rather the development and expansion of the completely independent sport of Rugby League.*

Rugby League will celebrate its Centenary in August of this year. It began in 1895 as "Northern Union" after a large number of Rugby clubs in Yorkshire and Lancashire voted to break away from the English Rugby Union over the issue of "broken time" payment. Rugby in those days was increasing in popularity and attracting large crowds on Saturday afternoons especially in the North of England. At the time the normal working week included Saturdays and many of the working men playing for the senior sides found themselves regularly out of pocket because they were forced to "break time" to play Rugby.

A conflict arose between clubs in the North with predominantly working class players and those in the South over a proposal to permit "broken time" payments to compensate players for loss of earnings in what was then an amateur game. The majority of the clubs in membership voted against the proposal and as a direct consequence, on 29 August 1895, the "Northern Union" clubs broke away. They introduced new rules designed to speed up the game and make it more spectator friendly and eventually changed its name to Rugby League.

What began as broken time payments eventually became professionalism in the top clubs but it is important to stress that *Rugby League has always had a majority of amateur clubs and players.* There are currently 32 professional clubs in the first and second division of the Rugby Football League but there are over 1,300 amateur clubs organised by the British Amateur Rugby League Association. Many of these clubs run several sides on a regular basis. While it is common to hear the London-based media refer to Rugby League as "the professional code" it is important to stress that *most Rugby League is played by amateurs.* The media also frequently quote Rugby Union officials' views that League is "parasitic" in terms of player recruitment from

Union. However, *the overwhelming majority of professional Rugby League players are signed from amateur Rugby League sides and not from Rugby Union.*

While a handful of First Division clubs employ full time players, the vast majority of Rugby League professionals are part-time with other employment. In the lower reaches of the Second Division, there are some teams paying little more than expenses.

The establishment of Rugby League as a completely independent sport with markedly different rules institutionalised the conflict with Union rather than ending it. The century-long antagonism between the codes stemmed from Union's concern at players being attracted to "professionalism" and League's belief that Union wanted to kill off Its development as a .completely Independent sport. More recently, as evidence has emerged of the extent of professionalism within Union, League followers and *this Group have become firmly of the opinion that the International Board of the Rugby Football Union's regulations on "Amateurism" are in practice applied to involvement in Rugby League rather than earnings or financial rewards in Union. This* question is the *heart of the current difficulties and the central issue which we believe should be addressed by the Select Committee.*

Until the 1980s, anyone who played Rugby League even as an amateur after reaching the age of 18 was banned for life from playing Rugby Union. I was personally subject to this ban which applied until pressure tun a number of MPs and the British Amateur Rugby League Association led to the establishment of a so-called "free gangway" between amateur Rugby League and Rugby Union. I am informed by MPs involved at the time that threats to access to public funding by Rugby Union bodies, via the Sports Council, played an important part in achieving the changes at this stage.

As well as operating such bans on individuals who have played Rugby League, even as amateurs, Union influence and actions have curtailed the development of Rugby League as a sport both in Britain and internationally. It is frequently said that Union is played world-wide while League isn't, but worth considering why this is the case. Union was spread world-wide through the British Armed Forces which until less than a year ago banned Rugby League as a sport.

This Group received representations from serving Forces personnel who were refused the right to play Rugby League. Formal representations to the Ministry of Defence by individual MPs and by this Group received the reply that there was no demand to play the game. When we demonstrated the extent of interest at a number of bases, we were then advised that it was not possible to fund the equipment necessary for the recognition of an additional sport-despite the fact that the pitches, balls and other equipment used were already available for Rugby Union! Pressure from the Group and support from the current Sports Minister Iain Sproat, eventually resulted in the game of Rugby League being recognised during 1994, after 98 years in existence.

Regrettably, similar progress has not been made in ending the blatant discrimination by the Rugby Union against players who have had associations of any kind with professional Rugby League clubs. The application of the "Amateurism" regulations by the International Rugby Football Board has resulted in many players over the years being disqualified from involvement with the sport of Rugby Union because of their involvement-even as amateur trialists-with professional Rugby League Clubs. Some of the more high profile cases have in recent times received extensive coverage in the press and have been the subject of Questions, Early Day Motions and Debates in both the House of Commons and the House of Lords. *The Group would strongly urge the Select Committee to examine the cases of some of the sportsmen directly affected* because *their treatment by Rugby Union is* in *our view inexcusable in a free society.*

We would draw particular attention to the fact that in one such case the Welsh Rugby Football Union and the International Board of the Rugby Football Union are currently subject to a legal action for "Restraint of Trade" by the imposition of a ban on a former professional Rugby League player. Mr Stuart Evans, the former Welsh Rugby Union player who subsequently played Rugby League for St Helens, is arguing that the Welsh Rugby Union ban on him returning to Union (under the International Rugby Football Board rules) preventing him earning money *from playing Rugby Union.* He believes he is able to prove conclusively that professionalism is so widespread in Rugby Union in Wales that the Welsh Rugby Union and the International Board are exercising restraint of trade by refusing his application to play.

I would draw the Committee's attention to the extensive evidence presented during debates on both the National Lottery Bill and the Sports (Discrimination) Bill to substantiate Mr Evans' claim about widespread professionalism in Rugby Union. This is allowed to continue while the Rugby Union act against those who have associated with Rugby League, even as amateurs.

Following increasing evidence of financial rewards within Rugby Union, the Group made a submission to the Inland Revenue regarding our concerns over the arrangement for taxation and national insurance within the sport. We took this step after parliamentary answers from Treasury Ministers had indicated that the Government regarded all Rugby Union players as amateurs. The Inland Revenue is now undertaking a wide-ranging investigation into tax evasion within Rugby Union and we understand that they have established that professionalism is widespread. *This Group believes it is absolutely essential that the Select Committee obtains evidence during its Inquiry from the Inland Revenue to substantiate this point.*

I am enclosing for your information copies of the Hansard report of a debate on a proposed amendment to the National Lottery Bill which took place during its Report Stage in the Commons on 28 April 1993 (not printed). The amendment, which was subsequently withdrawn, proposed that lottery funding should not be distributed to any bodies discriminating between players in amateur and professional sport.

I am also enclosing a copy of the Hansard report of the Committee Stage of the Sports (Discrimination) Bill which took place on 13th July 1994 (not printed). I introduced the Bill during the last session of Parliament in an effort to outlaw the current discriminatory practices by the various administrative bodies of the Rugby Union against those who have had past involvement in Rugby League. The Bill was blocked by the Government at Report Stage but is likely to be reintroduced in an amended form during this session of Parliament.

In conclusion, I would apologise for the length of this memorandum. My Group have attempted to summarise in as concise a form as possible the detailed concerns which we hope will be addressed by the Inquiry. In addition to the enclosed Hansard reports, we have in our Group's files numerous press reports and articles which substantiate these concerns. I will be happy to supply you with these or any other information that may be of help to the Committee in formulating its conclusions.

February 1995 (Italics as in original)

Appendix 3: The House of Commons Culture, Media and Sport Committee Report: The Future of Professional Rugby (December 1999)

Memorandum submitted by the All-Party Parliamentary Rugby League Group in June 1999

Introduction

1. The All-Party Parliamentary Rugby League Group welcomes the establishment of the Culture, Media and Sport Committee's Inquiry into professional rugby and the opportunity to set out our views on the issues being addressed by the Committee within its terms of reference. We have divided our evidence into two broad sections, firstly, that concerning the implications of Union's "professionalism" and secondly that concerning the internal arrangements, organisation and problems of the sport of Rugby League.

2. Our Group has been in existence since 1988 when it was formed to draw political attention to a range of issues of concern within both amateur and professional Rugby League. We currently have around 80 members in the Commons and Lords. Among the membership are individuals who have played the sport at an amateur and professional level or served in various capacities at club or higher levels within the game.

3. At the time of its formation, our Group wished in particular to address the blatant discrimination against our sport and its participants as a result of the so-called "amateurism" regulations then operating within Rugby Union. The efforts made by the group to bring pressure to bear on the Rugby Union authorities regarding the attitude towards Rugby League players, undoubtedly contributed to the decision of the Rugby Union International Board in 1995 to allow open professionalism in their game. We recognise that the conclusions of the 1995 Inquiry by the National Heritage Select Committee into relations between the two codes of
rugby played a very important part in the whole process of radical change within Rugby Union which, as we will set out, has also had significant implications for both amateur and professional Rugby League.

4. It is also worth recalling that during 1995 Rugby League, in its Centenary year, was itself undergoing a revolution within its professional arm following the Rugby Football League's contract with Sky TV and the move to summer rugby which began during 1996. Our Group
initiated a Parliamentary debate around the time of the proposals for Super League and members expressed serious concerns about both the implications of an apparent "take-over" of the professional game by News Limited and proposals that were then being considered to merge some of the game's most famous professional clubs.

5. While there were, and still are, differences of opinion within our Group, and the game as a whole, about the merits of the Super League development, the impact of the changes agreed in 1995 have undoubtedly been of great significance and we will discuss these later in this submission.

The implications of "Open" Professionalism In Rugby Union For Rugby League

6. At the time of the Rugby Union International Board decision, to allow "open" professionalism, there were many national "rugby" (i.e. Union) commentators predicting the demise of Rugby League as a direct consequence. Their assumption was that League had existed solely as an outlet and safety valve for a minority who wished to earn money from their rugby activities. They had also grossly over-estimated the importance of big name Union
converts to League, assuming that few would wish to change codes in future with dramatic consequences for League.

7. Such commentators totally failed to understand the fact that League has traditionally taken great pride in operating as a totally distinct independent sport with markedly different rules and a fundamentally different, much more inclusive, sporting culture. They also failed to appreciate the fact that the vast majority of British players recruited to professional Rugby League (over 95 per cent according to RFL evidence to the National Heritage Committee Inquiry) come from amateur Rugby League.

8. There have nevertheless been some very significant implications for professional Rugby League arising from Union's open professionalism.

9. Perhaps the main one has been the inflationary impact of the initial salary levels agreed by top Union clubs to recruit players in the first couple of seasons. There was, at first, serious concern within some professional Rugby League clubs that the rewards being offered by the likes of Sir John Hall's Newcastle Rugby Union club could lead to the loss of significant numbers of prominent Rugby League players.

10. While a number of former Union players were tempted back from League at the time, the game was able to retain the vast majority of its star players. Several of those who chose to play a winter season in Union whilst still contracted to Rugby League clubs, returned having learned that their handling skills were less valued in a 15-a-side code which, despite the adoption of several rules and practices from League, still emphasises the rucking, mauling and kicking game with which they were largely unfamiliar.

11. It may well be argued that the initial impact of Union's early attempts at professionalism could have had a more serious impact upon League if the Sky TV funding had not at that time enabled Rugby League clubs to enhance player contracts. In this respect there is a very real concern that the initial setting of what have subsequently proved to be frequently unsustainable salary levels in Union had the indirect effect of diverting resources received by League through the Sky deal into increased player rewards rather than important development work or ground improvements by professional clubs.

12. We welcome the steps taken by professional Rugby League clubs to introduce salary caps related to overall income but remain concerned that, in League as in Union, the payments being made to players are still frequently beyond the actual means of their clubs.

13. Obviously, in addition to income from television deals and sponsorship, the main revenue received by Rugby League clubs arises from spectator attendance at matches. In this respect our Group are concerned that the advent of Super League has not had the marked impact upon improved gates that its proponents anticipated. We believe that there are a number of possible reasons for this, some of which many relate directly to the changes that have occurred within Rugby Union.

14. Firstly, it is clear that open professionalism in Union and the increased emphasis on the importance of League and cup competition between clubs in that code has led to Union having its highest ever media profile. Our impression is that while Union's profile has increased, League's has generally decreased, with some national newspapers giving little, if any, coverage to the sport. In our view the poor media coverage given to Rugby League has a direct impact upon the game's failure to improve spectator attendances. We also recognise that the confinement of most of Rugby League's television coverage to Sky channels obviously results in less coverage elsewhere.

15. We strongly recommend the Committee to consider the reasons why League consistently receives a fraction of the coverage given to Union club rugby and have enclosed with our submission research evidence (Reference 1[1]) received recently from the House of Commons Library, outlining comparative attendances for the two codes for the most recent period available. Bearing in mind the fact that the average spectator attendance for both the professional divisions of Rugby League in England is clearly higher than those in Union, it is a matter of serious concern that media coverage is   not at the very least broadly comparable.

16. Obviously, there will be some who claim the discrepancy in media coverage arises from the perception of League's geographic concentration being primarily in the North of England. We

would strongly counter this point by drawing attention to the very marked expansion in active participation in the sport of Rugby League away from its traditional areas since the removal of the barriers to Union players also playing League. Perhaps the best example of this is the enormously successful Summer Conference League which has thriving clubs participating from numerous areas of the East and West Midlands, East Anglia, the Southeast and Southwest of England as well as more traditional areas in the North. Many of the players participating in these clubs are individuals who have only previously experienced Rugby Union that have been converted to League since the barriers were lifted in 1995.

17. While Sky and BBC TV coverage of Rugby League matches is seen nation-wide, we are concerned that the BBC and ITV companies regionalise their coverage of the sport to the detriment of coverage of League news and match highlights in areas outside the North of England. We recognise the difficulties a Super League contract with Sky TV poses for coverage by other broadcasters and welcome the recent arrangements whereby BBC TV can use Sky coverage to show recorded highlights. The recent half hour BBC 2 programme each Monday evening devoted to Rugby League is an important step forward but sadly this is confined only to the North of England and to Super League.

18. In addressing the implications of this perception of League as an exclusively Northern pastime, we were interested in the comparative coverage in national newspapers of the two codes' respective Cup finals which both took place during May of this year at stadia within London. Interestingly both finals featured teams from the North and South, with the London Broncos Rugby League side making its first appearance in a major final. Despite the obvious Southern interest in the League final, and the fact that this match attracted nearly double the number of spectators than its Union equivalent, the media coverage it received overall, especially in national newspapers, was considerably less.

19. The failure to accord the sport of Rugby League a similar status to Union in terms of media coverage is in our view a major factor in its inability to increase spectator attendances. Undoubtedly, with a media based primarily in the South, the "Northern" stereo-typing of League is an important factor in this problem but we believe that there are also other factors which have a bearing on the marked discrepancy in coverage of the two codes. As this Group pointed out in its submission to the 1995 National Heritage Committee Inquiry, throughout its history the sport of Rugby League has faced bigotry, discrimination and prejudice frequently as a consequence of the past social class divide between participants in Union and League. The game was until very recently banned within the British Armed Forces and within the education system is still the province primarily of comprehensive schools, rarely if every being played in grammar, private and public schools. Despite the progress made by League in colleges and universities, the impact of this continued exclusion of League from the sporting experience of vast numbers inevitably impacts on the outlook of many opinion formers, decision makers and commentators in the media.

20. In short, they are often ignorant of the strength and importance of the sport of Rugby League, a consequence of which is the frequent use of the collective term "rugby" to refer specifically just to Rugby Union. We consistently hear references in the broadcast media and newspapers to "rugby" correspondents whose brief is entirely to deal with just Rugby Union. Bearing in mind that there have been two distinct codes for 104 years and the fact that League's match attendances are at the very least broadly comparable to those in Union, we understand the concerns of League supporters over the use of the collective term "rugby" to refer only to Union. Such concerns are reinforced by the fact that a number of national "rugby" correspondents are well known for their dislike of Rugby League. It is a simple fact that not infrequently the only coverage given to Rugby League in some national newspapers and broadcasting media arises from derogatory reference to the sport by "rugby" (i.e. Union) correspondents. We hope the Committee will recognise the validity of our concerns in respect of this point and consider ways in which the merits of the completely independent sport of Rugby League might be properly and more fairly reflected within media coverage.

21. We make this point about League being a completely independent sport because we hope the Committee will accept that there is no desire among most Rugby League supporters for a merging of the two codes which has been muted among some commentators. While undoubtedly at club level relationships between the codes have considerably improved as a consequence of the International Rugby Union Board's 1995 decision, we are not aware of any serious proposals to develop just one common handling code.

22. Most people involved in Rugby League would, we believe, very strongly oppose any changes of rules geared to a process of merger. This view arises not just from a preference for the sporting spectacle resulting from their game's rules, but also from the legacy of Union's attitudes towards League over the past Century.

23. Such attitudes and concerns, however, will not prevent Union continuing to adopt League rules and practices which have clearly resulted in much more similarity between the codes. It should be remembered that the adoption of league table competition in Union is a relatively recent phenomenon which was opposed by those in that sport who believed it was moving them nearer to League. Union have taken numerous on the field rules directly from League including the adoption of knock-on rules, the kick to touch on the bounce from the 20 metre areas, the tap penalty and the sin bin. After 100 years of vilifying league for its professional elements, Union has allowed open professionalism and is adopting League's salary capping arrangements. And within the Union press, there continues to be vigorous debate about the possibility of reducing the number of players, possibly to 13, and over the possible abolition of the line out.

24. We hope the Committee will recognise that there is certainly no desire for a merged code among most of those involved in Rugby League. There remains however some nagging doubts that proposals for one game with common rules may be driven forward by the interests of TV companies. It should be noted in particular that Sky TV is now the main broadcaster for Union as well as League and in a key position to influence the future relationship between the two codes.

The internal arrangements, organisation and problems of the sport of Rugby League

25. In addressing the wider concerns of our Group regarding matters solely relating to Rugby League, we would wish to reiterate some of the points raised when the future of the sport was debated in Parliament during 1995.

26. At that time, there was considerable controversy within the game over the advent of Super League and its implications. Our Group remains of the opinion that Super League, rather than being simply a marketing arm of the game, as originally envisaged, has apparently broken away from the Rugby Football League's overall management of the game. While such a breakaway is continually denied we find it difficult to understand why Super League found it necessary to form a separate administration. They have their own separate headquarters, chairman and chief executive and in 1998 negotiated a contract with News Corporation worth £45 million over the years 1999 to 2003. This appears to be confirmation of an independent body.

27. The resources arising from the new contract are allocated solely to Super League Europe with nothing for the clubs outside Super League within the Northern Ford Premiership. We have very serious worries about the future of such clubs and share the views of many Rugby League followers that the apparent breakaway causing this problem is a betrayal of the real interests of Rugby League. Members of this Group recognise through contacts with their own local clubs that there is a belief in the game that some decisions already taken by Super League clubs may even have breached Rugby Football League bye-laws and we believe these concerns should be fully examined.

28. The Group also remains mystified over the circumstances under which the previous Chief Executive of the Rugby Football League was appointed as Chief Executive of Super League Europe, funded by the Rugby Football League. In view of the financial constraints facing Rugby League, as well as Rugby Union, we would be interested to establish why it was thought necessary to create a costly separate administration at Super League level. We would strongly urge the return of the Super League function and administration to the Rugby Football League to

end the current wasteful duplication within the professional game. We believe this would enable the best use of scarce resources and would urge the Committee to consider this specific point during its Inquiry.

29. We believe that in terms of the relationship between Super League Europe and the Rugby Football League, considerable lessons can be learned from the developments arising since 1997 in respect of the partnership between amateur and professional Rugby League. While retaining their separate identities, the partnership agreement between BARLA and the RFL has led to the successful operation of the Rugby League Joint Policy Board concerned with game wide development strategies. The original partnership agreement has been superseded by a further five year agreement and has brought to an end years of duplication and wasted resources which the game could ill afford.

30. We made reference earlier to the comparative attendances between top level Rugby Union and Rugby League clubs. As a Group we are concerned that the advent of Super League has not resulted in either the markedly increased attendances anticipated or improvements in the financial standing of individual clubs. With regard to attendances, we would urge the Committee to fully research and consider the implications for Rugby League attendances of the move to Super League and summer rugby. There is considerable debate within the game over trends in spectator attendances and a concern that the game's following at matches declines as each season progresses through spring and into the better summer weather. Figures for the most recent Super League attendances round by round during 1998, produced by the House of Commons Library, appear to confirm this trend.

31. In addition to the problems facing clubs outside Super League as a consequence of their exclusion from the new Sky contract, they face even more difficulties attracting spectators and have lost additional revenues through the abandonment of traditional cup competitions such as the Regal Trophy and County Cup competitions. We believe it is not in the interests of the game as a whole for a few clubs to be enjoying the benefits of sponsorship money to the detriment of the rest.

32. It is our impression that the vast majority of clubs are in no better financial position now than they were prior to the News Corporation contract. For reasons we have already set out relating to the open professionalisation of Union, much of this new resourcing appears to have found its way into player contracts with little apparent support for the regeneration of the structure of the game and capital investment in ground accommodation.

33. We know that the Committee will have received evidence regarding the serious difficulties facing individual professional Rugby League clubs as a consequence of safety at sports grounds legislation. It is unfortunate that a game which is noted for high standards of crowd behaviour has received only limited help from successive governments to undertake improvements required as a direct consequence of serious problems in soccer. While we believe that Rugby League clubs have a duty to improve spectator accommodation, we recognise the serious problems meeting the required changes have caused and hope the Committee will accept the need to consider improved levels of funding and other assistance to both Rugby League and other sports.

34. Finally we hope that the Committee will take the opportunity to consider the implications of the inclusion of increased numbers of overseas players in the game of Rugby League. While there is no doubt that some of these players do add to the quality of the sporting spectacle, we are concerned about their impact upon the development of home grown talent and would urge the Committee to consider the adequacy of current restrictions on overseas players.

June 1999

Appendix 4: The Sports (Discrimination) Bills

The 21 June 1994 Bill:

Sports (Discrimination)

A Bill to make it unlawful for any rule-making body for a sport to discriminate against persons who have participated, are participating or are expected to participate in any other lawful sport, and for connected purposes.

Be it enacted by the Queen's most Excellent Majesty, by and with the advice and consent of the Lords Spiritual and Temporal, and Commons, in this present Parliament assembled, and by the authority of the same, as follows:-

1. This Act shall apply to any sport or game which is played in public Application. and to which the public is or may be admitted, whether or not on payment
of a fee.

2. It shall be unlawful for any association (whether incorporated or unincorporated) which has responsibility for administering or making rules for the conduct of any sport or game, or any club affiliated to such an association, to discriminate against any person by reason solely of either-
(a) his past or present participation, or
(b) a presumption (whether reasonable *or* not) that he intends to participate
in any other lawful sport or game, whether as a player or otherwise.

3. (1) A claim by any person that an association has committed an act of discrimination against him which is unlawful by virtue of section 1 of this Act may be made the subject of civil proceedings in like manner as any other claim in tort or (in Scotland) in reparation for breach of statutory duty.

(2)Proceedings under subsection (1) above-

(a) shall be brought in England and Wales or in Northern Ireland only in a county court; and
(b)shall be brought in Scotland only in a sheriff court.

4.   For the purpose of this Act, to "discriminate" means either to treat any person less favourably than any other person or to make any rule which has the effect of so doing.

5.   This Act may be cited as the Sports (Discrimination) Act 1994.

The April 1995 Bill:

Sports (Discrimination) No. 2

A Bill to make it unlawful for any administrative or rule-making body for a sport, or any affiliated club, to discriminate against persons who have participated, are participating or are expected to participate in any other lawful sport; and for connected purposes.

Be It Enacted by the Queen's most Excellent Majesty, by and with the advice and consent of the Lords Spiritual and Temporal, and Commons, in this present Parliament assembled, and by the authority of the same, as follows:-

1. This Act shall apply to any sport or game which is played in public Application. and to which the public is or may be admitted, whether or not on payment of a fee.

2. It shall be unlawful for any association (whether incorporated or unincorporated) which has responsibility for administering or making rules for the conduct of any sport or game, or any club affiliated to such an association, to discriminate against any person by reason solely of either-
(a) his past or present participation, or

(b) a presumption (whether reasonable or not) that he intends to participate

in any other lawful sport or game, whether as a player or otherwise, where the reason for the discrimination is that the other lawful sport or game is not an amateur sport or game.

3. (1) A claim by any person that an association or club has committed an act of discrimination against him which is unlawful by virtue of section 2 of this Act may be made the subject of civil proceedings in like manner as any other claim in tort or (in Scotland) in reparation for breach of statutory duty.

(2) Proceedings under subsection (1) above-

(a) shall be brought in England and Wales or in Northern Ireland only in a county court; and

(b) shall be brought in Scotland only in a sheriff court.

(3) If a court before which proceedings are brought under subsection (1) above finds that an act of discrimination has taken place and that the association or club which has committed that act was acting in accordance with any rule it or any other body had made in so discriminating, it shall have power to declare such a rule to be void and unenforceable and to restrain that association or club (or any other association or club) from seeking to enforce or to act upon that rule.

4. For the avoidance of doubt, it is hereby declared that nothing in this Act shall affect any right which any rule-making body shall have in respect of the rules applicable to the sport or game for which it is a rule-making body, providing that nothing is done in contravention of any of the provisions of this Act.

5. For the purposes of this Act - an "amateur sport or game" is one in which no person is permitted directly or indirectly to-

(a) receive payment, benefit or other material reward, or

(b) accept promise of future payment, benefit or other material reward
for playing the sport or game; and to "discriminate" means either to treat any person less favourably than any other person or to make any rule which has the effect of so doing.

6. This Act may be cited as the Sports (Discrimination) Act 1995.

Bibliography

Collins, Tony — *Rugby's Great Split - Class, Culture and the Origins of Rugby League Football*, Frank Cass, 1998

Davies, Jonathan with Peter Corrigan — *Jonathan - An Autobiography*, Stanley Paul, 1990

Delaney, Trevor — *Rugby Disunion, Volume One -Broken Time*, 1993,

French, Ray — *My Kind of Rugby*, Faber & Faber, 1979

Gibbs, Scott — *Getting Physical, The Autobiography of Scott Gibbs*, Ebury Press, 2000

Holt, Richard — *Sport and The British - A Modern History*, OUP, 1989

Jones, Stephen — *Endless Winter - The Inside Story of the Rugby Revolution*, Mainstream, 1993

Kelner, Simon — *To Jerusalem and Back*, Macmillan, 1996

Lush, Peter and Dave Farrar (editors) — *A History of Rugby League in Wales*, London League Publications, 1998

Malin Ian — *Mud, Blood and Money*, Mainstream, 1997

Melling, Phil — *Man of Amman - The life of Dai Davies*, Gomer, 1994

Moorhouse, Geoffrey — *At the George - And other essays on Rugby League*, Hodder & Stoughton 1989

Moorhouse, Geoffrey — *A People's Game*, Hodder & Stoughton, London, 1995

Richards, Huw & Gareth Williams (eds.) — *More Heart and Soul - The Character of Welsh Rugby*, University of Wales Press, 1999

Schofield, Gary with Neil Hanson — *Gary Schofield's Rugby League Masterpieces*, Sidgwick & Jackson, 1995

Smith, David and Gareth Williams — *Fields of Praise, Official History of the Welsh Rugby Union 1881-1981*, University of Wales Press, 1980

Thompson, Cec — *Born on the Wrong Side*, Pentland Press, Durham 1995

Wheeler, Peter — *Rugby from the Front*, 1983

Williams, Gareth — *1905 and All That*, Gomer, 1991

Parliamentary reports:

National Heritage Committee: Inquiry into relations between Rugby Union and Rugby League (1995)

Culture, Media and Sport Committee: The Future of Professional Rugby (1999)

Footnotes

[1] p.116, *Encyclopaedia Britannica*, 15th edition, Macropaedia, volume 28, Chicago.

[2] p.13, quoted in *Rugby Disunion, Volume One - Broken Time*, Trevor Delaney, Keighley, 1993

[3] p.140, *Rugby's Great Split - Class, Culture and the Origins of Rugby League Football*, Tony Collins, London, 1998

[4] p.69, *A People's Game - The Official History of Rugby League 1895-1995*, Geoffrey Moorhouse, London 1995,

[5] *The Observer*, 17 April 1994

[6] Tony Collins: "Myth and Reality in the 1895 Rugby Split" , *The Sports Historian* No.16, May 1996

[7] *Rugby Union Handbook 1972-3*, p.234 para. 2.4

[8] Letter from M. Oldroyd, Huddersfield Rugby League Referees Society to Eldon Griffiths M.P., 18 October 1972

[9] Quoted in *Manchester Evening News*, article by Jack McNamara, 31 March 1987

[10] Quoted in p.24, *The Guardian*, 2 March 1979

[11] *BARLA Annual Report*, 1979

[12] Quoted in *The Times*, article by Keith Macklin, 27 February 1980,

[13] Ibid.

[14] Ibid.

[15] Quoted in "It's time to end the Union Slur" by Jack McNamara, *Manchester Evening News*, 11 March 1980

[16] *Open Rugby*, Opinion column, February 1981

[17] Letter from Brigadier D. Shuttleworth, President of the RFU to BARLA, 5 November 1985

[18] Quoted in letter of 7 January 1986 from John Cornwell, South Yorkshire County Council to Cyril Villiers, Regional Director, Yorkshire and Humberside Sports Council

[19] See "Politics wreck a rugby dream" by Paul Appandonato, Milton *Keynes Gazette*, 15 April 1983

[20] *Rugby from the Front*, Peter Wheeler, 1983

[21] "More socks for the union purists", Geoff Green, *Manchester Evening News*, 19 November 1983

[22] On Rugby, Clem Thomas, *The Guardian*, p18, 30 December 1983

[23] Letter from Ray Williams, Secretary WRU, 28 November 1983

[24] "WRU facing a dual threat", Steve Bale, *Western Mail*, 7 December 1983

[25] BARLA press release, 6 February 1984

[26] "Take them to court", Ray French, *Rugby Leaguer*, 16 February 1989

[27] Letter to T. Keaveney, secretary BARLA, from Ray Williams, secretary WRU on 19 March 1984

[28] Letter to secretary, RFU, from J. Stirling, assistant secretary, Civil Service Sports Council, 9 April 1984

[29] Letter from M. Oldroyd, BARLA to Mr Denzil Flannigan, HMI at Department of Education and Science, 13 July 1984

[30] "Freedom in Rugby", Trevor Delaney, *Open Rugby*, May 1984

[31] *Pontefract and Castleford Express*, 3 May 1984

[32] *Open Rugby*, September 1984

[33] Letter 20 November 1984 from M. Oldroyd, BARLA to T. Delaney

[34] Letter 20 November 1984 from M. Oldroyd to R. Weighell, RFU

[35] "Poaching? There is no need" Paul Fitzpatrick, *The Guardian*, 14 November 1984

[36] "RFU ban foxes French" Paul Fitzpatrick, *The Guardian*, 24 November 1984

[37] Paul Fitzpatrick, *The Guardian*, 13 December 1984

[38] *Rugby Leaguer*, 30 November 1984

[39] *Rugby Leaguer*, 3 January 1985

[40] *Lancashire Evening Post*, 19 January 1985

[41] See *My Kind of Rugby*, Ray French, London, 1979, pp.99-102

[42] p.146, *Born on the Wrong Side*, Cec Thompson, Durham 1995

[43] "League fury at RU pitch snub", Alun Thomas, *Daily Express*, 20 February 1985

[44] *Rugby Leaguer*, 28 February 1985

[45] "Rugby Apartheid - a case history", Paul Fitzpatrick, *The Guardian*, 8 March 1985

[46] Letter from David Pickett, Redditch Halcyon ARLFC to BARLA, 14 March 1985

[47] *Rugby Leaguer*, 28 February 1985

[48] "Cardiff's club for crackpots", Alan Thompson, *Daily Express*, 5 March 1985

[49] *The Guardian*, 8 March 1985, op cit.

[50] *Open Rugby*, March 1985

[51] Letter from J.G.M. Hart, IRB to BARLA, 1 April 1985

[52] *The Times*, 11 April 1985

[53] Minutes of inaugural meeting of Freedom in Rugby Campaign, 30 March 1985

[54] Letter from Lionel Hurst, LLb to BARLA 10 April 1985

[55] Letter from M. Oldroyd, BARLA to Lionel Hurst 23 April 1985

[56] *Relations between the Amateur Rugby League Association and the Rugby Football Union*, Sports Council Briefing paper, 24 May 1985

[57] Letter from Albert Agar, RFU, to Neil McFarlane M.P., Department of the Environment, 19 June 1985

[58] "Tackling Top Job", Roger Cross, *Yorkshire Post*, 2 July 1985

[59] Sports Council internal memorandum, 23 July 1985

[60] Letter from M. Oldroyd, BARLA to J.W. Smith, Chairman, Sports Council 9 August 1985

[61] Letter from Allan Scott, Scotswood ARLFC to John Wheatley, Director General, Sports Council. 21 August, 1985

[62] "Closed shop the Union must end", Patrick Collins, *Mail on Sunday*, 13 October 1985

[63] "Facing up to the facts", Tony Simpson, *Yorkshire Evening Post*, 23 October 1985

[64] Letter from R H G Weighell, Secretary RFU, to BARLA, 5 November 1985

[65] Letter from M. Oldroyd, BARLA to John Smith, Chairman, Sports Council, 13 November, 1985

[66] Letter from Dave Smith, Bristol ARLFC, to John Wheatley, Sport Council, 21 November, 1985

[67] "RL separate sport claims Oldroyd", *Yorkshire Post*, 28 November 1985

[68] Letter from Dr. Peter Harrison, Freedom in Rugby Campaign, to *Rugby World and Post*, 29 November 1985

[69] "The lost leader", Patrick Collins, *Mail on Sunday*, 1 December, 1985

[70] See p.169, *Jonathan - An Autobiography*, Jonathan Davies with Peter Corrigan, London 1990

[71] *Mail on Sunday* 1 December 1985, op cit.

[72] "Comment", *Sunday Telegraph*, 8 December 1985

[73] Early Day Motion 242, 1985-86 Parliamentary Session

[74] Parliamentary Question 234W, 16 December, 1985

[75] Yorkshire Post, 20 December, 1985

[76] Ibid.

[77] Ibid.

[78] *Rugby Leaguer*, 19 December, 1985

[79] Letter from Tommie Campbell, World Freedom in Sport, to Dr. Peter Harrison, Freedom in Rugby, 3 January, 1986

[80] "A different code of ethics", Bill Bridge, *Rugby News*, January, 1986

[81] Letter from R. Stott M.P. to R. Tracey M.P., Minister for Sport, 14 January, 1986

[82] See *Daily Express*, 7 January, 1986 and *Daily Mail*, 9 January, 1986

[83] "League and Union to clash head on", Raymond Fletcher, *Yorkshire Post*, 4 January, 1986.

[84] Ibid.

[85] "Welsh Rugby ban on Ford is unjust", *Daily Express*, 7 January, 1986

[86] Ibid.

[87] *Daily Mail*, 9 January, 1986

[88] *Yorkshire Post*, 10 January, 1986

[89] "No real surprise over Ford ban", *Yorkshire Evening Post*, 8 January, 1986

[90] See "Challenge to Union hypocrisy", Paul Fitzpatrick, *The Guardian*, 9 January, 1986

[91] Ibid.

[92] Ibid.

[93] Letter from M. Oldroyd, BARLA, to J. Wheatley, Sports Council, 15 January, 1986

[94] Yorkshire and Humberside Council for Sport and Recreation Press Release, 17 January, 1986

[95] Letter from J. Wheatley, Sports Council to M. Oldroyd, BARLA, 22 January, 1986

[96] "League inaccuracies camouflage", Roy Manock, *Yorkshire Post*, 21 January, 1986

[97] Letter from Mr. David Shaw, Sandal, Wakefield, to *Yorkshire Post*, published in part 7 February, 1986

[98] Internal memorandum from C. Villiers, Yorkshire and Humberside Sports Council to J. D. Wheatley, Director General on 29 January, 1986

[99] Letter from Richard Tracey, M.P., Parliamentary Under-Secretary of State, Department of Environment, to Roger Stott M.P., 31 January, 1986

[100] *Daily Telegraph*, 4 February, 1986

[101] *Western Mail*, 19 February, 1986

[102] Ibid.

[103] Ibid.

[104] Clause 8, Sports Council Financial Memorandum

[105] Letter from R. Stott, M.P., to J, Smith, Sports Council, 24 February, 1986

[106] Letter from J. Smith, Sports Council to R. Stott, M.P., 14 March, 1986

[107] Unpublished report of meeting with WRU on 11 March, 1986. WARLA

[108] Letter from R. Clive Millman, WARLA to M. Oldroyd, BARLA on 13 March, 1986

[109] See "Threat to amateurism is gathering impetus", David Hands, *The Times*, 23 April, 1986

[110] *The Times*, op cit.

[111] See "Lift amateur RL ban say Union", David Frost, *The Guardian*, 1 May, 1986

[112] *Rugby Leaguer*, 22 May, 1986

[113] See p.12, *A People's Game*, Geoffrey Moorhouse, London, 1995

[114] Letter from Earl of Arran to M. Rees M.P., 19, November 1989

[115] Letter from Earl of Arran to M. Rees M.P., 3 April 1990

[116] Letter from Earl of Arran to M. Rees M.P., 17 July 1990

[117] *Hansard*, co.694, 2 June 1992

[118] Letter from Armed Forces Minister A. Hamilton M.P. to I. McCartney M.P., 15 July 1992

[119] See p.25, *Getting Physical, The Autobiography of Scott Gibbs*, London, 2000

[120] *The Times*, Peter Bills 28 April 1993

[121] Ibid.

[122] Speech by Iain Sproat M.P., Under-Secretary of State, Department of National Heritage, at the launch of the National Coalmining Museum for England, 28 June 1995

[123] p.105, *Sport and the British - A Modern History*, Richard Holt, Oxford 1989

[124] p.124, *Fields of Praise, Official History of the Welsh Rugby Union 1881-1981*, David Smith and Gareth Williams, Cardiff 1980

[125] p.4, The 1895 Split and South Wales by Tony Collins and John Coyle in *Tries in the Valleys, A History of Rugby League in Wales*, edited by Peter Lush and Dave Farrar, London 1998

[126] Ibid.

[127] p.158, "How Amateur was my Valley" in *1905 and All That* , Gareth Williams, Llandysul,1991

[128] p.171, op cit.

[129] See p.27, *Man of Amman - The Life of Dai Davies*, Phil Melling, Llandysul, 1994

[130] Letter from Lord Brooks of Tremorfa to Doug Hoyle M.P., 16 August 1991

[131] p.33, *A People's Game*, Geoffrey Moorhouse, London 1995

[132] Report of Inquiry into the Involvement of Welsh Players in the Centenary Celebrations of the South African Rugby Board, August 1989, WRU, August 1991

[133] See p.22-23, *Endless Winter- The Inside Story of the Rugby Revolution*, Stephen Jones, 1993, Edinburgh

[134] "Tax probe on Rugby Perks", *South Wales Echo*, 3 September 1993

[135] *South Wales Echo*, op cit.

[136] "Across the Great Divide", *Rugby World*, pp.44-45, July 1994

[137] Quoted in *The Press*, p.37, Christchurch, New Zealand, 1 July 1994

[138] p.73, *Daily Mail*, 20 May 1994

[139] *The Sunday Times*

[140] "The Money Game", *Rugby World*, September 1994

[141] "Call off the battle, the enemy has long departed", p.9,*The Sunday Times*, 11 September 1994

[142] Ibid.

[143] "Hastings claims South Africans flout amateur laws", *Daily Telegraph*, p.21, 20 October 194

[144] Letter from Dudley Wood, Secretary RFU, to Iain Sproat M.P., Department of National Heritage,

29 September 1994

[145] "IB Chairman quick to play down "historic" talks", Steve Bale, *The Independent*, 9 January 1995
[146] Evidence to the Third Report of the National Heritage Select Committee, p.1
[147] Ibid. p.13
[148] Ibid. p.13
[149] *The Independent*, 15 March 1995
[150] *Yorkshire Post*, 15 March 1995
[151] *Western Mail*, 15 March 1995
[152] Evidence to the Third Report of the National Heritage Select Committee, p.23
[153] Ibid. p.26
[154] Ibid. p.26
[155] Ibid. p.30
[156] Ibid. p.4
[157] Preface of report of the International Rugby Board amateurism working party, page d, February 1995
[158] Ibid. page c
[159] Ibid. p..3
[160] Ibid.
[161] Ibid. p.11
[162] National Heritage Select Committee, op. cit. p.43
[163] Ibid. p.44
[164] Ibid. p.5
[165] p.13, IRB amateurism working party report
[166] National Heritage Select Committee, op. cit. P.54
[167] National Heritage Select Committee Report
[168] pp.162-3, *Endless Winter*, Stephen Jones, Edinburgh 1993
[169] p.163, op cit.
[170] Interview with Neil Fissler, *Total Rugby League*, 12 May 2000
[171] *League Express*, 22 May 2000
[172] *Yorkshire Post* 19 April 1995
[173] p. XViii Para 65, Third Report of the National Heritage Select Committee, 29 March, 1995.
[174] op cit.
[175] op cit.
[176] op cit.
[177] p.40, *The Independent*, 20 April, 1995
[178] "Shock for WRU as dome cash is threatened", *Western Mail*, 20 April 1995
[179] Editorial Comment, p10, *Yorkshire Post* 20 April 1995
[180] op cit.
[181] "League compete for moral low ground", Paul Hayward, p32, *Daily Telegraph* 20 April 1995
[182] p.119, *To Jerusalem and Back*, Simon Kelner, London 1996
[183] "Union split over pay for play plan", *The Guardian* 26 April 1995
[184] *The Guardian*, op cit.
[185] *The Guardian*, op cit.
[186] *The Times* 27 April 1995
[187] *The Times*, op cit.
[188] *The Times*, 24 May 1995
[189] *The Times*, op cit.
[190] *The Guardian*, 25 May 1995
[191] *The Times*, 24 June 1995
[192] *The Times*, op cit.
[193] *The Guardian* 24 June 1995
[194] *The Guardian*, op cit.
[195] *The Guardian*, op cit.
[196] *The Observer* 15 June 1995
[197] *The Guardian* 15 July 1995

[198] *The Guardian*, op cit.

[199] *The Observer* 16 July 1995

[200] M. Colman, op cit.

[201] M. Colman, op cit.

[202] "Rebels weigh up options", *The Guardian* 18 July, 1995

[203] *The Guardian*, op cit.

[204] *The Guardian*, op cit.

[205] *The Guardian*, 28 July 1995

[206] *The Guardian*, op cit.

[207] *The Guardian*, op cit.

[208] *The Observer*, 23 July 1995

[209] *The Observer*, op cit.

[210] *The Guardian*, 26 July 1995

[211] *The Scotsman*, 1 August 1995

[212] See *The Guardian*, 2 August 1995

[213] *The Guardian*, op cit.

[214] *The Guardian*, 3 August 1995

[215] *The Observer*, 6 August 1995

[216] *The Observer*, op cit.

[217] *The Observer*, op cit.

[218] "£40,000 deal cracks code", Robert Armstrong, *The Guardian* 25 August 1995

[219] See, for example, "Rugby Union abandons its amateurs only rule" by David Hands and Michael Horsnell, *The Times*, 28 August, 1995

[220] *The Times*, op cit.

[221] *The Times*, 29 August 1995

[222] *The Times*, op cit.

[223] *The Times*, 28 August 1995

[224] *The Times*, op cit.

[225] *Yorkshire Post* 26 April 1996

[226] *Yorkshire Post*, op cit.

[227] *Yorkshire Post*, 18 November 1995

[228] See comments in *The Times*, 2 October 1995

[229] *The Guardian*, 5 December 1995

[230] *The Guardian*, op cit.

[231] *Yorkshire Post*, 9 November 1995

[232] *Yorkshire Post*, op cit.

[233] *The Times*, 9 November 1995

[234] David Davies, *The Guardian*, 16 January, 1996

[235] Frank Keating, *The Guardian*, 16 January, 1996

[236] Ibid.

[237] *The Times*, 25 March 1996

[238] *The Guardian*, 26 March 1996

[239] *The Guardian*, 5 April 1996

[240] Ibid.

[241] *The Observer*, 7 April 1996

[242] *The Observer*, 14 April 1996

[243] *The Independent*, 17 April 1996

[244] *The Times*, 10 April 1996

[245] *The Guardian*, 5 April 1996

[246] Ibid.

[247] *The Guardian*, 13 April 1996

[248] Ibid.

[249] *The Times*, 16 April 1996

[250] *Yorkshire Post*, 26 April 1996

[251] *The Observer*, 28 April 1996

[252] *The Guardian*, 25 May 1996

[253] *Yorkshire Post*, 11 June 1996

[254] *The Times*, 15 July 1996

[255] *The Observer*, 21 July 1996

[256] Ibid.

[257] *The Guardian*, 21 December 1995

[258] Ibid.

[259] Ibid.

[260] p.14 *Super League 96*, Graham Clay and Tim Butcher, Bradford, 1996

[261] Quoted on p.68, *Gary Schofield's Rugby League Masterpieces* by Gary Schofield with Neil Hanson, London, 1995

[262] See unpublished memoir by Robert Fassolette, 1984, translated by Mike Rylance, and also *The Guardian* article, Nov. 1993 by Karl Spracklen and Chris Westwood, both quoted in Schofield with Hanson, ibid.

[263] See Mike Rylance, *The Forbidden Game*, p.140

[264] *Yorkshire Post*, 18 April 1996

[265] *Daily Express*, 9 May 1996

[266] Ibid.

[267] *The Times*, 27 May 1996

[268] *The Scotsman*, 27 May 1996

[269] Ibid.

[270] *The Observer*, 7 July 1996

[271] Ibid.

[272] Ibid.

[273] *The Guardian*, 13 August 1996

[274] Ibid.

[275] *The Observer*, 25 August 1996

[276] Ibid.

[277] *Yorkshire Post*, 8 April 1998

[278] *The Times*, 22 November 1996

[279] Quoted in *The Times*, 22 November 1996

[280] The Guardian, 21 November 1996

[281] *The Times*, 23 October 1996

[282] Bath RUFC chief executive Tony Swift quoted in *The Observer*, 16 February 1997

[283] *The Times*, 1 October 1996

[284] *The Guardian*, 4 October 1996

[285] *The Times*, 22 October 1996

[286] Quoted in *The Guardian*, 7 January 1997

[287] *The Guardian*, 29 November 1996

[288] Ibid.

[289] Mick Cleary and Norman Harris, *The Observer* 16 February 1997

[290] *Scotland on Sunday*, 2 February 1997

[291] *The Scotsman*, 22 February 1997

[292] *The Observer*, 16 February 1997

[293] *The Times*, 19 March 1997

[294] Quoted in *Yorkshire Post*, 29 March 1997

[295] *Yorkshire Post, op cit.*

[296] *The Times*, 11 July 1997

[297] Ibid.

[298] *Independent on Sunday*, 6 July 1997

[299] Ibid.

[300] *Independent on Sunday*, 28 September 1997

[301] *Financial Times*, 17 October 1997

[302] Quoted in *The Times*, 18 October 1997
[303] *Yorkshire Post*, 21 October 1997
[304] Ibid.
[305] *The Times*, 21 October 1997
[306] *The Sunday Times*, 26 October 1997
[307] *The Observer*, 14 December 1997
[308] *Independent on Sunday*, 14 December 1997
[309] *Yorkshire Post*, 12 December 1997
[310] *The Observer*, 14 December 1997
[311] *Yorkshire Post*, 12 December 1997
[312] *Yorkshire Post*, 14 January 1998
[313] *The Guardian*, 30 March 1998
[314] Ibid.
[315] *Yorkshire Post*, 26 February 1998
[316] *Independent on Sunday*, 8 March 1998
[317] *Yorkshire Post*, 10 March 1998
[318] *The Guardian*, 11 March 1998
[319] *Yorkshire Post*, 13 March 1998
[320] *Daily Mail*, 24 March 1998
[321] Quoted in *The Observer*, 29 March 1998
[322] *Yorkshire Post*, 6 April 1998
[323] Chris Rea, *Independent on Sunday*, 6 July 1997
[324] *The Times*, 10 September 1996
[325] Andy Wilson, *The Guardian*, 5 October 1996
[326] *Rugby Leaguer*, 30 June 1997
[327] *The Guardian*, 23 January 1997
[328] Ibid.
[329] *League Express*, 30 June 1997
[330] Andy Wilson, *The Observer*, 13 July 1997
[331] John Ledger, *Yorkshire Post*, 24 July 1997
[332] *Yorkshire Post*, 19 August 1997
[333] Robert Gate, *League Express*, 1 September 1997
[334] *League Express*, 1 September 1997
[335] *Rugby Leaguer*, 22 September 1997
[336] *Rugby Leaguer*, 1 September 1997
[337] Steve Brady, *Rugby Leaguer*, 22 September 1997
[338] *Rugby Leaguer*, 8 December 1997
[339] *Observer Sports Magazine*, May 2000
[340] *League Express*, 5 January 1998
[341] *Open Rugby*, March 1998, p.14 Dave Hadfield's "Independent View"
[342] *Independent on Sunday*, 11 January 1998
[343] Chris Rea, *Independent on Sunday*, 8 March 1998
[344] Quoted in *Rugby Leaguer*, 6 April 1998
[345] p.18, *Total Rugby League*, 4 August 2000
[346] p.8-9, "At the Millennium", Peter Stead and Huw Richards, *More Heart and Soul - The Character of Welsh Rugby*, edited: Huw Richards, Peter Stead & Gareth Williams, Cardiff, 1999
[347] Stephen Jones, *The Sunday Times*, 6 February 2000
[348] *The Guardian*, 17 December 1999
[349] *Western Mail*, 23 December 1999
[350] p.164, *Endless Winter*, Stephen Jones, Edinburgh, 1993
[351] Eddie Butler, *The Observer*, 30 April 2000
[352] Ibid.
[353] Ibid.
[354] Report of Culture, Media and Sport Committee: The Future of Professional Rugby

[355] The Future of Professional Rugby: Government Response to the Second Report from the Culture, Media and Sport Committee, Session 1999-2000

[356] Yorkshire Post, 26 August 2000

[357] See "Union no threat" by Graham Clay, *Rugby League World*, July 2000, p.10

[358] *The Times*, 6 December 1995

[359] *The Observer*, 21 January 1996

[360] *The Observer*, 21 January 1996

[361] See Ian Malin, *Mud, Blood and Money*, p.159, Edinburgh, 1997

[362] *Rugby Leaguer*, 28 August 2000

[363] Rugby League figures from *Rugby League 1999-2000* , Brighouse 1999. Rugby Union figures from *The Independent* 7 June 2000

[364] *The Times*, 27 May 1996

[365] *The Guardian*, 8 September 1995

[366] Ibid.

[367] *Independent on Sunday*, 21 September 1997

[368] *The Sunday Times*, 27 August 2000

[369] *The Times*, 6 October 1995

[370] Ibid.

[371] *Independent on Sunday*, 26 October 1997

[372] *The Observer*, 30 April 2000

[373] *Rugby League World*, July 2000 op cit.

[374] p.10, *At The George - And other essays on Rugby League*, Geoffrey Moorhouse, London 1989

Index

London League Publications Ltd
Rugby League Books

From Fulham to Wembley
20 years of Rugby League in London
Edited by Dave Farrar and Peter Lush
A celebration of 20 years of professional Rugby League in the capital. Includes profiles of the key players and coaches, match reports, and memories and recollections of people involved with the club.
Published in May 2000 at £8.75 Special offer £8.00

The Fulham Dream
Rugby League comes to London
by Harold Genders
The inside story of the creation of Fulham RLFC and the promotion winning first season. Told by the man who in 1980 set up the first new club outside the game's heartlands for nearly 30 years. With photos by the club's official photographer.
Published in September 2000 at £6.95.
Special offer £6.00

London Rugby League books special offer: **The above two titles for £12.00.**

Touch and Go
A History of Professional Rugby League in London
By Dave Farrar and Peter Lush with Michael O'Hare
Published in 1995 at £9.00. Special offer £5.00

Tries in the Valleys
A History of Rugby League in Wales edited by Peter Lush and Dave Farrar
Published in 1998 at £14.95. Special offer £8.00

Published twice a year. The magazine for the serious Rugby League supporter

Latest edition: £2.00   **Four issue** subscription £7.00
Special offer: Three issue subscription plus a copy of *Tries in the Valleys* £10.00

Order books and *Our Game* from: London League Publications Ltd, PO Box 10441, London E14 0SB. Cheques payable to London League Publications Ltd - no credit card orders. If subscribing to *Our Game*, please state with which edition the subscription should start.